Edmond de Goncourt and the Novel: Naturalism and Decadence

FAUX TITRE

264

Etudes de langue et littérature françaises
publiées sous la direction de

Keith Busby, M.J. Freeman,
Sjef Houppermans et Paul Pelckmans

Edmond de Goncourt and the Novel:
Naturalism and Decadence

Katherine Ashley

AMSTERDAM - NEW YORK, NY 2005

The paper on which this book is printed meets the requirements of
'ISO 9706: 1994, Information and documentation - Paper for documents -
Requirements for permanence'.

Le papier sur lequel le présent ouvrage est imprimé remplit les prescriptions
de 'ISO 9706: 1994, Information et documentation - Papier pour documents
- Prescriptions pour la permanence'.

ISBN: 90-420-1646-9
©Editions Rodopi B.V., Amsterdam - New York, NY 2005
Printed in The Netherlands

For my parents

Contents

Acknowledgements	9
References	11
I. Introduction	
Towards a New Novel	15
II. Paratexts	
Titles: Novel Transformations	35
Prefaces and Literary History	51
III. Facts and Fiction	
Documentary Processes	71
Les Frères Zemganno: Author as Acrobat	87
La Faustin: Origins and Heredity	107
Chérie: Female Documents	127
IV. Language and Forms	
Plot Development	149
Textual Voices	175
Language and the Literary Field	195
Natural and Artificial Expression	213
V. Conclusion	
Conclusion	227
Bibliography	235
Index	249

Acknowledgements

My interest in Edmond de Goncourt's novels was piqued half a dozen years ago, and since then several people have been instrumental in encouraging it. I extend my warmest thanks to Marion Schmid, whose knowledgeable and patient guidance proved invaluable. I apologise to my friends, who unwittingly found themselves immersed in late-nineteenth-century French literature, even though their own inclinations leaned towards such things as Gaullism, Nabokov and humour theory. I also wish to thank my family who shrugged their shoulders in bemusement as they watched this book come to fruition.

An earlier version of 'Prefaces and Literary History', entitled 'Authority and Intertext in the Goncourt Prefaces', appeared in *Trivium*, 32 (2000) 59-72. A modified version is reprinted here with the kind permission of the General Editor and the Editorial Board of *Trivium*.

REFERENCES

This monograph has been prepared using the *MHRA Style Guide* (London: Modern Humanities Research Association, 2002). In order to keep footnotes to a minimum, full publication details are only provided in the first reference to a work. Where possible, references have been incorporated into the body of the text. Due to the scarcity of the Slatkine edition of the complete works of the Goncourt brothers, unless otherwise stated all references to the novels refer to the following edition and will be made in the body of the text: *Les Goncourt: l'œuvre romanesque* (Paris: Bibliopolis, 1999) [cd-rom].

Short forms

Bibliothèque nationale de France, Manuscrits, Nouvelles acquisitions françaises will be abbreviated as B.N.F. M.S.S. N.A.F.

Correspondance de Jean Lorrain avec Edmond de Goncourt, suivie d'un choix d'articles de Jean Lorrain consacrés à Edmond de Goncourt, ed. by Eric Walbecq (Tusson: Du Lérot, 2003) will be abbreviated as *Corres. Lorr-Gonc*.

Correspondance Edmond de Goncourt et Alphonse Daudet, ed. by Pierre-Jean Dufief and Anne-Simone Dufief (Geneva: Droz, 1996) will be abbreviated as *Corres. Gonc-Daud*.

Edmond and Jules de Goncourt, *Journal: mémoires de la vie littéraire*, ed. by Robert Ricatte, Bouquins, 3 vols (Paris: Robert Laffont, 1989) will be abbreviated as *Journal*. Dated references will be made in the body of the text.

Gustave Flaubert-Les Goncourt: Correspondance, ed. by Pierre-Jean Dufief (Paris: Flammarion, 1998) will be abbreviated as *Corres. Flaub-Gonc*.

J.-K. Huysmans, *Lettres inédites à Edmond de Goncourt*, ed. by Pierre Lambert and Pierre Cogny (Paris: Nizet, 1956) will be abbreviated as *Corres. Huys-Gonc*.

INTRODUCTION

TOWARDS A NEW NOVEL

> Naturalists and decadents worked alongside each other as friends and collaborators.[1]

In comparison with other novelists of the second half of the nineteenth century, and regardless of their considerable reputation at the time, the Goncourt brothers have been all but ignored except in the context of their *Journal* and the Prix Goncourt, which has just celebrated its centenary. As one critic comments, 'on oublie souvent l'influence majeure [des Goncourt] sur la littérature de l'entre-deux-siècles'.[2] This is particularly the case of Edmond de Goncourt, who survived his brother by twenty-six years, during which time he continued to write prolifically. More often than not, he has been written into literary history as an acerbic whinger whose chief talent lay in annoying others, an 'emotional cripple' like his brother.[3] Alternatively, his novels, *La Fille Elisa* (1877), *Les Frères Zemganno* (1879), *La Faustin* (1882) and *Chérie* (1884) are simply grouped with the novels of the Goncourt brothers, the last of which, *Madame Gervaisais*, was published in 1869. There has been little attempt to distinguish between the pre- and post-1870 writings of the Goncourts, and few critics have paid much heed to the place of Edmond de Goncourt's novels in the literary field, despite the fact that they were extremely influential at the time of their publication, both in and outside the borders of France, as numerous requests for translation demonstrate. Yet, there are those

---

[1] Philip Stephan, *Paul Verlaine and the Decadence 1882-1890* (Manchester: Manchester University Press, 1974), p. 9.

[2] Philippe Chardin, 'Fins comparées de quelques artistes fictifs de la fin-de-siècle', in *Fins de siècle: terme-évolution-révolution? Actes du congrès de la société française de littérature générale et comparée, Toulouse 22-24 septembre 1987*, ed. by Gwenhaël Ponnau (Toulouse: Presses universitaires du Mirail, 1989), pp. 231-39 (p. 231).

[3] Roger Williams, *The Horror of Life* (London: Weidenfeld and Nicolson, 1980), p. 68.

who argue that *La Faustin*, along with Huysmans's *A Rebours* (1884), was a founding text of literary Decadence.[4]

The Goncourts prided themselves on their *jumellité*, on their *Charbovari*-like identity as *Juledmond*, and critics have tended to accept this, interpreting their novels as hybrid either because of the brothers' close relationship or because of their different artistic callings. For, in addition to being novelists, they were historians, biographers, journalists, artists, and diarists. Jules died in 1870, however, the same year that the Second Empire ended, and Edmond waited seven years – seven very long years in terms of the changes underway in French literature – before he published a novel under his own name. This monograph, therefore, aims to treat the Goncourts' writings as distinct. It will study Edmond de Goncourt's novels in their own right, in order to situate them within their historical period, the *fin de siècle*, which is an undeniably different environment compared to the one from which the joint novels sprang. It will study the aesthetic transformation that results from his changed circumstances, and note the similarities, but also the differences, between the pre- and post-1870 works.

Towards Naturalism

In the preface to their 1864 novel *Germinie Lacerteux*, the Goncourts elaborated their theory of the novel and violently broke with what had come before:

> Aujourd'hui que le Roman s'élargit et grandit, qu'il commence à être la grande forme sérieuse, passionnée, vivante, de l'étude littéraire et de l'enquête sociale, qu'il devient, par l'analyse et par la recherche psychologique, l'Histoire morale contemporaine, aujourd'hui que le Roman s'est imposé les études et les devoirs de la science, il peut en revendiquer les libertés et les franchises (p. 2).

One of the primary advances proposed in this preface is the prominence given to working class subjects, and it is in this respect that the novel splits with the tradition of, say, Flaubert, whose novels

---

[4] Sylvie Thorel-Cailleteau, *La Tentation du livre sur rien: naturalisme et décadence* (Mont-de-Marsan: Editions interuniversitaires, 1994), p. 200.

depict middle-class realities, and paves the way for Naturalism. Erich Auerbach, for one, argues that the Goncourts were in the 'extreme vanguard' with *Germinie Lacerteux*. 'Realism,' he writes, summarising and at the same time clarifying the position, 'had to embrace the whole reality of contemporary civilisation, in which to be sure the bourgeoisie played a dominant role, but in which the masses were beginning to press threateningly ahead'. Moreover, 'the common people in all its ramifications had to be taken into the subject matter of serious realism: the Goncourts were right, and they were to be borne out in it. The development of realistic art has proved it'.[5] Decades earlier, the Goncourts' celebrated contemporary, Emile Zola, had stated that '*Germinie Lacerteux*, dans notre littérature contemporaine, est une date' and added that a literary group had formed around its authors.[6]

The reference to 'Histoire morale contemporaine' in the preface to *Germinie Lacerteux* alerts the reader to correspondences between the Goncourt brothers and Zola, whose highly successful *Histoire naturelle et sociale d'une famille sous le Second Empire* deals with the effects of physiology, heredity and environment on the members of the Rougon-Macquart family. The *Rougon-Macquart* series is, in a sense, the *grand projet* of nineteenth-century French literature, perhaps a natural evolution from *La Comédie humaine*.[7] Zola's series springs from a tradition of sociological enquiry and categorisation in which the Goncourts themselves participate. According to the Goncourt *Journal*, Zola first explained the nature and structure of his project to Edmond on 14 December 1868, at which point he spoke of an 'histoire d'une famille' in ten volumes. By 27 August 1870, this had expanded to become an 'histoire naturelle et sociale d'une famille'. The Rougon-Macquart family tree was created in 1869 and first published in *Une page d'amour* in 1878, by which time Edmond

---

[5] *Mimesis: The Representation of Reality in Western Literature*, trans. by William Trask (Princeton: Princeton University Press, 1953), pp. 496 and 497.
[6] 'Edmond et Jules de Goncourt' [1875], in Emile Zola, *Du Roman: sur Stendhal, Flaubert et les Goncourt*, ed. by Henri Mitterand (Brussels: Complexe, 1989), pp. 247-84 (pp. 274 and 283-84).
[7] In the preface to *La Cousine Bette* (1848), Balzac refers to himself as a 'simple docteur en médecine sociale'.

de Goncourt was deliberately moving away from Naturalism and its subject matter.

The Naturalist novel is today virtually synonymous with Zola's *Rougon-Macquart* series, even though other authors, like Henry Céard, might be more representative of canonical Naturalism. In any event, due to the sometimes fraught relationship between the elderly Goncourt and the youngish Zola, literary critics seem almost driven to entrench themselves firmly in one camp or the other: there are partisans of Zola and partisans of the Goncourts, but rarely partisans of both. Marcel Sauvage provides a useful example of this: 'Des critiques ont longtemps refusé aux Goncourt,' he writes, 'd'avoir été les initiateurs du naturalisme littéraire, qui marque la fin du XIXe siècle. Emile Zola passe encore pour en avoir été le maître, il n'en fut que porte-drapeau et le théoricien un peu ridicule, après Taine'. Sauvage's disdain for Zola is barely concealed. Elsewhere, however, he launches an appeal to reinterpret literary history and to assign the Goncourts a substantial place in the emergence of Naturalism: 'Treize ans avant *L'Assommoi*r [...] depuis longtemps, les Goncourt revendiquent la paternité de cette expression, signe de ralliement de la nouvelle école, *le document humain*, qu'ils ont employée les premiers et qui leur revient en propre'.[8] Edmond de Goncourt would have approved, for he himself expressed a similar opinion in the preface to *La Faustin*. Both Goncourt's and Sauvage's assertions highlight the instability of the terms 'Naturalism' and '*document humain*' at the time.

> Cette expression très blaguée dans le moment, j'en réclame la paternité, la regardant, cette expression, comme la formule définissant le mieux et le plus significativement le mode nouveau de travail de l'école qui a succédé au romantisme: l'école du document humain.[9]

Goncourt makes his paternity quite clear. At the time of publication of *La Faustin* in 1882, though, rather than distinguish between Realism and Naturalism, he presents them as subsumed under the auspices of the 'école du document humain'. And, to be sure, the focus on the

---

[8] *Jules et Edmond de Goncourt: précurseurs* (Paris: Mercure de France, 1970), pp. 91 and 105.
[9] Edmond de Goncourt, *La Faustin* [1882], ed. by Jean-Pierre Bertrand (Arles: Actes Sud, 1995), p. 7.

document humain remains a common point between the joint and solo Goncourt novels.

The origins of the term Naturalism have been traced by Sylvie Thorel, who has evaluated the new meanings it acquired with the birth of the Zolian novel,[10] and Colette Becker has dated the 'grande période du naturalisme' as extending from 1876-84.[11] The different significations of the term are also analysed by David Baguley, who, in addition to assessing the artistic, philosophical and scientific interpretations of the movement, provides a framework by which to date it.[12] Three events are cited by him as central to the Naturalists: the Trapp dinner which first brought authors together in 1877; the *Soirées de Médan*, their joint publication in 1880; and the 'Manifeste des cinq' (1887), symbol of the internal rupture of the group. As an already established author, Goncourt did not write for the *Soirées de Médan*. It has, however, been repeatedly speculated that he masterminded the 'Manifeste des cinq'. Of interest to a study of Edmond de Goncourt's changing aesthetic in the tumultuous and choppy literary waters of the late nineteenth century is Baguley's conviction that by 1880 the group had peaked:

> If, as we can confidently state, the naturalist group, in so far as it had ever functioned in this way, was after 1880 no longer a coherent active force, then perhaps the greatest irony of the whole situation is the fact that its virtual disintegration coincided exactly with the beginning of a period of great productivity of naturalist texts in France and abroad.[13]

The irony of this situation in terms of Edmond de Goncourt's work stems from the fact that there is an increase in sales of his novels at the very moment that he begins to distance himself from Naturalism in a very public way. Even though his last three novels move toward a more rarefied aesthetic doctrine, their sales do not suffer too unduly, though they in absolutely no way compare to Zola's. *La Fille Elisa* was an enormous success at the cash registers and 6,000 of the first 8,000 copies of the now forgotten *Chérie* were sold on the day of its

---

[10] 'Naturalisme, naturaliste', *Les Cahiers naturalistes*, 60 (1986), 76-88.
[11] *Lire le réalisme et le naturalisme* (Paris: Dunod, 1992), pp. 61-64.
[12] *Naturalist Fiction: The Entropic Vision* (Cambridge: CUP, 1990), pp. 16-28, particularly p. 16.
[13] *Naturalist Fiction*, p. 24.

release.[14] The first edition of *Chérie* to be printed since the beginning of the twentieth century, apart from in collected works, has only recently appeared on shelves.[15] The initial success of the novel is arguably a direct result of Goncourt's association with the dominant literary force of the time. 1884, the year of *Chérie*'s publication, has been called 'une année de transition',[16] a year of transition, thus making Edmond de Goncourt's last novel and his subsequent decision to abandon fiction all the more central to a study of the changes underway in the literary field.

Aesthetically, it is the emphasis on the *document humain* and scientific method that would most seem to distinguish Naturalism from preceding literary trends. Gone are the days when authors could, like Baudelaire, launch invitations to imaginary voyages. The cult of the *document humain* advocated a scientific approach to literature, one in which fiction was allegedly rooted in empirical reality, rather than in the imagination. This is made clear in the preface to *Les Frères Zemganno*:

> Donc ces hommes, ces femmes, et même les milieux dans lesquels ils vivent, ne peuvent se rendre qu'au moyen d'immenses emmagasinements d'observations, d'innombrables notes prises à coups de lorgnon, de l'amassement d'une collection de documents humains, semblable à ces montagnes de calepins de poche qui représentent, à la mort d'un peintre, tous les croquis de sa vie. Car seuls, disons-le bien haut, les documents humains font les bons livres: les livres où il y a de la vraie humanité sur ses jambes (pp. 2-3).

Undeniably, Edmond de Goncourt worships at the fount of mimetic 'reality' rather than at the well of fiction.

Towards Decadence

There is, however, more to the Goncourts' novels – joint and solo – than documentary realism. There is more than working class characters plagued by hereditary flaws, and their influence extends

---

[14] François Fosca, *Edmond et Jules de Goncourt* (Paris: Albin Michel, 1941), p. 339.
[15] Ed. by Jean-Louis Cabanès and Philippe Hamon (Paris: La Chasse au Snark, 2003).
[16] Louis Marquèze-Pouey, *Le Mouvement décadent en France* (Paris: PUF, 1986), p. 105.

beyond the Naturalist movement. Writing in 1892, future member of the Académie Goncourt, Lucien Descaves, asserts that the Goncourts not only marked the beginning of Naturalism, but also foretold its end:

> Il semblerait que les Goncourt, après avoir déterminé le mouvement littéraire en avant, ont indiqué, dès 1869, la réaction inévitable, comme un mécanicien n'invente pas seulement une machine, mais le frein qui permet de l'arrêter au bord du fossé.[17]

What were they announcing? What happens after 1869, after Jules's death? While the publication of *Germinie Lacerteux*, for example, has been hailed as a red-letter day in the history of French Naturalism, the novel has also been linked to the Decadent aesthetic. David Weir uses *Germinie* as a base text in his comparison of Naturalism and Decadence, arguing that the Goncourt brothers simultaneously helped mould both movements. Decadence, according to him, can be defined as 'an aesthetic expression of naturalistic degeneration', rather than as an aesthetic only to be studied in relation to Romanticism.[18] To this view can be opposed the traditional belief of literary critics who have rather disapprovingly and reproachfully regarded Decadence as simply announcing another movement, Symbolism, or indeed as a lesser form of Symbolism, instead of as an aesthetic in its own right. In effect, Decadence has long had these negative undertones, a fact witnessed most obviously in Max Nordau's archly moralistic *Degeneration* (1892), which posits Decadence as an illness, and Decadent art as the product of deranged minds.

The choice of 'Decadence' as a term of reference is itself contentious, despite Paul Verlaine's apparent praise for it:

> J'aime le mot de décadence, tout miroitant de pourpre et d'ors, j'en révoque, bien entendu, toute imputation injurieuse et toute idée de déchéance. Ce mot

---

[17] Quoted in Pierre-Jean Dufief, 'Edmond de Goncourt et son cercle de "petits" naturalistes', in *Relecture des "petits" naturalistes*, ed. by Colette Becker and Anne-Simone Dufief (Paris : RITM, Université de Paris X, 2000), pp. 21-33 (p. 33).
[18] *Decadence and the Making of Modernism* (Amherst: University of Massachusetts Press, 1995), p. 48.

suppose au contraire des pensées raffinées, d'extrême civilisation, une haute culture littéraire, une âme capable d'intenses voluptés [...].[19]

'Décadentisme' and, in particular, 'décadisme' have been suggested as alternatives with less negative connotations – suggesting the birth of a new era rather than the end of another – but they have not been adopted.[20]

Dating of the Decadent movement has proved equally contentious. Henri Mitterand posits that 'dès avant 1870, les grands thèmes de la décadence sont en place'.[21] Yves-Alain Fabre extends the date marginally when he states that 'le terme décadent [...] s'applique à un certain état d'esprit qui apparaît vers 1875 pour se poursuivre jusqu'aux années 1900'.[22] Koenraad Swart, on the other hand, offers 1877-1905 as his timeframe.[23] So, in contrast to the argument that considers Decadence as present throughout the nineteenth century, though culminating in its final decades, it is arguable that it in fact coincided with the consecration of the Naturalist movement and was largely confined to the 1880s and 1890s – the main periods of Naturalist and Decadent creation appear to overlap, and indeed may be inseparable.

Regardless of these minor disagreements over dating, it is undeniable that the Decadent aesthetic, which at one and the same time prized the acceptance of modernity and mourned the contingent decline of past civilisations, was in full swing by the mid 1880s. Anatole Baju, founder of the journal *Le Décadent* – whose motto 'guerre au mercantilisme dans les Arts, place aux artistes' seems to be a direct reaction to Naturalism's popularity – defines the doctrine in 1886 by accentuating its modernity and anti-commercialism.[24] While

---

[19] Quoted in 'Les Influences d'un sentiment', <www.ac-reunion.fr/pedagogie/lyvergerp/FRANCAIS/2nde6/Cedric_symbolisme/influences.htm> [accessed 26 July 2004]

[20] Marquèze-Pouey, p. 10.

[21] *Le Regard et le signe* (Paris : PUF, 1987), p. 281.

[22] 'Vanités décadentes', in Ponnau, pp. 355-63 (p. 355).

[23] *The Sense of Decadence in Nineteenth-Century France* (The Hague: Martinus Nijhoff, 1964) contains a chapter entitled 'Fin de siècle 1877-1905'.

[24] *Le Décadent*, 1-15 February 1888; *L'Anarchie littéraire* (Paris: Léon Vanier, 1904), p. 10. In other respects, Baju's theories do not necessarily correspond to what modern critics view as Decadence. His opinion of literature as pursuing a social ideal rather

it would be impossible to pinpoint dates with respect to any artistic movement, those mooted above attest to a common belief that some sort of aesthetic change was taking place in the last decades of the century, at a time when Edmond de Goncourt was making his last literary stand.

Goncourt can be linked to Decadence from many perspectives. Aside from the value they attached to documentation and documentary realism, the Goncourt brothers asserted the primacy of 'nervosité', a term that they understood as a heightened artistic sensitivity to all sorts of stimuli and language. As Edmond himself famously commented: 'Les critiques peuvent dire tout ce qu'ils veulent de Zola, ils ne pourront pas nous empêcher, mon frère et moi, d'être les saints Jean-Baptiste de la nervosité moderne' (*Journal*, 23 April 1878). The more an author relied on nerves, so it went, the more refined his art. Or, as Williams would have it, 'the Goncourts defined true progress in civilization as the advance in sensibility. Thus, as humanity advances, it becomes increasingly neurotic and hysterical; and those who have nothing left but nerves are the finest of our flowers' (p. 72).[25] The Goncourts' nerves (and afterwards Edmond's alone) gave birth to an ornate, orchidaceous style that was thought to transform novels based on documents into works of art and to give their writing, in the words of Arthur Symons, a certain 'feverish beauty'.[26]

It was this style that was most appreciated by Decadent authors. In the 1884 novel, *A Rebours*, Huysmans's des Esseintes, the Decadent (anti)hero *par excellence* – whom critics have speculated could be modelled in part on Edmond de Goncourt –[27] places *La Faustin* firmly within his Decadent library precisely because of its fraught style:

---

than being disinterested is the antonym of current acceptances of French Decadent art and may have more in common with the English Decadence of Pater and Ruskin.

[25] Fittingly, a particularly rare flower is hyacinth 607, the 'Edmond de Goncourt', created for the author by the Dutch florist Krelage in 1895. B.N.F. M.S.S. N.A.F. 22466, fols 387 and 390.

[26] 'J.-K. Huysmans', *The Fortnightly Review*, March 1892, on <http://www.huysmans.org.uk/fortnightly.htm> [accessed 26 July 2004]

[27] Weir, p. 47; Swart, p. 163. The principal model for des Esseintes is, of course, Robert de Montesquiou.

> C'était un style perspicace et morbide, nerveux et retors, diligent à noter l'impalpable impression qui frappe les sens et détermine la sensation, un style expert à moduler les nuances compliquées d'une époque qui était par elle-même singulièrement complexe. En somme, c'était le verbe indispensable aux civilisations décrépites qui, pour l'expression de leurs besoins, exigent, à quelque âge qu'elles se produisent, des acceptions, des tournures, des fontes nouvelles et de phrases et de mots.[28]

The qualities mentioned by des Esseintes were also commented upon, esteemed, and sometimes imitated by contemporary authors. The mystical aesthete Francis Poictevin, whose own style is highly precious, dedicated his 1893 novel *Ludine* to Goncourt. There is a possible homage to Mlle and Mme Tony-Fréneuse, from *Chérie*, in Jean Lorrain's Duc de Fréneuse, the gem-obsessed protagonist of *Monsieur de Phocas* (1900). Goncourt is also quoted in the epigraph to Lorrain's 'Heures de villes d'eaux' (*Histoires de masques*, 1900). In addition, there were dedications from Belgian author Camille Lemonnier (*Le Mort*, 1887), Octave Mirbeau (*Sébastien Roch*, 1890), and Marcel Schwob, amongst many others. From the twentieth century, on the other hand, Marcel Proust's position of Goncourtian style is recorded for posterity in his pastiche of the *Journal*, where it is noteworthy that most references are to Edmond alone.[29] The pastiche is, Proust points out, 'laudative en somme'.[30]

Proust's opinion of the Goncourts has been usefully summarised in the following way: 'ce qui, pour les Goncourt, sépare la littérature du reportage, c'est "l'effort d'écrire", qui se marque dans le rythme, la cadence des périodes, "l'epithète rare", le néologisme: l'écriture artiste'.[31] For both brothers, style was synonymous with *écriture*

---

[28] J.-K. Huysmans, *A Rebours*, ed. by Pierre Waldner (Paris: Garnier-Flammarion, 1978), p. 208.
[29] *A la recherche du temps perdu* [1913-27], ed. by Jean-Yves Tadié, Pléiade, 4 vols (Paris: Gallimard, 1987-89), IV, pp. 287-95. See also *ALR*, IV, p. 488, n. 3. Annick Bouillaguet has studied the pastiche in 'Proust lecteur des Goncourt: du pastiche satirique à l'imitation sérieuse', in *Les Frères Goncourt: art et écriture*, ed. by Jean-Louis Cabanès (Bordeaux: Presses universitaires de Bordeaux, 1997), pp. 339-48.
[30] 'Les Goncourt devant leurs cadets', in Marcel Proust, *Contre Sainte-Beuve, Pastiches et mélanges, Essais et articles*, ed. by Pierre Clarac, Pléiade (Paris: Gallimard, 1971), pp. 641-43 (p. 642).
[31] Jean-Yves Tadié, *Introduction à la vie littéraire du XIXe siècle* (Paris: Bordas, 1970), p.80.

artiste, a highly personalised language, verging on the mannerist, evolved by them and used by writers of all persuasions. Not a specifically Naturalist or Decadent trait, it crossed the boundaries of literary movements. Like the Impressionist painters of the nineteenth century who, to a large extent, neglected or rejected the moralising narrative function of art in favour of perception and immediacy, *écriture artiste* draws attention not so much to the object being described as to its sensory effect. Its focus is inexorably on surfaces. This 'impresionnisme modernement suggestif', as Jean Moréas refers to it in 'Le Symbolisme, un manifeste littéraire', is primarily interested in sensation and the sensual.[32]

A characteristic trait of *écriture artiste* is its treatment of time. Philippe Desan, in his introduction to *Germinie Lacerteux*, for example, speaks of the distinctiveness of its temporal focus: 'les Goncourt ne s'intéressent guère au mouvement et au temps. La problématique de leur roman se situe ailleurs. Les descriptions de l'instant présent, pris sur le vif, sont le véritable objet de leur expérimentation romanesque'.[33] The style draws on nominal syntax and precious vocabulary to create literary tableaux, but these tableaux are quite unlike Zola's. They freeze images into a perpetual present, an isolated moment that defies reproduction. In this respect, *écriture artiste* is indissociable from the mediation between Naturalism and Decadence. So-called types are presented in all their momentary specificity and in all their temporality. This has led Jeremy Wallace, who has compared the Goncourts and La Bruyère, to state that 'l'écriture artiste cherche avant tout à traduire les sensations fugaces et à les figer dans le temps'.[34] The fixity evoked here has a large part to play in the stasis present in Edmond de Goncourt's solo novels, where language is rarely a utilitarian communicative tool.

The downside of this privileging of temporality, or what some consider the Goncourts' Impressionism, others their Expressionism, is that it contains the seeds of its own destruction. When the effect itself is overvalued, when style no longer seeks to render that which appears

---

[32] *Les Premières armes du symbolisme*, ed. by Michael Pakenham (Exeter: University of Exeter Press, 1973), p. 36.

[33] (Paris: Librairie Générale Française, 1990), p. xxix.

[34] 'Les Goncourt, La Bruyère et l'art du portrait', *Les Cahiers Edmond et Jules de Goncourt*, 6 (1998), 74-94 (p. 86).

to be, a Decadent style is born. Language becomes all-important, an end in itself, and words become separated from their referents, making visions anything but 'real'. This much was recognised by one of the pioneering *fin de siècle* theoreticians of Decadence, Paul Bourget, who in 1881 questioned the production of effects and suggested that the realism behind impressions was not what art was about in a Decadent aesthetic. Bourget's interpretation is now famous in its own right and is written in a clear, concise style that is generally accepted as being in no way redolent of the one he was dissecting:

> Un style de décadence est celui où l'unité du livre se décompose pour laisser la place à l'indépendance de la page, où la page se décompose pour laisser la place à l'indépendance de la phrase, et la phrase se décompose pour laisser la place à l'indépendance du mot.[35]

Coupled with a diminishing concentration on plot and a shedding of Naturalist analytical apparatuses, the foregrounding of style – both formally and thematically – orients Edmond de Goncourt's novels towards the Decadence of the 1880s and 1890s. The link between this movement and the Goncourts' shared style is so clear to Louis Marquèze-Pouey that he has referred to their writing, in particular the lessening role of plot and the increased importance of artistic language for its own sake, as 'le style même de l'époque' (p. 103). A similar attitude is, unsurprisingly, more or less held by Edmond de Goncourt himself, who, in the 1884 preface to *Chérie*, confessed that he had attempted to rid the novel of intrigue in order to focus on psychological analysis, to write, in effect, an anti-novel. In his four solo novels, narrative is downgraded in favour of a conception of analysis that relies on the disintegration of the novelistic whole. Rather than recount a linear story, the novels depict fragments that are bound together by their very disparity and their very particularity, rather than by strict cause and effect associations. This heralds an almost unavoidable deviation towards a Decadent aesthetic, where *mimesis* is supplanted by *poesis* and where Naturalism is overtaken by an aestheticised version of itself. It also, perhaps, reaches into the twentieth century and, as Weir suggests, paves the way for Modernism

---

[35] *Essais de psychologie contemporaine: études littéraires*, ed. by André Guyaux (Paris: Gallimard, 1993), p. 14.

(p. 48). Much as the Dandy sought to create effects through outward appearance often to the detriment of the inner self, in *écriture artiste* linguistic sensation was valued because of its ability to erect a tantalising façade, a mirage of words.

Edmond de Goncourt's style very much participates in the repositioning of views of the novelistic ideal at the end of the century. His characters' heightened interest in artistic refinement, and the linguistic rarefaction through which this is expressed, was crystallised by authors like Huysmans, Lorrain, Mirbeau, Poictevin and Rodenbach. Innovations in poetry have also been attributed to *écriture artiste*.[36] One eminent literary critic of Naturalism views the move from the Goncourts' *écriture artiste* to Decadence as a natural progression, arguing that 'une prose *décadente* [est] issue de la prose *artiste*'.[37] Remy de Gourmont, who first met Edmond de Goncourt in 1884, does not discuss the Decadence of the Goncourts directly, but the language he uses to discuss their joint stylistic innovation and the lessons it teaches highlights certain elements that have correlations in the movement. This supports the argument that the Goncourts' aesthetic, continued and expanded by Edmond de Goncourt alone, contributed to the elaboration of the Decadent mode that reached its pinnacle at the end of the nineteenth century:

> Trouver des phrases que nul n'a encore faites, en même temps claires, harmonieuses, justes, vivantes, émondées de tout parasitisme oratoire, de tout lieu commun, des phrases où les mots, même les plus ordinaires, prennent, comme les notes en musique, une valeur de position, des phrases un peu tourmentées, greffées adroitement de ces incidents qui déconcertent, puis charment l'oreille et l'esprit lorsqu'on saisit le ton et le mécanisme de l'accord, des phrases qui se meuvent comme des êtres, oui, qui semblent vivre d'une vie délicieusement factice, comme des créations de magie.[38]

Unlike Bourget, de Gourmont's own sentence is slightly tortuous and more than a little artificial, though it does effectively promote the view that the Goncourts were witchdoctors of words, or – perhaps an equally suitable analogy for a Decadent age – snake charmers

---

[36] Stephan, p. 106 *passim*.
[37] Mitterand, *Le Regard et le signe*, p. 271.
[38] Remy de Gourmont, *Le Deuxième Livre des masques* [1898] (Paris: Mercure de France, 1917), p. 266.

mesmerising readers with their evocative, suggestive style. It is a self-contained style that requires immense concentration on the part of the reader. It evokes Mallarméan poetics in which analysis is only permitted insofar as it is poetic and stylistic, insofar as it does not contribute to an understanding of a linear whole.

It is in the no man's land between Edmond de Goncourt's novels and the joint Goncourt novels that the seesawing between Naturalism and Decadence can be found. In terms of plot development, narrativity, representations of speech and conceptions of language and art, *La Fille Elisa*, *Les Frères Zemganno*, *La Faustin* and *Chérie* announce the emergence of a new literature that eschews unity and comprehension (even readability, at times). Instead, the novels adopt an aesthetic derivative of Naturalism, but based on a modified vision of the artistic ideal. This new aesthetic revolves around the failure of language as a medium of communication, which is possible because the form of the novels becomes inseparable from the increasingly Decadent themes that they depict.

Nonetheless, even though the novels of the Goncourt brothers, in particular *Germinie Lacerteux*, were crucial in the elaboration of a Naturalist aesthetic, and even though Edmond de Goncourt's novels were published during what most critics agree to have been a period marked by the climax of Naturalism and the birth of Decadence, no major critique of Edmond de Goncourt's four novels in relation to Decadence, or the relationship between Naturalism and Decadence, has been carried out. This is surprising given that, as Matei Calinescu forcefully states: 'During the early 1880s the Goncourt brothers themselves came to be regarded – and this was *before* the specifically "decadentist" movement started in 1886 – as *decadents*, and even more than that, as the foremost representatives of a contemporary decadent style'.[39] Moreover, the fact that Edmond de Goncourt was not averse to Decadence, or at least to Decadents, is attested to by the fact that two of the first ten members of the *Académie Goncourt*, who took up their seats in 1903 and who were chosen by him, are associated not only with Naturalism, but, also, with Decadence: Huysmans and Mirbeau. On top of this, many authors associated with

---

[39] *Five Faces of Modernity: Modernism, Avant-Garde, Decadence, Kitsch, Postmodernism* (Durham: Duke University Press, 1987), p. 169.

the Decadent movement and its move away from 'the masses', in both subject matter and audience, regularly attended Goncourt's weekly salon, the 'Grenier'. These included well-known dandy figures such as Reynaldo Hahn, Mallarmé, Montesquiou, Lorrain, Loti and Rodenbach.

Naturalism, Decadence, Fin de siècle

The problems of periodisation at the end of the nineteenth century are amplified by the common usage of the term *fin de siècle* to refer to the years 1880-1900. It has been successfully put forward that the term designates both a general and a specific period. Although *fin de siècle* can refer to any end of century, it is commonly employed to denote the end of the nineteenth century in France.

> Quand nous employons la formule fin de siècle, nous pensons d'abord à une époque précise: les années qui ont précédé la fin du XIXe siècle et qui ont été marquées par une esthétique précise, des débats et des options spécifiques. Nous confondons volontiers par ailleurs fin de siècle et décadence.[40]

That *fin de siècle* and Decadence are often treated as one and the same is apparent in one perhaps deliberately restricted view which sees the *fin de siècle* as beginning in 1892 when the *Rougon-Macquart* series was drawn to a close: 'La fin de siècle commence en 1892 avec l'élaboration des *Trois Villes* qui fait de Zola un romancier du présent'.[41] Present-day indecision over the terms Decadence and *fin de siècle* can be ascribed to the fact that both were in use in the late 1800s, the latter being referred to in the *Voltaire* as early as 4 May 1886, as well as in an 1888 play by Jouvenot and Micard.[42] Thus, not only has *fin de siècle* come to mean a specific period in the evolution of literature from Realism to modernity in the 1880s and 1890s, it is

---

[40] J.M. Goulemot and others, 'Les Siècles ont-ils une fin?', in *Fins de siècle: colloque de Tours 4-6 juin 1985*, ed. by Pierre Citti (Bordeaux: Presses universitaires de Bordeaux, 1990), pp. 17-33 (p. 21).
[41] Bertrand Marchal, 'Fin de siècle et temps nouveaux ou l'évangile selon Zola', in Citti, pp. 325-36 (p. 335).
[42] Daniel Mortier, 'Quelques questions posées au concept "fin de siècle"', in Ponnau, pp. 336-43 (p. 336).

also used to qualify novels and other artistic productions exhibiting thematic and stylistic tendencies of the period.

However, whereas Decadence corresponds to a particular aesthetic position or movement, for all intents and purposes *fin de siècle* corresponds to a fertile period of French literature in which movements rose and fell as regularly as tides. This is underlined in the (unintentionally ridiculous) title of Anatole Baju's 1892 publication, whose name more than adequately reflects the chaos of the late-nineteenth-century literary field: *L'Anarchie littéraire: les différentes écoles: les décadents, les symbolistes, les romaines, les instrumentistes, les magiques, les magnifiques, les anarchistes, les socialistes, etc.* The et cetera, here, speaks volumes. Another contemporary attempt at classification, found in Jules Huret's *Entretiens sur l'évolution littéraire* (1891), is equally entertaining in this regard. Amongst others, Huret opts for the headings Magi, Symbolists and Decadents, Naturalists (in which we find Goncourt), Neo-Realists, Parnassiens, and, somewhat incongruously within this frenzy of labelling, so-called Independents. These two accounts demonstrate the wealth of names used at the time to designate groupings of authors.

It is simplest, therefore, to consider the Decadent movement as forming a more or less coherent, though by no means exclusive, whole in the closing decades of the nineteenth century (the *fin de siècle*) and to explore the evolution of Decadent themes across the century, as this approach does not preclude Decadent themes or styles being present in the works of earlier writers, including the Goncourts. Thus, where Weir has argued that *Germinie Lacerteux* is both Naturalist and Decadent, this study will argue that it is in the *fin de siècle* novels of Edmond de Goncourt, written in the years around 1880, that the essential themes and styles of Decadence are elaborated. Although *Germinie Lacerteux* does elevate a base subject to the status of art, and does treat literature in a painterly fashion, it is with the advent of new, more aristocratic subjects that the elder Goncourt truly consecrates his works, both stylistically and thematically, to the cult of art. It is in the later novels that the characters themselves, who are no longer drawn exclusively from the Parisian working classes, pursue the cult of art, thereby mirroring the concerns of their author.

Late-nineteenth-century literature crystallised themes present much earlier. For instance, the cherished theme of disguise fascinated not only the Decadents, but Naturalists and earlier authors such as Champfleury, who, in the wake of Hoffmann, wrote several pantomimes while proclaiming the superiority of 'truth' over 'fiction' (Champfleury was also, of course, one of the first theorists of Realism as a genre). Subsuming Champfleury under the heading 'Decadent', however, ignores the particularities of his period and ignores the differences in treatment of the themes over the century. Likewise, considering an author such as Théophile Gautier as a Decadent – which would be possible if disguise, ennui, and masquerade were thematic requirements – ignores the changes in the literary field that took place in the second half of the century, and in particular ignores the democratisation, expansion and modernisation of French society and literature after 1870 and the birth of the Third Republic. Crucially, it ignores the complex relationship between Naturalism and Decadence. Nor does it take into account the particularities of Decadent style, such as the disintegration of syntax and increasing interest in foreign and ancient vocabularies that were distant from the everyday realities of the average late-nineteenth-century reader.

Fin de siècle civilisation was depicted in literature as decaying and certain themes and tones were invariably favoured over others, notably escape from reality, *ennui*, mysticism, Satanism, pessimism, idealism, sexual enslavement, eccentricity, and the primacy of art and artifice. A novel is not automatically Decadent for treating these themes, however, for they can be found in works considered to embody Naturalism. Zola's *Nana* (1880), for example, is the ultimate tale of sexual enslavement.[43] It portrays Decadence in a literal sense insofar as it tells the story of Nana's decline and fall, but importantly, this decline and fall is not aestheticised, and it is the aestheticisation of decline that fascinates Decadents. This illustrates the extent to which the two movements are interrelated, how works that are Naturalist are in many ways already Decadent, and how, to borrow David Baguley's term, Naturalism is 'entropic'. Naturalism deals with Decadent themes, Decadence with Naturalist ones: the relationship is symbiotic in more ways than one. Max Nordau, for instance, declared Zola, considered by many to be the quintessential Naturalist, a degenerate

---

[43] On Zola and Decadence, see Antoine Compagnon, 'Zola dans la décadence', *Les Cahiers naturalistes*, 67 (1993), 211-22.

author.[44] Nevertheless, by dissociating such themes from a pseudo-scientific Naturalist framework, Decadence is born. Effects are no longer only of interest because of their causes. As Marion Schmid has commented:

> It is undoubtedly in their shared obsession with degeneracy that Decadence and Naturalism overlap most – the crucial difference being that whilst Decadent writers accept and even celebrate degeneracy as a prerequisite of artistic refinement, Naturalist writers denounce it as a threat to civilization.[45]

In Decadent literature, the mechanisms and themes of degeneration are aestheticised and glorified. This rift is otherwise manifest in the rejection of the unrefined working classes as subject matter, in favour of refined artists and rarefied language.

The distance separating observed worlds and artificial ones, Naturalism and Decadence, is the focus here. An author like Edmond de Goncourt, who so valued both the *document humain* and individual expression in the guise of *écriture artiste*, must have been acutely aware of the constraints of the Naturalist ethos, or indeed of any system that became established and, as a result, risked becoming formulaic and programmatic. With this in mind, the gap that opens between the *document humain* and Decadence, in both language and themes will be probed. Beginning with paratextual writings, moving from there to a study of the necessities of documentation, and finishing with an analysis of various forms of linguistic paralysis, the present study intends to simultaneously explore how the imaginary interacts with the observation of nature and ascertain how the mimetic 'reality' of *La Fille Elisa*, *Les Frères Zemganno*, *La Faustin*, and *Chérie* is jeopardised by changing aesthetic values. Edmond de Goncourt's largely forgotten novels display many symptoms of Decadence, though they are rooted in Naturalism. In this respect, they are one of the chief intellectual and artistic examples of the literary evolution towards Decadence at the *fin de siècle* and deserve to be reappraised.

---

[44] See pp. 473-506, 'Zola and His School', of Max Nordau, *Degeneration* (Lincoln and London: University of Nebraska Press, 1993).
[45] 'From Decadence to Health: Zola's *Paris*', *Romance Studies*, 18-2 (2000), 99-111 (p. 103-04).

PARATEXTS

TITLES: NOVEL TRANSFORMATIONS

> A style means, among other things, a name; one clue to a writer's style is how he names his writings; and we have much personal documentation, casting light upon that process in some important cases, and even listing alternates considered and rejected. The prospect is not uninviting.[1]

The Goncourts grouped their biographies of eighteenth-century women into categories according to profession. They did a similar thing with their fiction. In the 1866 edition of *Henriette Maréchal*, they sorted their novels into three almost Balzacian headings that each correspond to different social realities:

Artistes
Les Hommes de lettres
L'Atelier Langibout

Bourgeois
Renée Mauperin
Madame Tony-Fréneuse

Peuple
Sœur Philomène
Germinie Lacerteux

Of the works listed in *Henriette Maréchal*, the two texts yet to be written – *Madame Tony Fréneuse* and *L'Atelier Langibout* – were renamed before publication, perhaps even before writing commenced. In 1867, *L'Atelier Langibout* would become *Manette Salomon*, while *Madame Tony Fréneuse* was not written until 1883-84, by Edmond alone, with *Chérie* as its title.

On one level, this points to a continuity between those novels written pre- and post-1870, a continuity evidenced in another manner by *La Fille Elisa*, which was researched by both Goncourts and published only in 1877, seven years after Jules's death and in the same

---

[1] Harry Levin, 'The Title as Literary Genre', *Modern Language Review*, 72 (1977), xxiii-xxxvi (p. xxxv).

year as the publication of Zola's *L'Assommoir*. On another level, however, the title alterations accentuate changes in Edmond's ideological and aesthetic concerns. While title modifications emphasise coherence between the joint and solo works, the nature of the modifications that titles undergo differs pre- and post- 1870. In the post-1870 names there is, from the outset, less emphasis on social realities and Naturalist types. This difference bears witness to shifts in the focus of Edmond's novels compared to those jointly authored. These differences, in turn, are telling in terms of the transformation of the literary environment over the course of the brothers' forty-year career.

The Goncourts sometimes referred to their novels by vague phrases that are not properly speaking formal titles. There is a clear difference between the titles, working titles, and descriptive phrases variously employed by them to designate their work; for instance, vague phrases can be used to refer to a novel. The essential difference between descriptive, conversational names and the titles that the novels were eventually given is that the former do not form part of the consecrated work itself; they are not part of the fiction presented in the novel, but only serve to denote the book within the authors' private environment.

There are numerous examples of this type of designation in relation to the Goncourts. The only alternative name for *La Fille Elisa* (1877), for instance, is more akin to a subject heading, or a generic indication, than to the title of a novel – 'roman de la prostitution' – and dates from before 1870. *Madame Gervaisais* (1869), the last of the novels written by both brothers, and thus chronologically closest to *La Fille Elisa*, also has a similar name: 'roman de ma tante'. Likewise, *Chérie*, which had several incarnations before it was formally christened, is referred to on one occasion as a 'roman d'amour. Ce serait l'amour d'une femme du monde' (*Journal*, 1 Feb. 1865). This reference dates from before work on the novel had actually begun. These descriptive yet vague titles seem to date, for the most part, from before 1870. Nonetheless, they must be distinguished from working titles insofar as the latter may well enter into circulation in the public domain. Four years after being described as a 'roman d'amour', for example, *Chérie* was referred to in the *Journal* as *Femmes du monde* (22 Sept. 1869), a more legitimate example of a working title.

Pre-1870 Titles

The name changes in the novels written prior to Jules's death are in the order of general to particular and confirm specific thematic choices. Each working title corresponds either to a type – for example, the man of letters and the bourgeois woman – or to a place or a given environment – for example, a masked ball or an artist's studio – indicating that the novels will present either tableaux of these environments or generalised portraits representative of certain types of people. In other words, use of this kind of title implies that the novel depicts shared or common characteristics of that class or professional group which it names, much as the eponymous bar gave Zola's *L'Assommoir* its name (*L'Assommoir*, incidentally, is an interesting comparison, for it went from the particular – *La Simple vie de Gervaise Macquart* – to the general).

By casting aside the working title and its type-centred focus, and by choosing instead to use a proper name – normally the protagonist's – as a title, the thematic axis shifts: types are sidelined in favour of individuals. Characters are no longer explicitly linked to a specific type, and are no longer simply presented as examples of a given noxious behavioural pattern. This is true insofar as *L'Atelier Langibout* becomes *Les Artistes*, but never becomes *L'Artiste*; instead, it is renamed *Manette Salomon*, a title that recalls at the same time Manet and the kingdom of Solomon, and reflects two of the thematic concerns of the novels, art and anti-Semitism. *Manette Salomon*'s title change was a public one: upon serialisation in *Le Temps*, it was *L'Atelier Langibout*. The change occurred in November 1867, when the novel appeared in book form.[2] Other titles went through similar transformations. *La Bourgeoisie* became *La Jeune bourgeoise* (*Journal*, 13 July 1862), before the latter was abandoned in favour of a proper name: *Renée Mauperin*. The individual has priority over the type here, and in general, interest in the species wanes. However, even if the individual is prioritised over the type, the character cited in the title is implicitly an example of the type, only an underhanded or surreptitious example, for the initial category remains unknown to the reader. At the same time, the title character is an individual who

---

[2] 'Chronologie', *Journal*, I, p. lxxxvi.

stands alone outside category boundaries and whose name will become associated with the given fictional reality to which it has lent its name. As such, the title name, even the title character, enters empirical reality as a manner of designating the book, but also belongs to the fictional realm of the novel. The name in this case is a form of exchange in the literary marketplace, but also signifies within the work of fiction itself.

This general-to-particular pattern of title revision reflects a much wider tendency of nineteenth-century 'titrology' (*titrologie*) pinpointed by Christian Moncelet: 'le titre se "personnalise" assez généralement au XIXème siècle'.[3] The eponymous titles favoured by the Goncourts are a 'désignation factuelle la plus directe', naming as they do specific objects, persons or themes (they are thematic titles – Genette's example is *Madame Bovary*), rather than categories (poem, novel of the people, etc., which would fall under the designation rhematic).[4] Readers, however, are to a greater or lesser extent unaware of this alteration in focus as far as individual Goncourt novels are concerned.

The planned titles of the novels written by both the brothers – *L'Atelier Langibout/Les Artistes*, *La Bourgeoisie/La Jeune bourgeoise*, *Au Bal masqué/Henriette Maréchal* – were all modified before publication. They are examples of private alterations, a form of self-editing. *Les Hommes de lettres* (1860) is a curious exception to the general pattern, though it does not deviate so dramatically from the norm as to negate it. On the contrary, it elucidates a first evolution in the Goncourt *œuvre*. In the case of *Les Hommes de lettres*, the name was not changed until the re-edition of the novel in 1868 as *Charles Demailly*. Initially published as the more general *Les Hommes de lettres*, the change to *Charles Demailly* took place wholly within the public domain. The book was openly renamed and reclassified. The reasons for this modification could be multiple – appealing to a wider audience, demonstrating how the authors' view of the novel had changed in reaction to the reception of the work, etc. – but it is undeniable that by making the choice public, the reader's interpretation of the novel is affected. As Charles Grivel comments in

---

[3] *Essai sur le titre en littérature et dans les arts* (Paris: BOF, 1972), p. 34.
[4] Gérard Genette, *Seuils* (Paris: Seuil, 1987), pp.74, 76, 82-85.

his theoretical analysis of titles, '*Le titre affiche la nature du texte*, et donc le genre de lecture qui lui convient'.[5] Titles tell the reader how the text can be read.

Regardless of the fact that *Les Hommes de lettres* was modified publicly, the change was still in the direction of general to specific. Jacques Noiray has argued that its new name invokes Charles Lassailly, a friend of Balzac's: 'Car le nom et la destinée du personnage éponyme rappellent de trop près le nom et la fin de Charles Lassailly, ami et collaborateur de Balzac, mort fou en 1843, pour qu'il s'agisse d'une simple coïncidence'.[6] This suggests that the revision is essentially a means of situating the novel within a 'real' world, a means of making the entire novel a *document humain* of external reality, rather than just a non-specific fictional *mise-en-scène* of men of letters.

That *Charles Demailly* was originally released as *Les Hommes de lettres* in 1860 ties it to the quasi-Balzacian classification seen in the third edition of *Henriette Maréchal*, and announces a shift towards a Naturalism that would culminate in Zola's *Rougon-Macquart* series. Genette touches on the difference between these two systems of classification, explaining that whilst Balzac hesitated and created the structure of *La Comédie humaine* as he wrote the novels, Zola's master plan was elaborated from the beginning of his project, even if it was subject to modification.[7] The *Henriette Maréchal* schema is midway between Balzac and Zola. It presents an *œuvre* that is from the outset simultaneously divided into types that the authors wished to study in their environment – 'Bourgeois', 'Peuple', 'Artistes' – yet evolved as individual titles (and, by extension, novels) were modified over time, and other new works were added to the overall structure.

---

[5] *Production de l'intérêt romanesque: un état du texte (1870-1880), un essai de constitution de sa théorie* (Paris: Mouton, 1973), p. 168.

[6] 'Déconstruction du romanesque: la subversion du modèle balzacien dans *Charles Demailly*', in Cabanès, pp. 167-80 (p. 167).

[7] *Seuils*, pp. 59-60.

Pre-1870 title modifications	
Publication Title	**Alternate Title**
Sœur Philomène (1861)	N/A
Renée Mauperin (1864)	*La Bourgeoisie*
	La Jeune Bourgeoise
Germinie Lacerteux (1864)	N/A
Henriette Maréchal (1865)	*Au bal masqué*
Manette Salomon (1867)	*L'Atelier Langibout*
	Les Artistes
Charles Demailly (1868)	*Les Hommes de lettres*
Madame Gervaisais (1869)	'roman de ma tante'

The central difference between these two authors and the Goncourts, however, is the presence of what could be termed a 'master title' to which the subsidiary titles conform. This stands despite the fact that Balzac's master title was only found retrospectively, in 1841-42.[8] Where many of Balzac's and Zola's works can be designated under the headings *La Comédie humaine* and *Les Rougon-Macquart* (even *Les Trois villes*), the Goncourts have a seemingly disparate collection of novels which were only regrouped publicly at one point, in February 1866, and then only on the *faux titre* of the third edition of a largely forgotten play. The news was by no means screamed from the rooftops. The Goncourts had a plan, but they had no genealogy, no family name for their *œuvre*. Whatever grandiose structure the authors had intended to give to their collected novels, it remained (and has remained) more or less concealed from the reader.

Three of the novels written in the 1860s do not appear to have had more than one title, descriptive phrases excluded: *Sœur Philomène*, *Germinie Lacerteux*, and *Madame Gervaisais*. The common ground between these three vastly different books is that the eponymous titles name the heroines of the narratives. Even if 'sœur' and 'madame' are not given names, they are the titles by which the protagonists are

---

[8] The title *La Comédie humaine* first appeared in the July 1842 preface to an edition of complete works. The evolution of the structure of *La Comédie humaine* is outlined in P.-G. Castex, 'L'Univers de *La Comédie humaine*', in Honoré de Balzac, *La Comédie humaine* [1831-47], ed. by P.-G. Castex and others, Pléiade, 12 vols (Paris: Gallimard, 1976-81), I, pp. ix-xix.

known in their fictional world. Of the remaining three joint novels, two of the titles evoke people with whom the Goncourts would have been familiar, Charles Lassailly (*Charles Demailly*) and Edouard Manet (*Manette Salomon*). The use of such names suggests a desire to merge fiction and reality, and this desire corresponds to the aesthetic beliefs of the period, where realism tended to be valued over other qualities. Furthermore, each title is bipartite: none diverges from the forename (or title)/surname model, and all of the modifications before Jules's death, from both working title and private descriptive phrase to consecrated title, move from the general to the particular. The situation is comparatively different as far as the post-1870 novels are concerned.

Post-1870 Titles

Strictly speaking, *La Fille Elisa* (1877) is the only post-Jules fictional work to which both authors actively and knowingly contributed: research was carried out in two main stages in the 1860s, and composition took place over the following decade. This is not to say that pre-1870 sources were not used in the later novels, for they were; but in this case it was Edmond alone who selected them and composed the stories. The idea for *La Fille Elisa* stems from 1862; the name Elisa stems from 1868-69. This much is known thanks to Robert Ricatte's intricately detailed *La Genèse de 'La Fille Elisa'* where he writes: 'Déjà, le 10 mars 1869, […] les voici occupés à saisir tous les gestes de l'accusé qu'ils pourront prêter à leur héroïne, déjà baptisée Elisa'.[9] Caution is called for, however. Despite the fact that the heroine's name was apparently settled on at this stage, it remains uncertain that this was the actual title of the novel, even if it is eponymous. The title *La Fille Elisa* first appears in the *Journal* in 1871 (24 Feb.) when Edmond confesses to being bitten by the urge to write. Tellingly, the novel he wished to sink his teeth into was '*La Fille Elisa*, ce livre que nous devions écrire, lui et moi, après *Madame Gervaisais*.' The fact that the desire to write is not simply a desire to write a novel about prostitute prisoners, but to write *La Fille Elisa*,

---

[9] (Paris: PUF, 1960), p. 18.

implies that the title was decided prior to his brother's death. The next direct reference to the novel occurs at the beginning of May 1875, when Alphonse Daudet mentions it in a letter as a book that is missing from Edmond's repertoire: '*La Fille Elisa*, et un roman de high life [*Chérie* doubtless], ces deux notes manquent à votre œuvre'.[10] This was almost certainly a means of encouraging his friend to write a novel that he had previously discussed, but it could also indicate that Daudet was aware of the framework within which Goncourt wished to operate. The prostitute novel is equally invoked by name by Flaubert, who, in a letter dated 31 December 1876, writes, presumably aware of the double entendre: 'Et, entre autres souhaits, que *La Fille Elisa* vous apporte beaucoup de gaieté!'.[11]

Post-1870 title modifications	
Publication Title	**Alternate Title**
La Fille Elisa (1877)	'roman de la prostitution'
Les Frères Zemganno (1879)	*Deux clowns* *Les Frères Bendigo*
La Faustin (1882)	*Le Théâtre* *Les Actrices* (1856)
Chérie (1884)	*Madame Tony Fréneuse* *Femmes du monde* 'roman d'amour' *Tony-Fréneuse* *Mlle Tony Fréneuse* *La Petite fille du maréchal*

In many respects, *La Fille Elisa* is the most atypical of the Goncourt novels, both pre- and post-1870: it was written partly by Jules, its title was in all likelihood fixed before writing commenced, and it is the only *roman-à-thèse*. Nor should it be ignored that its title qualifies the proper name it contains, by specifying that the eponymous Elisa is a 'fille', a prostitute. This links the individual to a type in a manner quite dissimilar to pre-1870 titles – 'sister' being a slightly more polite form of address than 'prostitute'. It is,

---

[10] *Corres. Gonc-Daud*, letter 13, May 1875, p. 23.
[11] *Corres. Flaub-Gonc*, letter 194, p. 253.

additionally, the only one of Edmond de Goncourt's fictional works not to have its title modified. In spite of these specificities, or perhaps because of them, the themes *La Fille Elisa* presents – particularly that of silence – are central to an understanding of the solo novels.

Both brothers contributed in one manner or another to *La Fille Elisa*, but their individual contributions are less clear in the three later novels. There is no concrete evidence that *Les Frères Zemganno* was a novel both siblings intended to write. As early as 1859 references to the circus are to be found in the *Journal*,[12] but the novel itself is only alluded to in 1877. This delay corresponds to the publication dates of Edmond's novels: *La Fille Elisa* appeared in 1877, *Les Frères Zemganno* in 1879, during which interval it would be safe to assume that the circus novel was being written. In October 1877, Flaubert inquired after his friend's 'histoire d'un clown […] ou plutôt ce roman sur les clowns' and Daudet wrote to Goncourt of 'vos clowns, vos clowns'.[13] On one occasion, the surviving brother refers to his novel as *Deux Clowns* (*Journal*, 29 July 1878). Did he intend this as a title, or was it simply an expedient way of referring to his work, as Flaubert referred to *Salammbô* as *Carthage*? Or is it a reference to Balzac's *La Rabouilleuse*, which was originally called *Les Deux Frères*?[14] In December of the same year, another *Journal* entry – on the 10th – baptises the novel *Les Frères Bendigo*, a name it would keep for several months.

Goncourt was some way into drafting the story before it was given its definitive title. It would appear that this was because he hesitated over the ultimate name, and that he in fact sought advice from a fellow writer on the matter, if the following note from Alphonse Daudet is anything to go by: 'Je suis si bien fait à Bendigo que je n'en vois plus d'autre. Zemganno a l'air fabriqué'.[15] This was apparently the right response. On 12 March 1879, Goncourt wrote to Julia Daudet and on

---

[12] The Goncourts confide: 'Nous pensons à faire sur toutes les choses de la société une satire, un roman philosophique, dans les trucs bêtes d'une féerie de cirque' (*Journal*, 28 Oct. 1859), though it does not seem that work on this project ever started in earnest.

[13] *Corres. Flaub-Gonc*, letter 201, 9 Oct. 1877, p. 259; *Corres. Gonc-Daud*, letter 71, mid-July 1878, p. 58.

[14] Maurice Hélin, 'Les livres et leurs titres', *Marche romane*, 6-3/4 (1956), 139-46 (p. 139, n. 3).

[15] *Corres. Gonc-Daud*, letter 82, Feb. 1879, p. 64.

17 March 1879 he wrote to Flaubert, referring in both letters to *Les Frères Zemganno*.[16]

For the first time in the Goncourt novels, a particular to particular title revision takes place, indicating an attention to detail and specific individualities which were not as pronounced in previous adjustments. The name Bendigo was the pseudonym of the English boxer William Thompson[17] and so, after much deliberation and dithering, Goncourt eventually settled on a curious and colourful name that 'a l'air fabriqué'. He chose a name that sounded false and unreal over a name that might have been recognised as representing a historical figure, and might consequently have added to the realism of the novel, as is the case with *La Fille Elisa*, where the name rather fittingly recalls 'la plus grande marchande de chair humaine de notre temps, Elisa, la Farcy II' (*Journal*, 26 March, 1858). Instead, the title of the 1879 novel conjures exotic images by means of a word that is phonetically unusual. In the story itself, a similar awareness is displayed: the clown brothers change their name from Bescapé to Zemganno. The title places emphasis on the siblings as extraordinary artists as opposed to ordinary French brothers. The modifications that lead to the title *Les Frères Zemganno* illustrate, to a great extent, Edmond de Goncourt's changing aesthetic concerns over the span of his career, as well as an evolution between the collective works and the solo works, in which there is more emphasis put on 'ce qui a l'air fabriqué'.

While not announced in *Henriette Maréchal*, the idea of penning a novel dealing with the world of theatre had long been mulled over by the Goncourt brothers. In 1859, this novel is referred to as *Les Actrices*, and in the following year, it is identified as *Le Théâtre*. *La Faustin* emanates from *Le Théâtre* and *Les Actrices*, but the latter was itself published as *Armande* in 1892. It is thus in and of itself a fine example of a Goncourtian title change.[18] Between 1862 and 1877, there is little evidence of thought given to the project. By the time

---

[16] *Corres. Gonc-Daud*, letter 83, p. 65; *Corres Flaub-Gonc*, letter 208, p. 267.
[17] See *Corres. Gonc-Daud*, p. 64, n. 2.
[18] See in this regard Dottin-Orsini's fine article '*La Faustin*, les paons blancs et l'agonie sardonique', in Cabanès, pp. 247-60. To clarify, *Les Actrices* was a novella written by the Goncourt brothers in 1856 and re-released by Edmond in 1892 with the new title, *Armande*. See Edmond and Jules de Goncourt, *Les Actrices (Armande)*, ed. by Mireille Dottin-Orsini (Toulouse: Editions ombres, 2000), pp. 21-22.

Edmond de Goncourt was again smitten with the idea, its name had reverted to *Les Actrices*. From the moment composition started, however, the single eponymous title that the novel had was *La Faustin*. There is a visible lurch from a subject-related title to a role-related title, which is suitable, given La Faustin's profession as actress. The fact that the story's title changed so frequently suggests that the so long as it remained an idea, its name vacillated between two imprecise appellations. In 1880, after *La Fille Elisa* and *Les Frères Zemganno* had been completed and Goncourt had time to devote to his next project, the novel became known under its consecrated title: 'Aujourd'hui, au milieu d'une forte migraine, *La Faustin* fait tout à coup irruption dans ma cervelle, avec accompagnement de fièvre littéraire' (*Journal*, 27 Aug. 1880).

Of special note in Edmond de Goncourt's two final books is the name chosen for the main character, and, therefore, the titles. The protagonist of the penultimate novel is Juliette Faustin, regularly referred to her by the epithet 'La Faustin'. As Sylvie Thorel-Cailleteau observes, 'le roman ne s'appelle pas *Juliette Faustin*'.[19] The 'la' links the woman to her profession. The addition of the article transforms the person into a thing; she is a part rather than a person, even though grammatically adding an article to a name is a fairly common way of referring to famous actresses. 'La Faustin', however, is more a legendary symbol than a Naturalist type, as Jean Richepin boldly notes: 'Ma foi, tant pis! Je lâche le mot. Elle est un symbole'.[20] Such an iconic nickname immediately summons comparisons with the notorious Faust. Comparisons with Faust, in turn, tie the novel to a long tradition of Faustian literature, by content or only by name, ranging from Elizabethan and German Romantic output through to Louis Bouilhet's *Faustine* (1864), and beyond into the twentieth century with Thomas Mann's *Doctor Faustus* (1947). Due to this observable tradition, the reader is alerted to the possible ruin of Juliette Faustin's soul: Faust is a conjurer, Juliette an actress, and both deal with the art of illusion to the detriment of reality. Moreover, the association between the names Jules (as in, de Goncourt) and Juliette

---

[19] *La Tentation du roman sur rien*, p. 203.
[20] 'Autour de *La Faustin*', *Gil Blas*, 1 February 1882.

alerts the reader to the perils of the Goncourts' own crusade in the name of artistic creation.[21]

In much the same way, the name Chérie is a diminutive that bestows certain qualities on the character, not the least of which is preciousness. The emblematic name, Chérie, imposes itself upon the novel, because the protagonist is presented as a creation based on the letters of Goncourt's female correspondents ('Cher M. de Goncourt'). It is a private name, as the women's letters were private. It is also a rather intimate expression of affection (cf. Colette's *Chéri*); Chérie could evoke all women, or any woman, but never simultaneously, due to its private nature. It is, in short, a beacon on the title page of the novel, warning the reader that the narrative deals with a closed and private world.

Chérie (1884) is the only text of Edmond's to be publicly forecast in *Henriette Maréchal*, yet nearly twenty years passed before the book came to be written, and, over this period, it took on several different forms. Referred to as *Madame Tony-Fréneuse* in *Henriette Maréchal*, the novel, as already mentioned, was referred to once, in 1869, by the title *Femmes du monde* (*Journal*, 22 Sept. 1869). That the author had decided to modify the title, and by extension the novel, is suggested by the fact that in 1878, six years before its publication and twelve years after its announcement, it is noted in the *Journal*: 'ma pensée allant au plan d'un roman qui raconterait la vie d'une jeune fille du second Empire' (14 Oct. 1878). This is without doubt a more precise guideline than simply writing a novel that falls under the heading 'Bourgeois'. Still, despite the fact that between 1878 and 1884 the *Journal* is teeming with information and anecdotes that would eventually contribute to Goncourt's ultimate novel, it was not until 1883 that the title was finalised. In 1882, Edmond notes: 'aujourd'hui, au milieu de mon malaise, écrit le titre du premier chapitre de mon roman de *Tony-Fréneuse* (titre provisoire)' (*Journal*, 16 Feb. 1882). At this stage, Tony-Fréneuse was a character in the novel, but her status was subject to ongoing change. This is another case of a particular to particular modification.

---

[21] See subsection 'Jules et Juliette' in Mireille Dottin-Orsini, 'Les Frères Goncourt et le "roman des actrices"', *La Revue des sciences humaines*, 259 (2000), 55-74 (pp. 70-74).

Through the title, it is possible to glimpse the processes of creation that culminated in the final novel. When compared to the details provided in *Henriette Maréchal*, it is significant that the surname is no longer preceded by a title, *Madame* having been dropped. This absence coincides with the first step in moving from a novel of a *femme du monde* to a novel depicting *filles du monde*. In fact, in 1884 Louis Desprez believed the book was called *La Petite-fille du maréchal*: 'Bientôt paraîtra un quatrième et peut-être dernier roman, une étude des plus nuancées qui a pour titre: *La Petite-fille du maréchal*'.[22] Two months after *Tony-Fréneuse* was announced as the provisional title, there was yet another refinement: the name Tony-Fréneuse remained unchanged, but the *Mademoiselle* replaced the original *Madame*. Goncourt told Alphonse Daudet: 'Oui, vraiment, *Mademoiselle Tony-Fréneuse*, ce n'est pas commode à faire, et je tourne autour du bouquin, sans oser entrer dedans'.[23] The title became more and more precise, and the main character grew ever younger. Eventually, Chérie usurped Tony-Fréneuse's position: the latter was relegated to a secondary status in the novel while the former assumed the title role. In June 1883, ten months before the book appeared on the shelves, Daudet wrote to Goncourt stating that 'l'on parlera beaucoup de *Chérie*'. Goncourt made it known that he wished, in writing *Chérie*, to write a novel devoid of plot and intrigues. The slow elimination of the proper name from the title of the novel confirms this desire, by giving the reader fewer and fewer points of reference. There are undoubtedly few greater proofs of an absence of story as the absence of individual identity.

In both the solo and joint works of the Goncourts, titles are not necessary to the writing of the novel, but they are central to an understanding of the finished product. While it cannot be concluded that the Goncourts needed a definitive name before work on a text could commence, it is evident that in the case of *Chérie*, for example, the title was modified as the central idea of the novel became more finely tuned. What seems vital in pre-1870 works is the category into which the novel falls, as is demonstrated by the preponderance of general to particular, or rhematic to thematic, changes. As concerns

---

[22] *L'Evolution naturaliste* (Paris: Tresse, 1884), p. 117.
[23] *Corres. Gonc-Daud*, letter 142, 29 April 1882, p. 103.

the question of continuity between the two halves of the Goncourt *œuvre*, the choice of subject matter, more so than the choice of title, connects the joint works to the solo ones. As far as post-1870 works are concerned, only one novel, *Chérie*, is projected in *Henriette Maréchal*, and it did not retain the title originally forecast. One other novel – *La Fille Elisa* – was planned by both Goncourts, and kept its name, perhaps because it was decided upon relatively early in the creative process. The remaining two novels – *Les Frères Zemganno* and *La Faustin* – deal with subjects dear to both brothers, but are solely Edmond's work, and thus the evolution of their titles is pertinent to a study of the elder brother's aesthetic. In the joint works, the title modifications are in the order of rhematic to thematic, and are always eponymous. Following Jules's death, titles are still chosen to reflect the central character of the novel, but they reflect a change in emphasis and a move away from strict representations of reality. *Les Frères Zemganno* replaces a title that designates an actual being, Bendigo; *La Faustin* has symbolic rather than realist resonance; and *Chérie*, while being the name of the protagonist, is also an intimate, yet universal, name, a 'nom de pure caresse' (*Chérie*, p. 32). Moreover, the post-1870 titles do not follow the bipartite formula of pre-1870 novels.

Conclusion

What remains to be undertaken is a comparative study of mid- to late-nineteenth-century *titrologie*, in order to ascertain how titles and title changes reflect the dominant Naturalist literary aesthetic, and tensions within this position. One important point is clear: whether representative of empirical beings or of imaginary creations, every Goncourt title is eponymous, a tendency that is almost unique to them. Although the choice of eponymous titles fits into a general pattern of nineteenth-century *titrologie* – earlier authors, including Balzac, Champfleury, Sand and Stendhal all use names – it in no way exactly mirrors the choices of Edmond de Goncourt's or his brother's contemporaries. Zola uses eponymous titles for certain works, but these are limited in number. *Thérèse Raquin* (1867) and *Madeleine Férat* (1868) are pre-*Rougon-Macquart* titles. *Madeleine Férat*, though, was originally serialised as *La Honte*. Apart from *Nana*, those *Rougon-Macquart* titles that do use names qualify them, as is apparent in *La Faute de l'abbé Mouret* (1875), *Son excellence Eugène Rougon* (1876), and *Le Docteur Pascal* (1893). Titles of works like *La Joie de vivre* (1884) and *Germinal* (1885) never focus on one character. Alternate titles included: for *La Joie de vivre*, *La Misère du monde*, *La Vallée des larmes* and *La Sombre Mort*; and for *Germinal*, *Le Sol qui brûle*, *Château branlant* and *La Maison qui craque*. Huysmans, before writing Decadent novels like *A Rebours* (1884) and *Là-bas* (1891), made use of eponymous titles like *Marthe: histoire d'une fille* (1876) and *Les Sœurs Vatard* (1879).

The titles of Edmond de Goncourt's novels bear witness to a desire to focus on individual realities, and not necessarily 'realistic' realities, over Naturalist categorisation of typical models of behaviour. The differences in the manner in which titles are modified in joint and solo works reveal important clues as to how his aesthetic concerns evolved after 1870.

Prefaces and Literary History

> Oui, oui, mon frère et moi avons mené un mouvement littéraire qui emportera tout, un mouvement qui sera aussi grand au moins que le mouvement romantique.
> – Edmond de Goncourt, *Journal*, 31 March 1877

The Goncourts, particularly Edmond, long asserted that they were 'chefs d'école'; yet, despite their bravado, they never wrote a manifesto proper. In this sense, their prefaces replace a more formal statement of literary aims. Edmond and Jules wrote six novels between 1860 and 1869. Of these, only one – *Germinie Lacerteux* – contained an original preface. Edmond's solo novels, on the other hand, are all preceded by prefaces. That he deemed these writings to be works of intrinsic value, outside any association with the novels in which they appeared, is proven by the fact that in 1888 they were collectively published in *Préfaces et manifestes littéraires*.

The theories expounded in the prefaces are of interest because they reflect the turbulence of the contemporary literary field, where one movement – Naturalism – was reaching its apex and others were being spawned. They were written at what Juin has called 'un moment crucial de l'évolution du naturalisme'.[1] Because of this upheaval, the Goncourt prefaces form part of a discourse on the evolution of literature and illuminate the transformation of Edmond's post-1870 aesthetic. Through continuous intertextual references, they furnish readings of the late-nineteenth-century literary scene and the author's position within it, rather than provide authoritative readings of the novels they allegedly introduce. They transmit a theory of literary history and a doctrine of literary creation to readers and writers alike. The upshot of this transmission was to guarantee not only a reading, but to encourage future writing that broke with established norms. To accomplish this, the prefaces function as both defences of the Goncourts' past works and offensives geared at consolidating the

---

[1] Edmond and Jules de Goncourt, *Préfaces et manifestes littéraires*, ed. by Hubert Juin (Geneva: Slatkine, 1980), p. 7.

future position of their author and initiating changes in the literary field.

The foremost critical study of prefaces is Gérard Genette's *Seuils* (*Paratexts* in English), which analyses them from philosophical, philological, historical, and cultural angles in order to determine their textual status. Using Genette's classification, the Goncourt prefaces would be authentic, authorial and assumptive, which is to say that the preface-writer is the author of both the primary text and the original preface but that 'the author feels no need at all to state positively what goes without saying; for him to speak implicitly of the text as his own is enough'.[2] In authorial prefaces, the prefacer's textual authority is born of his dual role as both fiction and non-fiction writer.

There are grounds for arguing that this authorial power was increased in the nineteenth century due to a faith in science and consequent respect for non-fiction. As Teresa Bridgeman points out in relation to Zola's prefaces, the positivist celebration of science meant that an aura of authority was attached to the author who linked himself to the supposedly more analytically rigorous task of writing non-fiction.[3] The 1877 preface to *L'Assommoir* is a fine example of this: after partial serialisation, Zola countered critics by questioning why they took issue with the language of his novel when no one grumbled about the existence of dictionaries devoted to the same language. This allowed him to align his work as author to that of a historian of language: 'ma volonté était de faire un travail purement philologique, que je crois d'un vif intérêt historique et social'.[4] Elsewhere, in *Thérèse Raquin* (1867), his task is more scientific: 'J'ai simplement fait sur deux corps vivants le travail analytique que les chirurgiens font sur des cadavres'.[5]

Since prefaces are discourses on fiction, rather than part of the fictions themselves, they benefit from this faith in scientific and social

---

[2] *Paratexts: Thresholds of Interpretation*, trans. by Jane E. Lewin (Cambridge: CUP, 1997), p. 184.

[3] *Negotiating the New in the French Novel: Building Contexts for Fictional Worlds* (London and New York: Routledge, 1998), p. 103.

[4] *Les Rougon-Macquart: histoire naturelle et sociale d'une famille sous le Second Empire*, ed. by Armand Lanoux and Henri Mitterand, Pléiade, 5 vols (Paris, Gallimard, 1960), II, p. 373.

[5] *Œuvres complètes*, ed. by Henri Mitterand, 15 vols (Paris, Cercle du livre précieux, 1966-69), I, p. 520.

analysis. By virtue of their physical position, they stand between an author and a text, and between a reader and a reading, thereby exerting a potentially enormous influence over the primary narrative. In authorial prefaces, implicit ownership of both text and paratext carries with it an authority to comment on, defend, praise, disown, mock, deprecate, justify, define, pre-empt, or otherwise interpret and protect the primary text. Indeed, it was defensiveness that led Marcel Rouff to label the preface to *La Vie et la passion de Dodin-Bouffant, gourmet* (1924) a 'justification' of transcendental cookery.[6]

Pre-1870 Prefaces

In 'La préface et ses lois: avant-propos romantiques', Henri Mitterand convincingly argues that prefaces as discourses are 'document[s] sur la théorie du genre romanesque' that aim to transmit a given ideology. According to him, the transmission of the ideological or aesthetic message takes the following form: 'La littérature doit *être* ou *faire* "x". Or ce roman a fait "x"; Donc toi, lecteur, tu dois le tenir pour un livre de valeur universelle'.[7] The truth of this statement is evident in the Goncourts' sensationalist preface to *Germinie Lacerteux*. The didactic message here is that 'Literature must be modern, scientific. This book is scientific in its method and modern in its subject matter'. That it had universal value was implied.

The preface to *Germinie Lacerteux* is addressed to 'the average reader' and calls for two things: firstly, the author's right to portray the lower classes in the novel ('ce livre vient de la rue'); secondly, the importance of scientific analysis and documentation to the realism of the novel ('le Roman s'est imposé les études et les devoirs de la science'). Realism is a recurring theme in prefaces of the period. *Thérèse Raquin* refers to 'la copie exacte et minutieuse de la vie'. Huysmans, in *Marthe: histoire d'une fille* (1876), confesses that it is a realist text: 'Je fais ce que je vois, ce que je sens et ce que j'ai vécu, en l'écrivant le mieux que je puis, et voilà tout'.[8] In his preface to

---

[6] (Paris: Serpent à Plumes, 1994), pp. 9-14.
[7] *Le Discours du roman* (Paris: PUF, 1980), pp. 21 and 25.
[8] *Marthe: Histoire d'une fille; Les Sœurs Vatard*, ed. by Hubert Juin (Paris: Union générale d'éditions, 1975), p. 26

Thérèse Raquin, Zola also states that in the scientific analysis that he had attempted to apply could be found 'la méthode moderne, l'outil d'enquête, dont le siècle se sert avec tant de fièvre pour trouver l'avenir'. In the preface to *L'Assommoir*, on the other hand, he alleges that the novel is 'le premier roman sur le peuple, qui ne mente pas et qui ait l'odeur du peuple'. Nonetheless, the Goncourts' 1864 claims were so strenuous that Hubert Juin has gone so far as to argue that all post-*Germinie Lacerteux* prefaces 'perpétuent et accusent les proclamations contenues dans *Germinie Lacerteux*'.[9] By this token, the preface is nothing if not a literary manifesto that trumpets the revolutionary nature of the novel, and this message was plainly picked up on by other authors of the period.

The Goncourts, in a case of author knows best, write that *Germinie Lacerteux* does not conform to readers' tastes, but to what ought to be their tastes, given that they live in an age of progress. The implied faith in progress was undoubtedly an authorial ruse – Edmond de Goncourt was also the author of the enticingly titled, though ultimately unsuccessful, play, *A bas le progrès!* (1893). All the same, certain passages of the 1864 preface accentuate the modernity and actuality of the novel. No mention is made of the particulars of plot. Indeed, with the notable exception of *Chérie*, none of the novels' intrigues is explicitly revealed in their prefaces. In *La Fille Elisa*, Goncourt writes at length about prostitution and the penal system in general, but never truly announces the plot of the novel, or the fact that the (anti)heroine is an imprisoned prostitute. In much the same manner, *Les Frères Zemganno* is only mentioned in passing at the end of its preface. Nowhere is it suggested that the novel could be read as a transposition of the Goncourts' life onto the life of two circus performers. This avoidance of plot allows the novels to be situated within a literary framework that can explain how and why they came to be, without ever calling into question the texts themselves. Importantly, it draws attention away from the fictions and centres it firmly on the person of the author, focussing interest on his personal literary history and his interpretation of the cultural environment of his day.

---

[9] In Goncourt, *Préfaces et manifestes littéraires*, p. 1.

Post-1870 Prefaces

More often than not, in the later (post-1870) prefaces, Goncourt provides a model of the ideal novel, only to claim that this model does not correspond to the novel that is about to be read (it is thus the opposite of the tactic used by Racine in the preface to *Phèdre*, where it is claimed that the play adheres to the three classical unities, but where the text itself contradicts these assertions). In the prefaces to *Chérie*, *La Faustin* and *Les Frères Zemganno*, the reader is told what is wrong with novels to date and is presented with wish lists of what could have been – and can still be – done differently to improve them. The last paragraphs of the preface to *Les Frères Zemganno* offer advice to aspiring authors to the effect that documentation is what makes good books: 'disons-le bien haut, les documents humains font les bons livres' (p. 3). While echoing *Germinie Lacerteux*, this penultimate paragraph also explains the motivation behind the preface and makes it clear that it is targeted at other authors as opposed to disinterested readers: '[…] cette préface a pour but de dire aux jeunes, que le succès du réalisme est là, et non plus dans le *canaille littéraire*, épuisé à l'heure qu'il est, par leurs devanciers' (p. 3). In the remaining lines, however, it is stated that the novel about to be read is, in fact, 'une tentative dans une réalité poétique' (p. 3), a category not discussed in the rest of the text.

Insofar as these prefaces ignore the very theories they present, it is necessary to refine Mitterand's syllogism. Only his core phrase – '*La littérature doit être "x"*' –[10] holds true as far as the later Goncourt prefaces are concerned. The ideological message has evolved: 'literature should be x. This novel is y. But I, the prefacer/author, nevertheless remain the theoretician of x'. The author's influence is in the realm of the theoretical as much as the fictional. One obvious consequence of this refusal to write a novel that adheres to the outlined theory is that the prefacer/author and his work are presented as entirely original and individual, in as much as they cannot be categorised or taken as examples of a given literary aesthetic. This protects the work from criticism according to certain aesthetic precepts by suggesting that either the prefacer/author occupies such a

---

[10] *Le Discours du roman*, p. 24.

position of authority that he can stray from his own theories, or that the author is a writer of inferior quality who cannot write the proposed ideal novel. The latter is implied, but only, one suspects, out of false modesty.

By not commenting on the novels, but on the Novel *per se*, Goncourt acts as a guide who magnanimously discloses where progress can be made, while bequeathing the work to a younger generation. He establishes a theoretical model for future creation while ignoring the imminent reading. It is a model of transcendence, if not rupture, where an individual author moves beyond the theories of a group (even if this group purportedly follows in his footsteps, as Goncourt is wont to suggest), so that he does not participate in the institutionalisation of his theories (even if this is arguably the goal of anyone who assumes the role of mentor). Goncourt distances himself from his own fiction in order to assert his authority over the consecrated aesthetic theory. The preface-writer is nevertheless ever-present, because displacing attention from the novel places it firmly on the theories. This prefatorial tactic mirrors the role of the quintessentially nineteenth-century omnipresent and authoritative – if not authoritarian – narrator, who is not necessarily a character in his story, but is always lurking in the shadows.

The notion of the divided prefacer caught between, on the one hand, consecration, and, on the other, revolt (and between fiction and non-fiction), is significant because, as Christophe Charle comments in his study of the literary crisis during the Naturalist period, 'l'afflux le plus important de nouveaux venus [à la littérature] se situe pendant la période 1876-1885'.[11] These dates correspond almost exactly to the chronology of Edmond de Goncourt's solo novelistic career: 1877-84. They thus go some way to explaining the ideological focus of the prefaces, as well as why most prefaces were written after Jules's death: 'Jules est mort avant toute polémique'.[12] This interpretation is all the more credible as the second half of the nineteenth century witnessed the beginning of mass market production and promotion of books – Zola, it should be remembered, was once publicity officer at

---

[11] *La Crise littéraire à l'époque du Naturalisme: roman, théâtre et politique: essai d'histoire sociale des groupes et des genres littéraires* (Paris: Presses de l'Ecole Normale supérieure, 1979), p. 48.

[12] Juin in Goncourt, *Préfaces et manifestes littéraires*, p. 2.

Hachette. The paratexts, which display a keen awareness of the literary field, are therefore just as much examples of a revolt from within against popular, accessible and commercially successful books in favour of more elitist output.

Intertext

Goncourt's prefaces subtly skirt issues relating to the fiction ostensibly being presented, but they do deliberate at length on the position and influence of the authorial prefacer. In addition, they relate to each other through constant coming-and-going. Intertext is a fundamental tool in Goncourt's writing on the evolution of the literary field.

Central to an understanding of the preface to *La Fille Elisa* (and perhaps the novel), is an acquaintance with the literary crusade that is referred to in its opening lines. It begins by cueing a past preface and quoting from it: 'Mon frère et moi, il y a treize ans, nous écrivions en tête de *Germinie Lacerteux* [...]' (p. 1). *La Fille Elisa* is presented as the culmination of a decade-old literary struggle to make literature more scientific and analytical. This inter-prefatorial jousting brings into focus not so much Goncourt's fiction, but his paratextual assertions. Interpretation of his position – and his ability to comment on matters literary and aesthetic – depends, therefore, on acceptance of the authorial reading of the *œuvre*, both textual and paratextual. The resulting implication is that the enlightened reader who wishes to fully understand this 1877 preface must be aware of the literary struggle that is alluded to. This presentational mode consolidates the author's position: his status as high priest and magus of literature is certified by virtue of the existence and influence of past works. What is more, the preface to *La Fille Elisa* makes reference to the 'jeune et sérieuse école du roman moderne' (p. 1), a school in which the author situates himself, thereby linking his production to the successes of an entire movement.

The prefaces to *Germinie Lacerteux* and *La Fille Elisa* both claim the right to feature ignoble subjects in a refined style, to base novels on documentary evidence while presenting them artistically. *La Fille Elisa* even has a Fourieresque social shade to it: it is called a 'plaidoyer' intended to 'donner à réfléchir' on the abject state of French prisons. This social focus is completely absent in later paratextual writing where art for art's sake wins out over art with a social function. The divide between scientific method and social impact and aesthetic representation haunts all of Goncourt's subsequent output.

The three final prefaces discuss the importance of moving beyond these early aesthetic guidelines towards a literature that is refined in more than just language. Interestingly, this change coincides with the consecration of the Naturalist movement: *La Fille Elisa* sold 10,000 copies in a few days and was in its thirtieth edition by 1890.[13] The fact that by 1884 Naturalism was the literary movement *par excellence*, accounts for the fact that the three later prefaces continue to cite Goncourt's Naturalist novels, while focussing more on how literature can change and on justifying a move away from works like *Germinie Lacerteux* and *La Fille Elisa*. This line of argument is consolidated in the preface to *Les Frères Zemganno*, which is addressed to 'jeunes' and which discusses, from the outset, the author's past:

> On peut publier des *Assommoir* et des *Germinie Lacerteux*, et agiter at remuer et passionner une partie du public. Oui! Mais, pour moi, les succès de ces livres ne sont que de brillants combats d'avant-garde, et la grande bataille qui décidera de la victoire du réalisme, du naturalisme, de l'étude d'après nature en littérature, ne se livrera pas sur le terrain que les auteurs de ces deux romans ont choisi. Le jour où l'analyse cruelle que mon ami, M. Zola, et peut-être moi-même, avons apportée dans la peinture du bas de la société, sera reprise par un écrivain de talent, et employée à la représentation des hommes et des femmes du monde [...] – ce jour-là seulement, le classicisme et sa queue seront tués (p. 1).

These opening lines can be likened to a war cry, so military is the vocabulary: 'combats', 'victoire', 'avant-garde', 'bataille', 'terrain', 'tués'. Like Hugo's *Cromwell* (1828), this preface aims at toppling literary convention and precipitating literary (r)evolution. The war in question is the battle waged by Zola, in *L'Assommoir*, and the Goncourt brothers, in *Germinie Lacerteux*, against Romanticism. These two works, as the reference to 'des *Assommoir*' and 'des *Germinie Lacerteux*' indicates, are treated as defining a specific brand

---

[13] *Journal*, I, lxxxxvi.

of fiction. *Germinie Lacerteux*, and by extension the Goncourts' entire *œuvre*, is linked to the rollicking success of *L'Assommoir*, which had sold over 100,000 copies by 1882 (considerably more than *La Fille Elisa*).[14] Goncourt asserts, however, that while these two novels may have been successful, the battle for the soul of Realism, Naturalism, and studies after nature, should not end with them. By invoking the spectre of literary schools like Realism and Naturalism, Goncourt draws on the public's knowledge of contemporary literary and aesthetic crusades and situates his work – past, present, and future – within these parameters. Consequently, his audience is prompted to consider his works as exerting influence beyond the here and now.

Having presented the reader with a battlefield, it is left to the commanding officer to name an enemy, and to lead troops into battle. The enemy is defined as Classicism, but, as some might consider this phenomenon as belonging solely to the seventeenth century, Goncourt adds 'et sa queue'. This has the effect of prolonging Classicism into the present day and insinuates that this pernicious genre, replete with outdated rules and unities, has never entirely faded. Is this perhaps a jibe at the established literary and cultural order, a criticism of the conservative notions and received ideas that the Goncourts and other authors felt pervaded the Académie française and the *Revue des deux mondes*? Traditional literary critics felt threatened by new novelistic forms because 'they felt that legitimate literature was under threat from a literature that appealed to a wide audience without abandoning its literary pretensions or social implications'.[15] Ferdinand Brunetière, star critic at the establishment *Revue des deux mondes*, went as far as to state that 'c'est une préoccupation mauvaise et prétention systématique de bouleverser les règles éternelles de l'art'.[16] Without doubt a revolt against the established aesthetic order was underway.

Once the problem had been presented, and the enemy named, the next step was to establish how to banish it. The solution: to put an end to Classicism was by applying the same techniques and devices used to popular acclaim in *Germinie Lacerteux* and *L'Assommoir*, but to use *écriture artiste* to write about 'ce qui est élevé, ce qui est joli', 'ce qui sent bon', '[des] êtres raffinés et des choses riches' (p. 1). In

---

[14] Charle, p. 43.
[15] Translated from Charle, p. 84.
[16] *Le Roman naturaliste* (Paris: Calmann Lévy, 1892), p. 2.

anticipation of the Decadent movement, elegance and refinement are put forward as replacements for the 'vérité trop vraie' (p. 4) and the 'réalité brutale' (p. 3) of traditional Naturalist working-class subject matter. By insisting that the 'cruel analysis' of these two novels was the weapon with which to wage the final literary combat ('la grande bataille'), Goncourt sets them on a pedestal and insists on the fact that firstly, they founded a genre – be it Realism, Naturalism, or studies after nature – and secondly, as a result, they are the central canonical works from which all new fiction must spring and differ.

That said, the reference to *L'Assommoir* might be nothing more than false flattery. Goncourt-the-diarist thought that it was entirely derivative of his novel: 'J'ai donné la formule complète du naturalisme dans *Germinie Lacerteux*, et *L'Assommoir* est fait absolument d'après la méthode enseignée par ce livre' (*Journal*, 1 June 1891). (Zola, of course, had already studied high-class life in the 1871 novel, *La Curée*, by this point, so the extension of the Naturalist project is not so clear-cut). Either way, the intertextual reference makes another of Goncourt's novels an essential point of departure for the reader of *Les Frères Zemganno*. As such, Goncourt becomes a standard bearer for two movements: the one founded on *Germinie Lacerteux* and the one yet to be founded. It is interesting to note that in the following year, 1880, Goncourt's unsolicited advice was flatly ignored by the authors of the key Naturalist text *Les Soirées de Médan* (1880), who wrote in their preface that 'notre seul souci a été d'affirmer publiquement nos véritables amitiés et, en même temps, nos tendances littéraires'.[17]

The preface to *Les Frères Zemganno* provides both a reading and a suggested writing, but not of the text it allegedly introduces. If the reader accepts Goncourt's interpretation of *Germinie Lacerteux* and its preface, as well as his take on *L'Assommoir*, then his suggested writing (what sort of novels should be written and how) would hold true. The 'êtres raffinés' and the 'femmes et hommes du monde' that Goncourt refers to make their first appearance in 1882, in *La Faustin*. The theories of literary evolution put forth in *Les Frères Zemganno*, and which are based on prior works, find their expression in Goncourt's last two novels. The 1879 preface thus looks to the future

---

[17] Emile Zola and others, *Les Soirées de Médan* (Paris: Grasset, 1955), p. 19.

– Derrida would contend that all prefaces 'rend[ent] présent l'avenir' – and to the past.[18] Goncourt-as-prefacer is portrayed as having a global view of both a body of work that is not yet completed, and a movement that has not yet reached its end. Once again, there are obvious parallels to be drawn with the omnipresent narrator.

Unsurprisingly perhaps, the preface to *La Faustin* also looks forward. Almost exclusively concerned with an anticipated, future project, it is mum on the novel itself. No reading of *La Faustin* is offered. The entire preface, from the intimate tone to the discussion of historians, is geared towards producing writing. The writing sought is manifold: women will write to the author offering their intimate memories, and the author, in turn, will use these confessions to write his novel. Other writers will follow suit and collectively they will renew the Novel.

This particular preface is remarkable for its intimacy with, and proximity to, both readership and contemporary literary debates. In order to instigate the desired change, the prefacer must know and understand his public, and that this is the case is evidenced by the possessive 'mes lectrices'. The familiar, spoken language that predominates creates a sense of confidentiality: individual readers are addressed directly by the confiding author. Studies written by men about women are presented as missing essential ingredients – female contributions and female points of view – just as the middle of Goncourt's sentence is hiding something in its ellipsis: 'Les livre écrits sur les femmes par les hommes, manquent, manquent... de la collaboration féminine et je serais désireux de l'avoir cette collaboration' (p. 1). The intimate tone fostered by the use of such expressions as 'oui' and 'eh bien' gives the impression that collaboration will begin, or, at the very least, that acquiescence to the author's desires is taken for granted. Readers are lulled into complicity by this tone and by frequent reference to the prefacer's 'je'. Female readers who have been faithful in the past are implored to be so in the present, by sending juicy personal stories of childhood and adolescence to contribute to a planned book. If readers comply with these demands, they themselves will become authors, and will share in the preface-writer's authority. The consecration of the author –

---

[18] *La Dissémination* (Paris: Seuil, 1972), p. 13.

attested to by the fact that he has a devout readership – is itself a springboard for change, a point of departure for a revolt against the literary machine, and for a renewal of literature by using, in this case, readers' letters as part of the text.

The last and longest of the original prefaces belongs to *Chérie* and at times it strays wildly outside the bounds of the imagined category 'preface to *Chérie*'. This is demonstrated by the fact that in 1884 it appeared in *Le Figaro* (17 April), independent of the novel. The preface gained autonomy and was arguably the source of as many polemics as the novel itself.[19] In a mirror move, the novel itself was serialised, without the preface, in the newspaper *Gil Blas*, from 11 March to 17 April of the same year. Add to this the fact that the preface contains in its pages the preface to another book, and there is a lot to contend with.

Unlike the prefaces to *La Fille Elisa* and *Les Frères Zemganno*, which only introduce their subject in their closing lines, the 1884 preface begins with a discussion of the fiction at hand. To emphasise the tight link between the two final novels, the opening sentence of the paratext makes explicit reference to *La Faustin* and the work carried out in the two years since its publication: 'Voici le roman que j'annonçais dans l'introduction de *La Faustin*, et auquel je travaille depuis deux ans' (p. 1). The presentation of *Chérie* is undertaken by referring to a past novel – indeed, like *La Fille Elisa*, to a past novel's preface – suggesting that the reader will already be acquainted with the subject matter of the book, as well as with Goncourt's historic mission. It also implies that Goncourt as preface-writer is a persuasive propagandist because his request for female collaboration issued in 1882 did not, presumably, go unheeded, since the novel announced then was now being presented. The intertextual play between the two prefaces breaks down the barriers separating past, present and future texts.

The preface to the 1884 novel is not simply a play between two paratexts, a play between past and present. It is, in fact, two distinct texts. In a highly unusual move – original prefaces are normally

---

[19] Four articles are of particular interest: Georges Duval, 'Le Roman nouveau', *L'Evénement*, 22 April 1884; Quidam, 'Les Goncourt', *Le Figaro*, 25 April 1884; Francis Enne, 'Au hasard: la préface de *Chérie*', *La Nation*, 27 April 1884; Gustave Geffroy, 'Revue littéraire: les Goncourt', *La Justice*, 10 November 1884.

written after the primary text – the preface to *Chérie* contains the preface to the Goncourt *Journal*. In terms of Edmond de Goncourt's *œuvre*, this firms up the inter-prefatorial relationships that exist between his publications, and reinforces a sense of continuity. *La Fille Elisa* cites the preface to *Germinie Lacerteux* and comments on it, rather than on *Germinie* the novel. The preface to *Les Frères Zemganno* includes lengthy passages on the topic of *Germinie Lacerteux* and *L'Assommoir*, and thereby places the so-called fictional autobiography on a literary timeline and establishes its worthiness. In contrast, the novel *La Faustin* is not once mentioned in its preface. Rather, this penultimate preface discusses an entirely different work, a work that did not yet exist in 1882. The preface to *La Faustin* can be more aptly interpreted as a supplementary preface to *Chérie*. On top of this, the preface to *Chérie* refers to *La Faustin*'s preface and includes in its pages the preface to a non-fiction work-in-progress that was begun by the Goncourt brothers and that could only be published, at the earliest, twenty years after Edmond's death.

By including this preface within the preface to *Chérie*, Goncourt consolidates the play of past-present-future and fiction/non-fiction in his prefaces: he wrote a preface to a work that he co-authored and published it before the work was completed, so that in the eventuality that the *Journal* itself did not reach the printing presses, 'ce sera toujours ça au moins de sauvé' (p. 7). In terms of Goncourtian paratext, it is entirely consistent that the 1884 preface appears to drift outside the normal bounds of the category 'preface to *Chérie*', as one of their striking characteristics is that they elude the temporal as well as textual boundaries imposed by the fictions they accompany. It is entirely consistent that the present, by virtue of the blurring of the boundaries between *Chérie* and the *Journal*, is infused with references to both the past and the future, references which cement Goncourt's seminal role in the development of the nineteenth-century novel and accentuate the supremacy of the prefacer-theoretician.

Canonical Change

When, in the preface to *Chérie*, the subject leaps from a discussion of the early-nineteenth-century novel to a prediction of what the novel might be at the end of the same century, there can be no doubt that the assessment of the evolution of the Novel imagines the genre as occupying a predetermined, or fixed, timeframe. It presents a reading that is somehow fatalistic, foreseeing as it does the death of the Novel in much the same way as Nietzsche would tell of the death of God and Barthes of the death of the author. How else to interpret 'la dernière évolution du roman' (p. 2) than as a warning of the end of the progress of the traditional novel through literary history? To arrive at the end of its literary history, the novel must become 'le grand livre des temps modernes' (p. 2) by growing into a plotless text, a work of pure analysis, a pure document. In Goncourt's story of the future of (the history of) literature, it is at this point that the Novel will cease to exist.

In *Théorie des genres*, it is suggested that in order to define a genre, you must already have written its history,[20] and this is precisely what is taking place in this instance: Goncourt, as prefacer, is writing a predictive history of the novelistic genre, in order to define its limits and its place in literary history. In so doing, he assesses the extent of his influence. 'Se combinent ici,' writes Thorel-Cailleteau, 'un esprit critique aigu, un souci de modernité, et la volonté de se démarquer par des œuvres originales d'une tradition jugée épuisée'.[21] By switching between the roles of historian and fortune-teller, the public is offered a reading of literary history as well as suggestions as to how one author's *œuvre* could be changed or reinterpreted in order to better correspond to (advance, announce, anticipate) a development that he predicts. While Goncourt's works cannot be rewritten, because the author cannot regain his youth, a younger author may one day stumble upon the new novel for which Goncourt was searching.

Goncourt's role is limited to that of mentor; he states that he is drawing his writing days to a close. In a magnificently Decadent gesture, he (prematurely) terminates his literary line: 'cette préface étant la préface de mon dernier livre, une sorte de testament littéraire'. Nor is he above melodramatic interjection: 'Maintenant, toi, petite CHÉRIE, toi pauvre dernier volume du dernier des Goncourt, va où sont allés tous tes aînés' (p. 9). Like a parent whose child leaves

---

[20] Gérard Genette and Tzvetan Todorov, *Théorie des genres* (Paris: Seuil, 1986), p. 34.
[21] *La Tentation du livre sur rien*, p. 105.

home, Edmond de Goncourt releases his final offspring into the harsh world of literary competition, where every book must fend for itself. Novels are his children: procreation has been replaced by literary creation, the body has been denied in favour of the word.

In actuality, since the preface to *Les Frères Zemganno*, Goncourt had been publicly complaining about his physical state of health. He was 'veillisan[t]', 'maladi[f]', 'lâch[e] devant le travail' (p. 4). Naturalist truths made him 'malad[e] nerveusement' (p. 3). This neurosis is one of the most well documented features of Decadence. To escape from the troubling reality of Naturalism was to write 'de l'imagination dans du rêve mêlé à du souvenir' (p. 4), to depict 'un type à la distinction plus profondément ancrée dans les veines, à la distinction perfectionnée par plusieurs générations' (*Chérie*, p. 1). One of the professed aims of *Chérie* was to evoke 'le joli et le distingué' (p. 2) of its subject. This form of 'réalité élégante' parallels that mentioned in the preface to *Les Frères Zemganno*. The ambition presented in *Chérie* is to write a stylistically beautiful novel devoid of the novelistic, devoid of drama, to write a novel that could replace everyday reality in its very uneventfulness, in its very banality. The suggestion is that even if another author created or named a new genre, it would only be completing work begun by a mentally and physically ravaged Goncourt, and fulfilling a prophecy foretold in these paratextual writings. This being the case, *Le Figaro*'s opinion that the preface to *Chérie* was the Bible of Naturalism is surprising, to say the least.[22]

The discourse contained in these prefaces is, in effect, a more or less sophisticated analysis of the processes governing literary evolution. It is by situating himself within a wider literary debate that Goncourt establishes his authority and attempts to break with Naturalism. Underpinning the prefacer's view of his personal authority in matters of literary doctrine is the belief that, with regard to changes in what is today referred to as the literary field, the actions of a powerful, influential, and above all, insurgent, few – among whom he includes himself – exert enormous influence on the behaviour of the many. 'Le public [...] trois ou quatre hommes, pas plus, tous les trente ans, lui retournent ses catéchismes du beau, lui

---

[22] Ignotus, 'Goncourt', *Le Figaro*, 4 March 1885.

changent, du tout au tout, ses goûts de littérature et d'art, et font adorer à la génération qui s'élève ce que la génération précédente réputait exécrable' (*Chérie*, p. 3). Linking art to religion, or perhaps more accurately, linking established art to dogma, artistic norms are called the 'catéchismes du beau'. There are rules governing tastes, but these rules vary according to a pattern: every thirty years they are toppled in favour of new beliefs. Art exists in a state of perpetual change – 'la marche et le renouvellement incessants et universels des choses du monde' (*Chérie*, p. 3) – that negates the idea of permanence and fixed beliefs (and ties in quite nicely with the fleeting nature of much *écriture artiste*).

This unstable transience allows Goncourt-as-prefacer to position himself as both canonical author and instigator of change. The idea that he is at the heart of the current literary movement – Naturalism – yet on its margins because he foresees its end, is reinforced by the reading of literary evolution offered in his paratextual writings. However, the discourse on the evolution of literature does not simply discredit literary norms outright. In *Les Règles de l'art*, Pierre Bourdieu writes that:

> L'action subversive de l'avant-garde, qui discrédite les conventions en vigueur, c'est-à-dire les normes de production et d'évaluation de l'orthodoxie esthétique, faisant apparaître comme dépassés, démodés, les produits réalisés selon ces normes, trouve un soutien objectif dans l'*usure de l'effet* des œuvres consacrées.[23]

The reason that it cannot be argued without reservation that the Goncourt prefaces unequivocally discredit contemporary aesthetic orthodoxy is that this orthodoxy, according to at least two of the prefaces (*La Fille Elisa* and *Les Frères Zemganno*), is founded on the works of Edmond and Jules de Goncourt. In these two texts, it is suggested that *Germinie Lacerteux* – both novel and preface – was central to the Naturalist movement in France. This is corroborated by Remy de Gourmont who believed that 'tout le naturalisme, en sa partie populaire, vient de *Germinie Lacerteux*'.[24] The only thing to have lost its effect is the subject matter of the 1864 novel, hence the

---

[23] (Paris: Seuil, 1992), p. 352.
[24] *Le Deuxième Livre des masques*, p. 265.

advice to young authors to concentrate on refined subjects while simultaneously making use of the stylistic lessons taught in *Germinie Lacerteux*. One part of the consecrated work has been superseded (subject), but the other remains contemporary (style and composition).

Conclusion

Over the span of his novelistic career, Edmond de Goncourt distances himself from a movement that he implies in these very paratexts is born of his work. He is, for that reason, presented as a visionary and an authority in the theory and the practice of late-nineteenth-century literature (like the narrator, the preface-writer is omniscient). He is set up as a canonical author who incites others to move beyond the dominant literary doctrine towards something more aesthetically refined.

Facts and Fiction

DOCUMENTARY PROCESSES

> Police reports, lists of imposts, tables of commerce, statistics of crimes and suicides, information on the prices of provisions, salaries, the mean duration of human life, the marriage rate, the birth rate, legitimate and illegitimate – these are 'human documents.' [...] The history of civilization, when it wants facts, puts M. Zola's entertaining novels aside of no account, and has recourse to tedious statistical tables.
>
> – Max Nordau, *Degeneration*[1]

In the use of documentation, and the conception of reality, truth, and fiction that it both underpins and supports, lies one of the keys to the evolution of Edmond de Goncourt's literature, methodology and themes in the late 1870s and early 1880s. By examining the role of the author, and how data of various sorts is collected and deployed in supposedly realist novels, the relationship between the literature of *fin de siècle* France and the output of one writer can be clarified.

The somewhat ambiguous term *document humain* refers to at least two distinct concepts: the first pertains to the process of literary creation and the status of the document as material to be exploited in a novel; the second pertains to the result of the process of observation and the accumulation of data. The document is many things to the Naturalist author, both a means and an end, as David Baguley has rightly observed: 'Le propre du mot "document" dans le lexique naturaliste est l'extraordinaire flexibilité de son application, car il en vient à désigner toutes les étapes de cette méthode, toutes les phases de l'élaboration du roman'.[2] The document is, on the one hand, a material trace of a present or past empirical reality. According to Pierre Sabatier, 'le document c'est un témoignage d'une habitude, d'une mode, d'un sentiment, d'un drame du passé ou présent; c'est une lettre, un dessin, un moulage, un mouchoir, une étoffe, une robe, un meuble, en un mot, c'est la preuve matérielle d'un fait susceptible de devenir la matière d'un objet d'art'.[3] Written, oral, or painted

---

[1] p. 489.
[2] 'Le *Journal* des Goncourt, document naturaliste', in Cabanès, pp. 105-14 (p. 109).
[3] *L'Esthétique des Goncourt* (Geneva: Slatkine, 1970), p. 141.

'documents', in the form of letters, memoirs, diaries, library research, or field work, were acquired, noted, observed or carried out by the industrious author in order to fuel the creative process and generate what can, given the dual meaning of the term, be considered a new document: the novel. Indeed, in keeping with this interpretation, texts written according to a documentary process could themselves be interpreted as documents of their time. Future readers should be able to approach document based Naturalist novels as pieces of fictionalised truth about the nineteenth century.

Science and Fiction

In practice, of course, this position resulted in several confusions of reality and fiction, where fiction was taken for either reality or scientific fact, due to both the mimetic qualities of texts and the intellectual posturing of authors and their narrators. While Zola is well known to have read Bernard, Charcot, and Lucas, it was not unthinkable for scientists to attempt to draw on fiction for their studies. In a wonderful reversal of roles, Edmond de Goncourt was interviewed by a doctor for an article that appeared in the *Chronique médicale* about his insights into female madness as presented in his novels.[4] What is more, a medical intern rather naïvely approached him wishing to quote a passage from *La Faustin* as evidence for his study on sexual anomalies. The intern, Paul Sérieux, writes:

> Je fais en ce moment un travail sur les anomalies de l'instinct sexuel; je serais heureux de pouvoir vous emprunter l'observation complète de Georges Selwyn si, comme j'en ai la conviction, il s'agit là d'une description faite d'après nature, avec une précision toute scientifique.[5]

---

[4] Dr. Cabanès, 'La Documentation médicale dans le roman des Goncourt', *La Chronique médicale*, 1 August 1896; Dr Cabanès, 'Journal médical des Goncourt', *Journal de médecine de Paris*, 22 March 1891.

[5] B.N.F. M.S.S. N.A.F., 22475, fols 427-28. Pierre-Henri Castel has studied the author-doctor relationship with regard to the Goncourts in 'Des Goncourt à Huysmans, entre littérature et histoire de la médecine', in Sylvie Thorel-Cailleteau, ed., *Dieu, la chair et les livres: une approche de la décadence* (Paris: Champion, 2000), pp. 509-49.

For the Naturalist writer, acquiring documentation is equivalent to carrying out a scientific experiment. Evidence is gathered and then tested, but the confusion between fact and fiction on the part of scientists is perhaps attributable to, if not excused by, the way that the use of documentation leads novelists to compare their work as authors with other more empirical and analytical forms of writing. One of the most famous analogies of this type is contained in 'La Formule critique appliquée au roman' (1879), where Zola compares the author's role with that of the critic, stating that 'le romancier part de la réalité du milieu et de la vérité du document humain; si ensuite il développe dans un certain sens, ce n'est plus de l'imagination à l'exemple des conteurs, c'est de la déduction, comme chez les savants'. He goes on to highlight the similar role of the document in both critical and fictional texts:

> Le romancier et le critique partent aujourd'hui du même point, le milieu exact et le document humain pris sur nature, et ils emploient ensuite la même méthode pour arriver à la connaissance et à l'explication, d'un côté de l'œuvre écrite d'un homme, de l'autre des actes d'un personnage, l'œuvre écrite et les actes étant considérés comme étant les produits de la machine humaine soumise à certaines influences.[6]

Documents are material signs of a life subjected to environmental pressures at a particular moment in time. The novelist, like the critic, studies documents in order to analyse a given environment. The resulting novel is the conclusion of this critical study. The subtitle to the *Rougon-Macquart* series – *Histoire naturelle et sociale d'une famille sous le Second Empire* – provides further insight into the system of belief underlying the collection of novels. For Zola, the novelist, theoretically at least, was much like a scientist, and the novel an 'histoire' as natural as it was social, where characters bore the burden of Hippolyte Taine's three determining factors: *race*, *milieu* and *moment*. Insofar as this is the case, there is a difference between Naturalism and Decadence:

> Naturalism and decadence are not at all the same thing, since the former proposed to analyse contemporary society (in Zola's case, the recently contemporary society of the Second Empire) with scientific rigour and, it was

---

[6] Zola, *Du Roman*, pp. 51-58 (pp. 54, 55-56).

implied, little sympathy, and the latter sought to express the sentiments of 'modern' man, who was likened to the ancient Romans of the decadence.[7]

Like Zola, Goncourt's novels rely on the *document humain*, but their central focus is characters who are haunted by a desire for modernity in all areas of life.

History and Story

The Goncourtian stance does not differ unduly from Zola's positivist formulation of the novel 'pris sur nature', but Edmond de Goncourt, as has been mentioned, gives the novelist's role a different twist by arguing that '[un romancier...] n'est au fond qu'un historien des gens qui n'ont pas d'histoire' (*La Faustin*, p. 1). This could mean several things, all of which rely on the double meaning of 'histoire' as both history and story. Firstly, that the novelist ought to concentrate on those who have historically been ignored by both the novel and by official history. This interpretation matches statements made in the preface to *Germinie Lacerteux*. Alternatively, the historian-novelist analogy can be interpreted as an insight into the Goncourtian method of creation: fiction produced in the same manner as history. This analogy ties in with the Goncourt brothers' own shared interest in history, particularly the history of the eighteenth century, and their research into female historical figures. They state in the 1856 preface to *Portraits intimes du dix-huitième siècle* that they consider their historical study to be a 'roman vrai que la postérité appellera peut-être un jour l'histoire intime'.[8]

During their early career in the 1850s, most of the Goncourts' writing was historical in nature: *Histoire de la société française pendant la Révolution* (1854), *Histoire de la société française pendant le Directoire* (1857), *Sophie Arnould d'après sa correspondance et ses mémoires inédites* (1857), *Histoire de Marie-Antoinette* (1858). The brothers wrote no major novels at this time. In the 1860s, however, they wrote successful novels and historical studies simul-

---

[7] Stephan, p. 10.
[8] *Œuvres complètes*, 21 vols (Geneva: Slatkine, 1985-86), XXXVIII-XXXIX, p. 9.

taneously. Pierre Martino believes that thanks to their 'double' career, history and fiction would henceforth be inseparable to them:

> Les Goncourt [...] transportèrent de l'histoire au roman; et comme ils continuèrent, après 1860, leurs recherches et leurs publications historiques, en même temps qu'ils écrivaient des romans, ils n'établirent point, entre ces deux modes d'activité, de différences autres que celles qui étaient commandées par la nature des sujets et les conditions de la documentation.[9]

No doubt this is a slight exaggeration of the situation, but it does impart the idea that the truth the Goncourts were searching for was 'le "vrai" auquel aboutissent les recherches historiques'.[10] Their conception of history, however, is not typical: it is grounded in the particular, in intimacies, much like their conception of the novel.

The fundamental and inescapable conundrum here is that this method of creation is entirely appropriate as far as historical discourse is concerned, documents can be used to support an argument and in attempts to recreate historical events (though recent historiography has successfully done away with the notion of there being one, decisive version). In a work of fiction, however, the so-called argument is always an invention, the characters and the world they inhabit do not exist, and documents merely contribute to the author's vision rather than to any empirically verifiable past reality. In order to establish *vraisemblance* and plausibility, historical texts must adhere to established documentary processes. This is not the case for the novel. The view of the Goncourts' novels as pieces of history, or as accounts of events that have occurred, in anything other than an extremely specific or narrow sense is troublesome. An insoluble tension exists between literary and historical discourse and this cannot simply be erased by claiming the novelist as a historian.

The literature-history parallel is more or less upheld in pre-1870 novels (though it doesn't do to be dogmatic about this), and to a certain extent in *La Fille Elisa*, where the mimetic representation of the Goncourts' immediate environment of Second Empire Paris predominates. Enzo Caramaschi points out as much when he states in general terms that 'le roman sera pour les Goncourt de l'histoire contemporaine: le récit se présentera chez eux comme le moyen de

---

[9] *Le Roman réaliste sous le Second Empire* (Paris: Hachette, 1913), p. 231.
[10] Martino, p. 236.

livrer au lecteur, au lieu d'une invention, une réalité transposée, caractéristique d'un moment de l'actualité ou d'un aspect du monde actuel'.[11] This assessment seems accurate as far as the joint novels are concerned. All of these texts, save *Madame Gervaisais*, are set primarily in Paris (and *Madame Gervaisais* is the story of a Parisian in Rome). All of the joint novels are clearly set during either the Second Republic or the Second Empire. Secondary characters born in the eighteenth century provide background for the stories and furnish the characters with a lineage: Mlle de Varendeuil in *Germinie Lacerteux* is born in 1782 and watches the Restoration and the fall Louis-Philippe; Germinie herself, who is born circa 1824 and dies in the early 1860s, shares her history with Rose, the Goncourts' servant; Renée Mauperin's father is born in 1787, and Renée herself is born in 1835. The story takes place during her adolescence. Most of the 1860s characters have real-life antecedents that were either known to or by the Goncourts, and it has been pointed out that this distinguishes them from their contemporaries: 'Flaubert, Zola puisent autour d'eux dans la vie réelle, bien sûr; mais les Goncourt, eux, opèrent dans un cercle plus étroit, celui de leur famille et de leurs plus intimes relations'.[12]

La Fille Elisa: *Transitional Novel*

After 1870, the novels unashamedly advertise their documentary nature, without it always being clear what the reality they are allegedly describing is. Documents are drawn upon to construct the novels, but they lack the homogeneity of source or subject matter of previous texts. Whereas Renée Mauperin is based on Blanche Passy, and Germinie Lacerteux on Rose Malingre, the heroine of *La Fille Elisa* is based on some combination of Jules's mistress Maria's two daughters, a woman described in the *Gazette des tribunaux*, and one observed during the Goncourts' 1862 visit to the prison, La Charité, in Clermont d'Oise. The story itself is the result of years of note-taking that spans the Second Empire and the Third Republic, so much so that in *La Genèse de 'La Fille Elisa'*, Ricatte divides the textual genesis

---

[11] *Réalisme et impressionisme dans l'œuvre des frères Goncourt* (Pisa: Libreria Goliardica, 1971), p. 31.
[12] Ricatte, *La Genèse de 'La Fille Elisa'*, p. 56.

into four categories according to theme: the brothers' visit to Clermont d'Oise, which provides the background for the second half of the novel, as well as setting up its ending; the information on the midwife provided by Maria, which gives Elisa a past; the world of prostitution; and the crime and trial. He also divides its genesis into several phases.[13] In addition, Gabrielle Houbre has noted that the debate on the French system of incarceration was relaunched in 1871 and that it could only have been at this time that the judicial side of the novel was 'found' and the plot elaborated.[14]

La Fille Elisa is very much an exception in the overall Goncourt *œuvre*, for, although it was written by Edmond alone, much of the thematic focus of the story was established jointly with Jules. Prior to his death, the brothers found material relating to prostitution, the trial, and the prison the novel describes. The all-pervading theme of social injustice likely stems from the fact that exactly one month before the initial visit to the prison they were busy reading *Les Misérables*.[15] It is only following Jules's death, however, that the issue of the Auburn system of incarceration re-enters public consciousness and winds its way into the novel. The process of finding (rather than inventing) the story is spread over upwards of two decades and deals, unlike subsequent novels, with topical issues of contemporary relevance. *La Fille Elisa* is, thus, in many ways unlike Edmond de Goncourt's three subsequent novels, though it does undeniably introduce themes that resurface in them in dramatically different contexts.

Research for *La Fille Elisa* and *Germinie Lacerteux* was carried out at the same time in the early 1860s, and certain documentary details from this period appear in both novels: one reality is transformed into two distinct fictions.[16] In addition, passages in the *Journal* that relate to orgies and homosexuality within the female religious orders that ran prisons were omitted from the novel, though observed in reality.[17] Either this particular point was deemed too scandalous for fiction, or the author was aware of the political and

---

[13] *La Genèse de 'La Fille Elisa'*, pp. 29, 56-57, and 21.
[14] 'Le Mauvais procès de *La Fille Elisa*', *Francofonia*, 21 (1991), 87-96 (p. 90).
[15] Ricatte, *La Genèse de 'La Fille Elisa'*, p. 55.
[16] Ricatte, *La Genèse de 'La Fille Elisa'*, pp. 10-11.
[17] Houbre (p. 91) cites entries in the *Journal* on the following dates: 30 Dec. 1876, 21-23 and 28 March 1877, 3 Oct. 1876.

legal dangers of including such scurrilous allegations in a novel. Goncourt deforms the historical and political reality of the French prison system and presents highly biased readings of the source texts pertaining to prostitution that were consulted (notably Parent Duchâtelet's *De la prostitution dans la ville de Paris*, 1837 – also used by Alexandre Dumas for *Filles, lorettes et courtisanes*, 1843 – and Joséphine Mallet's, *Les Femmes en prison*, 1843). He merges two distinct systems of incarceration under one name in order to accentuate the evils of state-imposed silence. Whatever is thought of Houbre's suggestion that Goncourt's choices were erroneous, her comments are more than worthy of note: 'Entraîné par sa volonté de convaincre l'opinion, Goncourt commet une faute grave dans sa préface: par maladresse ou par mauvaise foi, il déforme et détourne le sens original des ouvrages cités comme caution à ses propos. La scientificité affichée par la préface est donc fallacieuse' (p. 91). This much is known about the choices that went into *La Fille Elisa*; a similar form of selection is manifest in the three later novels, but these are also influenced by a thematic focus that no longer prioritises such Naturalist concerns as the portrayal of the hereditary and environmentally imposed decline of the Parisian underclasses.

La Faustin and *Chérie,* unlike *La Fille Elisa*, scarcely seem to fulfil Caramaschi's dictum that the Goncourtian novel applies to the 'monde actuel'. Indeed, the latter two (if not three) novels, in addition to being distinctly otherworldly at times, are not explicitly based on Second Empire characters or events. They do, on the other hand, describe fin de siècle neuroses. Ironically, this non-homogeneous nature stems from the documentation itself, which appears to be deployed according to anti-mimetic, rather than mimetic, ends. Caramaschi is, however, accurate in arguing that 'dans leur œuvre de romanciers [les Goncourt] traitent l'imaginaire en historiens dans la mesure où ils exigent d'abord, des faits qu'ils chargent de symboliser la réalité de leur temps, d'être arrivés quelque part à quelqu'un, d'être "authentiques"' (p. 32). The 'authenticity' and 'truth' of the later novels is disrupted by the conflicting times, places, people and sources that are drawn upon and surreptitiously represented in the novels, thus putting an end to any claim of Naturalist documentary accuracy or relation to any external reality (there are no more *romans-à-clef* in the style of *Charles Demailly* and *Manette Salomon*). This change in process (and the ever-diminishing place of narrative) is connected to the changing thematic focus of the later novels. François Fosca believes that 'Edmond revenait de plus en plus à ce travail d'assemblage de documents qui convenait si bien à son tempérament; et de *La Fille Elisa* à *Chérie*, on voit peu à peu l'historien éliminer le romancier' (p. 340). This is true in terms of the creative process: the later novels are more historical in approach than in subject matter. The subjects they deal with renounce Naturalism and move into the realm of the unknown and the unverifiable to become, at times, eccentric and digressive anti-novels.

La Fille Elisa is the only one of Edmond's solo novels to be placed in an unambiguous historical moment, and the only one in which this really matters. Nonetheless, at least one of his novels, *Chérie*, is based on a conspicuously historical creative process. This process is referred to in the text by a narrator who alleges to have documents to support his narrative (which is presented as a fictionalisation of the truth). Statements such as 'Mme Michelet dit quelque part...' (p. 41) attest to this. Allusions to the documentary process, coupled with the discussion of the genesis of the novel in the preface to *La Faustin*, begs an interrogation of the nature of documents, especially given that an enormous distance separates the milieus of the 1877 and 1884 novels.

Interestingly enough, it is at the very moment that Goncourt is composing *Chérie*, with its pseudo-documentary focus, that he bequeaths his papers to the Bibliothèque nationale de France: 'Cette correspondance des littérateurs et des artistes du jour où mon frère et moi avions commencé à faire de la littérature jusqu'au jour de ma mort, je la lègue au département des manuscrits de la Bibliothèque pour être mise immédiatement à la disposition du public. Le 19 décembre 1882'.[18] The relationship between documentation and the composition of the novel is thus all the more tightly intertwined. It is at this point of transition, when Goncourt, using the tools of the historian, is composing a documentary novel so unlike his earliest solo work, that the correspondence is bequeathed to posterity, with, as Genette would have it, 'la part d'intention qui s'attache à un tel

---

[18] B.N.F. M.S.S. N.A.F., 22479, fol. 404.

geste'.[19] Quite apart from the insights this offers into Goncourt's fondness for documentation, the author's swansong itself speaks of decadent sterility: it coincided with the decision to abandon literary creation, which for the deliberately celibate Goncourts was in many ways a substitute for procreation. Work on the *Journal*, however, continued.

The Journal

According to Baguley, the Goncourt *Journal* constitutes 'un vaste dossier préparatoire de leurs romans'. 'Le *Journal* des Goncourt', he writes, 'est comme une immense machine à transformer instantanément le vécu en documentaire'.[20] Given the nature of the *Journal* as a repository for notes of all kinds, everything was susceptible to becoming a 'document' and of, therefore, being fictionalised. It follows, then, that the process of creating fictional texts need not start with a plan. Because of the *Journal*, the documentary process was ongoing and all consuming. The topic of a novel was not necessarily fixed before research was unconsciously begun. Information gathered without reference to a particular novel could be used towards any future endeavour. In this sense, the *Journal* is an 'aide-mémoire' and a 'forme d'épargne'.[21] It was the author's personal savings account where he invested for the future. The *Journal* is a resource that furnishes both eyewitness accounts and more reflective writings. It is, to borrow Béatrice Didier's terms, both 'intime' and 'externe', for considerations of self go hand in hand with reporting on the external world (p. 30). It provides both objective and subjective documents, by recording well-anchored specific social facts that can be transposed into novels, in addition to documents of a more psychological nature, which establish lyrical rather than actual historical parallels between empirical and fictional realities. It is entirely consistent with Edmond's project that something as personal as the *Journal* should eventually be published – particularly given the

---

[19] *Seuils*, p. 364.
[20] 'Le *Journal* des Goncourt, document naturaliste', pp. 111 and 107.
[21] Gérard Genette, 'Le Journal, l'anti-journal', *Poétique*, 47 (1981), 315-22 (p. 319); Béatrice Didier, *Journal intime* (Paris: PUF, 1976), p. 52.

similarities between the author and his characters – as fragments of it were used in the creation of novels destined for public consumption.

The genetic study of *La Fille Elisa* confirms how both objective and subjective documents from the *Journal* were drawn upon during the creative process. Descriptions of the prison (in the novel called 'Noirlieu') and the brothels that Elisa visits, for instance, refer to an observed reality: following visits to these places, observations were noted in the *Journal* by the brothers, only to be later used in the novel. The final chapter of the novel is essentially a rewriting of their visit to Clermont: 'Il y a des années, je passais quelques semaines dans un château des environs de Noirlieu. Un jour de désœuvrement, la société avait la curiosité d'aller visiter la Maison de détention des femmes' (p. 196). The actual account of the Goncourts' tour is described on 28 October 1862 in the *Journal* and a note in the carnet makes it clear that this conflation was planned: 'Fin à l'hôpital de la prison de Clermont'.[22] On the other hand, states of mind and moods attributed to Jules de Goncourt in the *Journal* are transposed into the 1877 novel and applied to the main character, particularly in the final chapters where his deterioration becomes Elisa's.[23] A similar process is found in *Les Frères Zemganno*, where the text can be considered a 'document', or fictionalised account, of Edmond and Jules de Goncourt's artistic quest, due to the manipulation of documents of a psychological nature, called 'témoignages'.[24] In this latter case, however, the thematic focus is vastly different and the documents are used in a text that has overtly Decadent overtones, something that cannot be said of *La Fille Elisa*, which deals with two hypotheses, both of which would have been subversive at the time of its publication: firstly, that prostitutes could love, yet refuse sexual relations with their lover; secondly, that the sentence of perpetual silence reduced women to little more than imbeciles.[25]

---

[22] Ricatte, *La Genèse de 'La Fille Elisa'*, pp. 183-84. The passage continues: 'Visite de gens qui, voyant sur la figure de la mourante un désir de parler qu'elle comprime quand elle voit le directeur'.

[23] Ricatte, *La Genèse de 'La Fille Elisa'*, p. 132.

[24] Genette, *Seuils*, pp. 363-64.

[25] See Katherine Ashley, 'Policing Prostitutes: Adaptations and Reactions to Edmond de Goncourt's *La Fille Elisa*', *Nineteenth-Century French Studies*, 33-1/2 (2004-05), 135-46.

Once noted in the *Journal*, episodes drawn from reality become the material of future literary productions. Sylvie Thorel-Cailleteau brings this interpretation to its inevitably extreme, yet somehow compelling, conclusion by proposing that the *Journal* is not merely the source of the Goncourts' fiction, but is itself the fiction. This is accomplished by an aesthetic that, as time goes by, approaches collage:

> On est tenté de lire le *Journal* des Goncourt comme une grande somme de documents humains, qu'il est bien sûr, comme l'avant-texte des romans. En réalité, la pratique des Goncourt (et surtout d'Edmond) est peut-être inverse: de *Germinie Lacerteux* à *Chérie*, déjà *Charles Demailly* (la genèse de *En 18...* est, pour cause, plus obscure), le roman goncourtien semble une coupe de plus en plus brute du *Journal*, une mise en forme de plus en plus légère et souple de sa matière.[26]

This emphasises the extent to which documents are used to different ends in post-1870 than they were pre-1870. In Edmond's solo novels, the use of documents goes some way to undermining the Naturalist ends according to which they are (or were at the beginning) collected and assembled. By 1884, novels are cut and pasted together into what is sometimes a discontinuous assemblage of fragments.

This cut and paste aesthetic could be – indeed, has been – interpreted as a sign of fading literary prowess, of Edmond de Goncourt's lack of compositional talent compared to his brother. It could also be argued that Edmond's use of the *Journal* is the supreme incarnation of the *document humain*, and of Naturalist fiction reflecting reality. It could be argued that there is no more Naturalist method of creation than the daily transformation of reality into a document so that it might be used in fiction. It cannot be reasonably argued, however, that Edmond de Goncourt's novels are the most Naturalist of the Goncourts' collective *œuvre* due to the fact that the details from the *Journal* included in them are not subjected to rewriting. This interpretation would discount the extent to which extracts are apparently selected according to increasingly Decadent thematic concerns and are less rooted in a unified historical reality. It also sidesteps the question of mimetic representation.

---

[26] *La Tentation du livre sur rien*, p. 182.

Forms of Collaboration

One of the key areas of change in the documentary process post-1870 is evident in terms of book research. *La Fille Elisa*, it should be stressed, is the only novel of Edmond's for which a full manuscript and preparatory notes exist. Much of the story was elaborated jointly by Edmond and Jules, but each brother had his own role, Edmond's being book research: 'il est assez curieux que, sauf les notes de lecture qui figurent dans le carnet de *La Fille Elisa*, nous n'ayons dans ce carnet aucune indication sur le travail d'Edmond seul'.[27] In the case of *La Fille Elisa*, the reading notes are Edmond's alone, whereas for previous novels both brothers undertook the task:

> Il est un fait: toutes les notes de lecture du carnet d'*Elisa* sont prises par Edmond; or, dans les autres carnets destinés à la documentation de leurs romans, *Manette Salomon*, *Madame Gervaisais*, on voit les deux frères se partager ce dépouillement ingrat des ouvrages techniques. Si Edmond s'en est ici chargé tout seul, on peut penser que seule la mort de son frère l'a privé du secours qu'il en pouvait attendre.[28]

In effect, *La Fille Elisa* is a novel of two parts in more than just structure. The details pertaining to the far from racy story of the prostitute all stem from pre-1870 sources (discussion with Jules's mistress Maria about her daughter, readings on the history of prostitution). The story of the prison, on the other hand, relates to the brothers' visit to the women's detention centre in Clermont-d'Oise, to Edmond's readings, and to the re-emergence of the debate on incarceration. It seems, then, that a good deal of the pre-writing work was carried out by both brothers. This would coincide with what is known about the Goncourts' collaborative writing, which Emile Zola, before their relationship soured, described with much aplomb and obvious traces of affection:

> Ils amassaient surtout un nombre considérable de notes, voyant tout sur nature, se pénétrant du milieu où les épisodes devaient se dérouler. Puis, ils causaient le plan, arrêtaient ensemble les grandes scènes, jalonnaient ainsi l'œuvre entière. Enfin, arrivés à la rédaction, à cette exécution qui ne

---

[27] Robert Ricatte, 'Autour de *La Fille Elisa*', *La Revue d'histoire littéraire de la France*, 48-1 (1948), 69-83 (pp. 82-83).
[28] Ricatte, *La Genèse de 'La Fille Elisa'*, p. 7.

comporte plus le débat oral, ils s'asseyaient tous deux à la même table, après avoir une dernière fois préparé le morceau qu'ils comptaient écrire dans la journée; et là, ils rédigeaient ce morceau chacun de son côté, ils en faisaient deux versions, selon leur façon personnelle de voir. Ces deux versions, qu'ils se lisaient, étaient ensuite fondues en une seule; on conservait de part et d'autre les choses heureuses, les trouvailles; c'étaient les apports de deux esprits libres, comme le meilleur d'eux-mêmes qu'ils écrémaient et dont ils faisaient un tout solide.[29]

In Edmond's and Jules's case, the studies of paratextual documents such as letters unsurprisingly point to a clear change in creative process following 1870. The Goncourt correspondence (letters sent to and, to a lesser extent, from the brothers) suggests that more use was made of third party sources and research after Jules's death than before. There appear to be few pre-1870 letters that deal with the details of a novel before its publication. Two from the same correspondent, Georges Ponchet, exist and both somewhat improbably provide information about a monkey at the Jardin des Plantes for the novel *Manette Salomon* (1867).[30] The number of letters received by Edmond in connection with the process of literary creation increases for the three later novels (there are letters to and from Alphonse Daudet that deal with the *La Fille Elisa*, but these are more letters of encouragement than of documentation).[31] In the correspondence received by Goncourt, there are two letters pertaining to *La Fille Elisa*, nine pertaining to *Les Frères Zemganno*, nine dealing with the writing of *La Faustin*, and ten relating to *Chérie*.[32] These numbers alone testify to the changing circumstances of literary creation as far

---

[29] 'Edmond et Jules de Goncourt', pp. 267-68.
[30] B.N.F. M.S.S. N.A.F., 22473, fols 162-63. This is not to mention an irresistible missive from the *Société protectrice des animaux* awarding Edmond the *médaille de Vermeil* for taking up the cause of animals in the same novel: B.N.F. M.S.S. N.A.F., 22463, fols 26-29.
[31] See, in particular, letters 22, 33, 36, 41 and 43 of the *Corres. Gonc-Daud.*
[32] All references are to B.N.F. M.S.S. N.A.F. *La Fille Elisa*: 22460, fol. 2; 22461, fol. 1. *Les Frères Zemganno*: 22454, fol. 208; 22462, fols 514-15; 22464, fols 251-52; 22464, fols 320-21; 22464, fols 322-23; 22469, fol. 308; 22471, fols 546-47; 22475, fol. 233; 22477, fol. 79. *La Faustin*: 22457, fols 132-36; 22462, fols 75-76; 22462, fol. 77; 22465, fol. 248; 22473, fol. 53; 22473, fol. 55; 22473, fol. 176; 22473, fols 178-79; 22478, fol. 155. *Chérie*: 22459, fol. 35; 22459, fol. 40; 22461, fols 138-39; 22462, fol. 52; 22465, fols 252-53; 22471, fol. 292; 22471, fols 293-94; 22474, fol. 356; 22477, fols 252-53; 22478, fols 47-48.

as post-1870 novels are concerned. Again, once the brotherly collaboration was brought to an untimely end, letters relating to works in progress increase in number, suggesting that Edmond requested the assistance of others as a means of replacing his absent writing partner.

Conclusion

Many of the issues at stake in *Les Frères Zemganno*, *La Faustin* and *Chérie* are already present in the 1877 work. Indeed, some of the fundamental documentary practices of the later novels are perceptible in *La Fille Elisa*, which incorporates letters into the body of the text (though changing their function and significance) and draws on past sources including, it has been suggested, the Goncourts' own *Histoire de la société française* (both of the Revolution and the Directory).[33] Documents – both fiction and non-fiction – are preserved by the author and are integrated into his novels. The creative process, Naturalist in essence, is based on use of documents, but as the following chapters hope to make clear, there is a transformation in the treatment of themes and an evolution toward Decadence that is reflected in the documentary choices made.

---

[33] Ricatte, *La Genèse de 'La Fille Elisa'*, pp. 182 and 191.

LES FRÈRES ZEMGANNO: AUTHOR AS ACROBAT

> O poëtes heureux! comme dans votre esprit,
> Le même ardent rayon sur vos lèvres fleurit,
>
> Et, par un double effort, vos âmes fraternelles
> Vers le même Idéal ensemble ouvrent leurs ailes!
>
> – Théodore de Banville, 'A Edmond et Jules de Goncourt'[1]

Les Frères Zemganno (1879) is a very different novel from *La Fille Elisa* in terms of subject matter and themes. It is also the novel where, through its melancholy description of fraternal love, Jules de Goncourt's absence is most potently felt. Based on documentary research, it is commonly regarded as providing an accurate picture of the nineteenth-century French circus. At the same time, though, the portrayal of circus performers introduces themes distant from Realism and Naturalist experimental heredity. Add to this the fact that *Les Frères Zemganno* has been somewhat problematically interpreted as a fictional autobiography, and the role of the *document humain* in it is doubly complicated.

The Goncourts and the Zemgannos

The term 'fictional autobiography' implicates both historical reality and a given set of biographical details, and suggests that biographical information is disguised within a fictional framework. The figures said to represent Edmond and Jules de Goncourt – Gianni and Nello Bescapé/Zemganno – are gymnast-acrobats, and the choice of profession to illuminate the lives of the two authors must be questioned with regard to criteria of realism and *vraisemblance*. *Les Frères Zemganno*, it turns out, does not so much represent the Goncourt brothers as their struggle for artistic innovation: similarities,

---

[1] *Œuvres poétiques complètes*, ed. by Peter J. Edwards, 8 vols (Paris: Champion, 1994-2001), II: *Odelettes*, p. 117.

while present in specific incidents, are much more apparent on the level of artistic creation. At first, the transposition from novelist to circus performer can be interpreted as alluding to the Goncourts' preoccupation with the working and lower classes (extended here to include low culture as opposed to high culture), but in fact it highlights the extent to which Edmond de Goncourt is concerned with art that is ripe with mimetic detail within stories that are themselves far from the realist prerogatives of mid-nineteenth-century literature. Documentary realism can therefore be scrutinised from the perspective of both autobiography and the circus.

There are similarities between the fears and memories of the clowns and the fears and memories of the Goncourts. Indeed, at the time of publication, informed readers recognised the Goncourts in the Zemgannos. Julia Daudet, who never met Jules, described *Les Frères Zemganno*, which is dedicated to her, as a novel about Edmond de Goncourt's love for his sibling: 'c'est un monument d'amour fraternel et l'histoire de la collaboration des Goncourt brisée par la mort du plus jeune'.[2] In confusing the name of the author with the name of a character (either deliberately or not), one correspondent draws attention to the similarities between fiction and reality: 'C'est bien Gianni lui-même qui raconte la vie et la fin prématurée de son cher Nello'.[3] It should be remembered that whereas Jules de Goncourt died at the age of 40 from syphilis, in the novel, Nello does not die: he is paralysed. In this respect, the extent to which the demon of Jules's death is exorcised is left open. Instead of describing the successful renewal of art, the author presents an inability to create, ostensibly caused by a physical impediment. The end of the Goncourts' joint artistic creation is caused by death; Nello's paralysis is as good as death as it ends the Zemgannos' creative life.

Recently, Michel Caffier has noted the similarity between Edmond and Jules and Gianni and Nello in terms of artistic initiation: Gianni introduces Nello to the world of gymnastics just as Edmond initiated Jules into the world of writing.[4] Pierre-Jean Dufief is more assertive in making the link between fact and fiction, and calls the book an

---

[2] *Souvenirs autour d'un groupe littéraire* (Paris: Charpentier, 1910), pp. 111-12.
[3] B.N.F. M.S.S. N.A.F., 22464 fol. 253 (25 June 1879).
[4] *Les Frères Goncourt: un déshabillé de l'âme* (Nancy: Presses universitaires de Nancy, 1994), p. 210.

autobiography: '*Les Frères Zemganno* sont un roman autobiographique, un récit constellé de petits faits vrais, fruits non plus de l'observation mais du souvenir'.[5] The distinction between observation and memory is all-important here and is at the heart of the debate surrounding the nature of realism and memory, and Naturalism and Decadence. While many details derive from the Goncourts' life, and while the story may be inspired by it, the change in social context between the author and his characters is enormous, and requires a substantial leap of faith on the part of the reader.

Nello is the younger brother, born twelve years after Gianni; Jules is eight years younger than Edmond. The Bescapés' hands are joined by their mother upon her death: 'sans une parole, sans une caresse, sans un baiser, elle prenait la petite main de Nello qu'elle mettait dans la main de son aîné, et ses doigts déjà froids serraient les mains des deux frères dans une étreinte que la mort ne desserra pas' (p. 69). Edmond recounts a similar occurrence involving himself and his brother in the *Journal*: 'Ma mère, sur votre lit de mort, vous m'avez mis la main de votre enfant chéri et préféré dans la mienne, en me recommandant cet enfant avec un regard qu'on n'oublie pas' (*Journal*, 18-19 June 1870, 10 heures du matin). The two travelling gymnasts, like the two well-to-do Goncourts, are united by their mother.

The acrobats' absolute love for each other is one explanation of their celibacy, which is both artistic and sexual: in the end, they produce no children and no lasting work. Their all-consuming bond grows into a quest for artistic refinement and innovation, which is, ultimately, destructive. Nello suffers from an injury that prevents him from performing again. Gianni agonises and blames his brother's downfall on his own desire for artistic novelty. Meanwhile, the injured brother's dedication to art is presented as a manifestation of filial love worthy of Plato:

> Et longtemps, songeant à l'épanouie jeunesse de son frère, à l'indolence et à la paresse de sa nature, à la pente de son caractère à se laisser doucement vivre, sans effort et sans recherche de gloriole, il se remémorait tout ce que lui avec son exemple, son vouloir de célébrité, son dur célibat, avait contrarié, gêné, empêché dans cette vie toute sacrifiée à la sienne, et cela jusqu'au moment, où

---

[5] Edmond de Goncourt, *Les Frères Zemganno* [1879], ed. by Pierre-Jean Dufief (Geneva: Slatkine, 1996), p. 14.

au milieu de sa songerie, s'échappait de la bouche de Gianni avec l'accent d'un remords: '[...] Je suis foutûment coupable!' (pp. 231-32).

The echoes of Edmond's own guilt at working his brother to death in the name of literature are audible: 'A cette heure, je maudis la littérature. Peut-être, sans moi, se serait-il fait peintre. Doué comme il l'était, il aurait fait son nom sans s'arracher la cervelle... et il vivrait' (*Journal*, 18-19 June 1870, 10 heures du matin). Certain details have indisputable antecedents in the Goncourt *Journal* and little seems to have changed in the transplanting of these documents of a psychological nature ('témoignages') to the realm of fiction. Still, the chasm of social difference between the Goncourts and the Zemgannos cannot be overlooked.

While it is implied that Gianni's and Nello's 'confiance morale' (p. 86) is a result of what could be called their 'confiance physique', their closeness is dependent on sentimental as well as physical causes. In contrast to the explanations of the brothers' physical affinity to their mother, the bonds that bind them to each other are not explained in medical or scientific terms; rather, they are 'liens mystérieux, des attaches d'atomes crochus de natures jumelles' (p. 162). The impulses behind their performances are also shrouded in mystery. Gianni becomes so absorbed in gymnastic creation that he performs all other functions like a machine: 'L'existence animale, ses actes, ses fonctions, semblaient s'accomplir chez lui, comme par la continuation d'une mécanique remontée pour quelque temps, et sans qu'il y eût en rien une participation de son individu' (p. 152). Artistic creation transforms him into an automaton. Unlike in *La Fille Elisa*, however, his animal-like behaviour is not presented as degraded, but as an indication of his preoccupation with matters of a higher order. Nello, on the other hand, is subject to 'impulsions de courants magnétiques biscornus' (p. 144) when preparing to perform. His features are distorted 'dans une sorte de dilatation extatique' (p. 145) and he is no longer master of his actions ('gestes dont il n'avait pas l'absolue volonté', p. 144). Although these conditions could very well lead to something more malign in the novel, in the end the failure of the Zemgannos' revolutionary performance has little to do with their physiological predispositions and everything to do with a *femme fatale*. Needless to say, red herrings of this sort are distinctly un-

Naturalist and have no antecedent in the Goncourts' life (unless it is a clumsy metaphor for syphilis).

Fictionalised Circuses Past and Present

Les Frères Zemganno is not only a representation or interpretation of the Goncourts' lives. It has also been read as a faithful portrayal of the circus, particularly the circus of the Second Empire, so much so that one English admirer wrote to Goncourt, with undoubtedly dubious motives, requesting not only a photograph of the Zemganno brothers, but a special performance of 'young men of about 21'.[6] Anecdotes aside, the accuracy of the circus details is attested to by the many letters, both of praise and of information, that Goncourt received regarding specific circus issues.

Edmond collected documents about the circus and drew on them to give citational authority to his text. For example, a letter from the celebrated engraver Félix Braquemond, who, according to Dufief 'vécut jeune dans un manège', reveals that Ernest Renan, author of *La Vie de Jésus*, was a source of information on the circus (and, therefore, a man of many interests).[7] Braquemond's note reveals that Edmond was an author-historian in search of specific documentary evidence on *saltimbanques* upon which to build a fiction that in some ways represented his own life. Other letters serve a similar function. The Zemganno brothers are hired by the 'directeur-gérant des Deux-Cirques' (p. 121). Charles Franconi, director of the 'Société des deux cirques de Paris (Cirque d'hiver/Cirque d'été)', educated Goncourt on trampolines and rehearsals.[8] The lancewood trampoline mentioned in Franconi's letter is found in the novel where his terms are reiterated almost verbatim: 'un tremplin où il substituait au sapin "le frêne des îles", le bois désigné par les Américains sous le nom caractéristique de *lance-wood*' (p. 197). The presence of the exotic apparatus is enough to convey the brothers' intrepidness, but adds little to the overall narrative.

---

[6] B.N.F. M.S.S. N.A.F., 22464, fols 270-71.
[7] Edmond de Goncourt, *Les Frères Zemganno*, ed. by Pierre-Jean Dufief, p. 20; B.N.F. M.S.S. N.A.F., 22454 fol. 208. Letter dated 'Paris Auteuil 11 9bre 1878'.
[8] B.N.F. M.S.S. N.A.F., 22462, fols 514-15. This letter is dated 24 March 1879.

Additionally, in a revealing note in the preface to *Les Frères Zemganno*, Goncourt acknowledges the assistance of several contemporary circus professionals in providing a 'reality' in which to ground his fiction:

> A propos de la réalité que j'ai mise autour de ma fabulation, je tiens à remercier hautement M. Victor Franconi, M. Léon Sari, et les frères Hanlon-Lees qui ne sont pas seulement les souples gymnastes que tout Paris applaudit, mais qui raisonnent encore de leur art comme des savants et des artistes.[9]

This statement of thanks (for which the English Hanlon-Lee brothers in turn thanked Goncourt)[10] draws attention to the realist aspects of the text. Indeed, it anchors the novel firmly in a 'real' world external to the story. It also establishes the authority of the novel by giving it a stamp of approval from experts in the circus. In this way, the part of reality in the 'fabulation', or fantasising, is made explicit before the reader has begun the story, even though, in truth, the thematic thrust of the text verges on the Decadent by virtue of the selfsame fantasising, which permeates the characters themselves.

It is not only contemporary circus that is mentioned; past circus traditions are also alluded to.[11] Information on the circus of yore is gleaned from Archangelo Tuccaro's *Trois dialogues de l'exercice de sauter*. This much is revealed in the novel itself:

> Gianni, un liseur de livres dans les boîtes des quais, et que l'on voyait, à l'étonnement de ses camarades, souvent arriver au Cirque, un bouquin sous le bras, descendait parfois dans le pavillon de musique un vieux volume: un gros in-quarto, relié en parchemin, aux coins écornés, aux armoiries lacérées pendant la Révolution, et où la main et le crayon d'un enfant de nos jours avaient mis des pipes à la bouche des personnages du seizième siècle. De ce livre portant sur son dos: TROIS DIALOGUES DE L'EXERCICE DE SAUTER ET DE VOLTIGER PAR ARCANGELO TUCCARO 1599, et apprenant que le Roi Charles IX, *s'adonnoit à toute espèce de sauts et s'y montroit fort adextre et dispos*, Gianni lisait à son frère (p. 160).

---

[9] *Les Frères Zemganno*, ed. by Pierre-Jean Dufief, p. 36.
[10] B.N.F. M.S.S. N.A.F., 22465, fol. 93.
[11] Frédéric Masson supplies information about the the circus of old, describing different types of jumps and tightrope acts. His information is drawn from an encyclopedia of 'Art. Sauts'. B.N.F. M.S.S. N.A.F., 22469, fol. 308.

Citing actual texts in a novel is far from unusual, but while the documentary detail contributes to establishing a level of realism by describing the book as a material object with a referent, it also makes surreptitious reference to the creative process. Tuccaro's text is listed in the catalogue of the sale of Goncourt's books, thereby linking the fictional and historical brothers by means of a shared object.[12] Both Edmond and Gianni use Tuccaro in their artistic creations: writing is linked to the act of creating acrobatic stunts.

Gianni's fascination with Tuccaro points to a more distant past: certain words, such as 'saltarine' and 'saltatoire', bear the stamp of the Romans, for whom 'saltation' was a spectacle mixing dance, theatre, and pantomime. As such, it is highly appropriate to Gianni's and Nello's art. Although the mix of dance, theatre and pantomime does correspond to the Zemgannos' art, it also refers to a more 'refined' past, of which the average reader may be unaware. Likewise, 'sauts épheristique', 'orchestique' and 'cubistique' (p. 160) point to Greek Antiquity and the gymnastic-like dances of the Bacchantes. This cross-cultural borrowing is itself characteristic of Decadent literature, which perceived many parallels between nineteenth-century France and the decadence of the Roman Empire.[13] Here it is particularly significant as the Bacchantes were quite possibly the first Decadents. Yet, while the Zemgannos perform jumps related to Bacchus, it is confusingly specified that they sustain a 'privation "de Bacchus et de Vénus": tradition venant en droite ligne... des artistes du muscle de l'antiquité' (pp. 170-71). The gymnasts deprive themselves of physical, sexual pleasure in what may be a case of two sides of the same coin, total abstinence being, in fact, closely related to the total indulgence of the Bacchantes. Goncourt is documenting decadence.

Places and People

In *Les Frères Zemganno*, which paints ancient and modern circus arts, and is realistic in its particularities if not in tone and overall mood,

---

[12] Alidor Delzant, *Bibliothèque des Goncourt, livres modernes. Vente à Paris, Hôtel Drouot 5-10 avril 1897* (Paris: Imprimerie de Motteroz, n.d.), p. 174, number 1087.

[13] Désiré Nisard was extremely influential in this respect in the early part of the century. See Swart, p. 7.

seemingly insignificant details seem to be of inordinate importance. This is clear from the evidence that Goncourt sought specific information relating to relatively small points of historical interest. It is obvious in autobiographical terms in as much as the novel deviates substantially from the events of the Goncourts' life.

When they were young, the Goncourt brothers toured France and Algeria before devoting their lives to writing. The Zemgannos also travel, but not to any of the countries that the Goncourts visited, and not for the same reasons. After spending their childhood roaming Europe with their family's travelling circus, the Zemgannos (still the Bescapés at this point) embark on a journey of discovery to Britain, where they hope to unravel the secrets of the British circus. Although Edmond himself had never been to Britain, his gymnasts are sent there in the aim of studying foreign circuses 'd'après nature'. Mimicking Naturalist authors and impressionist painters, Gianni exclaims that it would be 'un joli *travail* à aller étudier sur place et dans l'endroit' (p. 101). Edmond, however, deviates from Naturalist practice by moving the intrigue to an environment that had not been observed first-hand (though some British performers were in Paris at the time). Characters study 'd'après nature' for the same creative reasons that are shunned by their author; the novel deviates from the very processes to which its semi-autobiographical characters profess to adhere.

In terms of foreign circuses, Goncourt documented his novel from texts recommended to him by peers. Frédéric Masson directed him to a study by Boz (Dickens) about a Covent Garden clown, *The Life of Joa Grimaldi*.[14] He was also encouraged to read such weighty tomes as *Modern Boxing*, *Manly Exercises*, and *Boxiana*.[15] Goncourt pillaged one of the recommended texts, *Circus Life and Circus Celebrities* by Thomas Frost, and passages are incorporated into the novel without significant transformation.[16] The route that Gianni and Nello follow on their journey of discovery through Britain is similar to the one described in Frost's account of Alhambra Joe, as both share the unlikely destinations of Greenock and Carlisle: the fictional

---

[14] B.N.F. M.S.S. N.A.F., 22469 fol. 308.
[15] B.N.F. M.S.S. N.A.F., 22464 fols 320-21. B.N.F. M.S.S. N.A.F., 22464 fols 322-23.
[16] See pp. 225-27 of Thomas Frost, *Circus Life and Circus Celebrities* (London: Tinsley Brothers, 1875) and p. 104 of Goncourt's novel.

clowns 'allaient *étoiler* douze nuits à Greenock en Ecosse' (p. 108) and début as clowns in Carlisle.[17] The Zemgannos' lives, and by implication the Goncourts', are mapped onto the life of actual circus performers. Their fictional autobiography merges details of their life and the lives of others. *Les Frères Zemganno* is, in this regard, realistic in its representation of the peregrinations of circuses. The choices made in the use of documentation establish how fiction and reality converge in the process of writing. Documents are culled from non-fiction texts, one written under a pseudonym by a novelist, and inserted almost verbatim into a work of fiction that uses them to establish its *vraisemblance* and corroborate its fictional and autobiographical 'argument'.

The need for detail to contribute to the realism of the text is equally apparent in the names of the characters. As states previously, the novel was originally named after a circus performer and was changed at the last minute for one that sounded 'fabriqué': Bendigo becomes Zemganno (and there are no traces of documentation relating to this name). A similar thing happens in the novel: when Gianni and Nello are ready to present their act to the public, they change their last name from Bescapé to Zemganno. The director of the circus reflects: 'Zemganno... mais il est vraiment original votre nom... il possède un diable de Z au commencement qui est comme une fanfare... on dirait une de nos ouvertures, vous savez, où il y a une sonnerie de clochettes dans une batterie de tambours' (p. 207). Apart from its bizarre sonority, the name evokes distant lands and the hybrid origins of the brothers. Despite the fact that nothing has been mentioned about this before, Gianni wistfully makes the vague pronouncement that 'c'est le nom que nous avions là-bas' (p. 208). Nor is it clear what Gianni is referring to when he says 'là-bas'. Noiray speculates that the name evokes 'tzigane', 'zingane', or 'zingaor', all of which relate to travelling gypsies.[18] Interestingly, it is only when the brothers abandon the travelling life that they adopt a mellifluous and unusual name associated with travellers. Their pseudonym erects a barrier between the brothers and their art, while highlighting the changing nature of

---

[17] Frost, pp. 230-33.
[18] 'Tristesse de l'acrobate: création artistique et fraternité dans *Les Frères Zemganno*', *La Revue des sciences humaines*, 259 (2000), 91-110 (p. 105).

their performances, which are becoming less realistic and more 'original'.

Even if the stage name Zemganno is a fabrication, first names are not. Although this confessional novel is the most personal of Goncourt's texts, he resorts to research to name his fictional family. There is no information relating to Edmond's own alter ego, Gianni, but the names of his brother Lionello (Nello), and his father Tommaso, can both be found in an 1878 letter dealing with Tuscan names.[19] Fittingly, Tommaso Bescapé winters in Italy and returns 'avec l'hiver dans son pays natal, et travaill[e] pendant le mauvais et dur temps en Lombardie et en Toscane' (p. 19). Ivan Turgenev (1818-83), a faithful member of the 'groupe des cinq', wrote to Goncourt regarding famous Russian bohemians, and the Zemgannos' mother is modelled on one of them.[20] In the novel, Turgenev's words are reiterated: 'Stépanida, en notre langue Etiennette, et qu'on appelait par le diminutif de son nom de là-bas, Steuchâ' (p. 20). Compared to the original, the similarities are startling: 'je pourrais vous citer des noms (diminutifs caressants) des bohémiennes célèbres en Russie. "Steucha" - (dim. de Stepanida, Etiennette). Elle a fait tourner les têtes de plusieurs générations entre 1820 et 1830'.[21] A historical figure is thus inserted into the novel. This contributes to *vraisemblance* in terms of the representation of the world of the circus, but also has thematic resonance, since Steuchâ's foreignness is used as an explanation of her mysticism and her inability to love her husband, an inability that is passed on to her sons whose deliberate celibacy is presented as an artistic necessity.

Another historical figure introduced by stealth into the novel is Adah Isaacs Menken.[22] Menken was an American rider who first performed in Europe at the Astley circus in London, a circus that is mentioned in *Les Frères Zemganno*. She later went to Paris where she was acquainted with George Sand, Dumas père, Swinburne, Dickens and Gautier. There can be no doubt that Goncourt knew of her. Floyd Zulli reports that Menken served as a model to Goncourt for 'la'

---

[19] B.N.F. M.S.S. N.A.F., 22464, fols 251-52.
[20] B.N.F. M.S.S. N.A.F., 22477, fol. 79.
[21] B.N.F. M.S.S. N.A.F., 22477, fol. 79.
[22] Floyd Zulli, 'Edmond de Goncourt's American Equestrienne', *French American Review*, 3 (1978-79), 53-56.

Tompkins. There are no traces of documentation on Menken – there is only the extreme coincidence between the bizarre fictional performer and the equally outlandish historical one. With the appearance of Tompkins, though, the novel's Decadent leanings are confirmed.

Tompkins is one of very few women in the novel, a fact that a proudly misogynist Huysmans praised as 'merveilleux'.[23] She is, however, a *femme fatale*. Her status is related to the transformation of the role of riders in literature and the circus, identified by Louisa Jones, who has forcefully argued that as the nineteenth century progressed and the circus became more elitist, the pantomime figures of Columbine and the bare-backed rider (which both Menken and Tompkins are), were depicted as being as dangerous in literature as they were on stage: in all of the arts, pantomime became permeated by death.[24] Fittingly, Tompkins is the prime destructive force in the novel. Her very presence leads to a dramatic change of events.

There are many *femmes fatales* in the works of the Goncourts, yet the themes associated with these earlier examples are not entirely the same as those associated with Tompkins. Manette Salomon, for example, stifles and eventually destroys male artistic power, but is not associated with the cult of eccentricity or refinement (at least not on her own). Tompkins, on the other hand, thrives on her fetish for disaster and travels Europe in search of hangings and natural catastrophes. She is driven by 'l'ambition de faire de l'impossible, du surhumain, des choses défendues par la nature et Dieu' (p. 174). She seeks out the unusual, buys expensive pieces of art only to lock them in a room that she never enters. Like des Esseintes after her, she is guided by the 'plaisir solitaire de la possession secrète de belles et uniques choses inconnues à tout le monde' (p. 180). Her fetishes provide a useful framework within which to study the potentially Decadent nature of circus and pantomime, not to mention the reasoning behind the transposition of the Goncourts' life as authors pursuing artistic perfection onto the Zemgannos' life as performers pursuing the same goal in a different arena.

---

[23] *Corres. Huys-Gonc.*, letter 4, 2 May 1879, p. 54.
[24] *Sad Clowns and Pale Pierrots: Literature and the Popular Comic Arts in Nineteenth-Century France* (Lexington: French Forum, 1984), pp. 51 and 187.

Low Lives and High Culture

It is worth reiterating that Gianni and Nello begin their lives and careers as *saltimbanques* in their family's travelling circus. From the outset of the novel they are closely associated with 'the people' and with a gypsy lifestyle. At this stage they are very distant from the high culture so beloved of rarefied *fin de siècle* Decadents, but it should be remembered that there was also a pronounced taste for the *canaille* at the time.

The choice of a 'low' art form to represent the Goncourt brothers seems to transpose into fiction not only specific lives, but the entire Naturalist movement. There are many Naturalist novels that are set in working-class districts; there are many novels that situate one character's life within a much wider framework and study the effect of environment and family on that character (consider not only the novels of Zola, Maupassant and the Goncourts, but the novels of lesser-known authors such as Henry Céard and Paul Bonnetain); there are also a number of novels that represent undistinguished characters from ignominious backgrounds. Yet, the Zemgannos are set apart from their peers by their refined artistic quest – they thrive on disguise and on performance. They abandon the boredom of the travelling circus because it does not offer sufficient opportunity for artistic innovation. Eventually, they join a more metropolitan and more 'civilised' environment: the Parisian circus.

Gianni's and Nello's change of direction is representative of a wider change in the Goncourt *œuvre*. The solo novels concentrate on more refined environments than the joint ones. There is a palpable difference in focus from *Germinie Lacerteux* and *La Fille Elisa* to *La Faustin* and *Chérie*. Analogous repositioning from working to upper class subject matter can be observed in the works of other authors of the period. Most notably, Huysmans began his career with Naturalist influenced novels like *Marthe, histoire d'une fille* (1876) and *Les Sœurs Vatard* (1879), only to later write *A Rebours* (1884) and *Là-bas* (1891). Christopher Lloyd believes that *Germinie Lacerteux* and *La Fille Elisa* are to *Marthe* and *Les Sœurs Vatard* what *La Faustin* is to *A Rebours*.[25] In his later career Huysmans, much like Goncourt,

---

[25] *J.-K. Huysmans and the fin de siècle Novel* (Edinburgh: EUP, 1990), p. 28.

rejected Naturalist subjects and environments outright and turned to a refined, aestheticised art, permeated in his case by an incense-suffused version of Catholicism.

The end of the century saw an enormous shift in aesthetic focus, and this shift is already under way in *Les Frères Zemganno*, as Zola rightly points out in *Le Voltaire*:

> M. Edmond de Goncourt dans *Les Frères Zemganno* a eu la caprice originale de sortir de la réalité immédiate pour entrer dans le domaine du rêve. Après le roman technique de *La Fille Elisa*, il a voulu montrer qu'il pouvait échapper à l'observation exacte. Son nouveau livre est de la psychologie poétique, si l'on me permet ce terme.[26]

Zola's term 'poetic psychology' can be adopted as highly appropriate to the 1879 novel, which recreates the Goncourts' motivations, as well as the nervous psychological state that breeds and feeds artistic creation. While this psychological state was perhaps observed by Edmond with regard to his own circumstances (as the 'souvenirs' evoked earlier imply), it is hardly empirically verifiable 'evidence'. Once again, the distinction between fiction and external reality is problematically blurred, as are the two meanings of 'document humain'.

Les Frères Zemganno paints the psychological disposition of two poets of gymnastics. It can be read as an analogy for a much wider cultural swing, and as a representation of the psychological disposition of a generation fearful of the unstoppable push of progress and modernity, basking in neurotic pre-millennial tension. In this sense, the novel leaves behind its roots in observed reality and instead focuses on interiority and internalised psychological states. In 1884, Louis Desprez deemed it 'une sorte de poème en prose' (p. 116), drawing attention to the extent to which, as a whole, observed reality was at the very least sidelined, if not abandoned, in favour of poetry – there were no constraints on poetry to accurately represent a world external to it – despite the realist details that appear in the text.

None of this offers an adequate explanation as to why the circus was chosen as the medium through which to paint the tribulations of

---

[26] 'Revue dramatique et littéraire', *Le Voltaire*, 25 March 1879. Zola was, in fact, defending his aesthetic against the perceived criticism of Naturalism contained in the preface to *Les Frères Zemganno*.

two authors in search of novelty and ingenious artistic modernisation. The difference between the descriptions of two performances in the novel sheds light on the choice of transposition and explains why it functions as an effective analogy of the literary field in *fin de siècle* France. Tommaso Bescapé's 'pantomime sautante', *Le Sac enchanté*, is succinctly outlined in a plot summary:

> 1. - Aux environs de la ville de Constantinople, représentée par un paravent, avec le haut découpé dans des formes de minarets, promenade du vieux Bescapé travesti en Anglaise, avec les lunettes bleues de rigueur, le voile feuille morte, une toilette britannique ridicule.
> 2. - Rencontre par l'Anglaise de deux eunuques noirs.
> 3. - Pantomime enjôleuse et immorale des eunuques dénombrant à l'Anglaise tous les avantages et les plaisirs qu'elle trouverait dans le sérail du Grand Turc […] (p. 45).

This pantomime is performed with acrobatics, not words, but is clearly structured around a central narrative, and this narrative is clearly designed to amuse with its bawdy humour.

The situation could not be more different by the time Gianni and Nello perform their own 'invention sautante' at the end of the novel. Gianni is described as 'surexcité par une singulière activité cérébrale […], à l'invention abstraite de conceptions gymnastiques presque toujours irréalisables' (p. 135). In contrast to their earlier performance, the brothers' long-awaited and innovative abstract jump is described anything but succinctly, and is the focal point of ten chapters (56-66), in which the 'débuts des Frères Zemganno' (p. 211) are announced and speculated upon by the audience. At the premiere, they eschew the 'fabulation' or narrative framework that was integral to both their father's performances and their own until this point. The new jump is audaciously devoid of points of reference external to the act itself. Like many the authors of the *fin de siècle*, Gianni and Nello eventually reject representational and story-driven performances in favour of non-communicative and non-referential ones. The new jump is purposely empty of storyline; its focus is the poetry of the jump. Their bodies are the sole focal point:

> Il y avait encore la recherche de l'invention scénique, dont ils voulaient selon une ancienne habitude enguirlander leur gymnastique. Et Nello, le poète ordinaire des exercices fraternels, avait trouvé d'aimables imaginations, un

cadre d'un fantastique souriant et des musiques qui étaient à la fois des échos d'ouragans et de soupirs de la Nature. Mais au dernier moment les deux frères faisaient la remarque que *l'osé* de leur tour disparaissait dans l'enjolivement de la mise en scène. D'un commun accord, ils se décidaient à être cette fois des gymnastes, uniquement des gymnastes, quitte plus tard pour redonner du nouveau à la chose vieillissante, à l'agrémenter de leur petite fabulation poétique (p. 200).

Nello, Jules's stand-in, and not Gianni (Edmond's), is 'le poète ordinaire des exercises fraternels', the storyteller. Could this be an explanation of Edmond's apparent change of aesthetic approach after his brother's death? No story is needed to give context to the clowns' artistic derring-do, and this is itself innovative. By having the Zemgannos discard the ancient habit of dressing art up in stories, the scene functions as a metatextual comment on the changes in the Goncourts' pre- and post-1870 writing. In this evolution lies a move from popular culture to so-called high culture, which can allow itself abstractions. The gymnasts move beyond representation and are left with only the act itself, or art for art's sake. The abstract acrobatic act endeavours to surpass the physical limitations of the body and the earth, by jumping ever higher. The difference between the two performances sheds light on how developments in the circus, which was recognised at the time as the lowest of popular art forms,[27] mirror developments in the literature of the *fin de siècle*. Gianni and Nello abandon narrative in the same way that Edmond de Goncourt attempts to in his solo novels.

At the same time as the nature of their performances is modified, the Zemgannos' costumes become more elaborately adorned. What they abandon in storytelling, they make up for in external appearances. When Nello is presented with his first costume at a young age, 'il prenait entre ses bras son aimable travestissement' (p. 57), as if the costume itself were alive. As time goes by, his disguises become more ostentatious and self-indulgently sumptuous. Already, distance from the self is critical. Other worlds are evoked, as are metals drawn from the centre of the earth:

---

[27] Jones, pp. 14-16; Hugues Hotier calls it the 'spectacle le plus populaire'. 'Le Vocabulaire du cirque et du music-hall en France' (unpublished doctoral thesis, Université de Lille, 1972), p. 2.

Il était vêtu de couleurs de fumée et d'ombre aux sombres fulgurations des métaux cachés dans les entrailles de la terre, des nacres noires dormant au fond des Océans, et que, dans les cieux sans clartés, agitent sur leurs ailes les papillons de la nuit (p. 129).

The descriptions of Nello in costume are disturbing and foreshadow trouble that stems from his divided nature and the abdication of his own personality in favour of his 'autre lui-même du soir' (p. 143). Changes are due to art rather than heredity. In these descriptions, it is Nello, rather than the costume, who is lifeless, Nello who is turned to stone, Nello whose eyes glaze over, Nello who is frozen, petrified. With white paint he creates a deathly 'visage de statue' (p. 143), rather than a typical Pierrot mask. He is transformed into 'un homme-statue du pays sublunaire' (p. 143) and his body obeys 'l'impulsion de courants magnétiques biscornus' (p. 144):

Puis peu à peu, en un état à la fois vague et exalté, et comme au milieu d'un léger effacement autour de lui de la réalité [...] le clown arrivait à n'avoir plus que le reflet de sa blanche figure renvoyée par les glaces, les images des monstres que rencontraient ses yeux sur son habit, et encore le murmure resté dans ses oreilles de la musique diabolique de son violon (p. 144-45).

Nello is pushed towards actions 'de somnambule et d'halluciné [...] gestes dont il n'avait pas l'absolue volonté [...] et cela sans but, pour se faire plaisir à lui tout seul' (p. 144). Alterity is the governing force of the Zemgannos' art, escape from the pedestrian one of their principal objectives. Here, life is art, and art is something to be lived by the artist, not something to observe others living. What is being described is Nello's own decadence, for his fall from artistic glory concludes the novel.

The Circus and 'Cultivated' Authors

Jones posits the history of the nineteenth-century French circus as a 'constant interaction throughout the century between the popular forms of circus and pantomime and the ever more elite forms which assimilated, adapted and interpreted them' (p. 11). This argument refers principally to the assimilation of English-style equestrian arts into the circus and pantomime in France, and accordingly, the

Decadent *femme fatale* of *Les Frères Zemganno* is an American equestrian. *Les Frères Zemganno* is an example of another form of assimilation, as well, one in which the dying circus becomes a theme of literary exploitation.

Concomitant with the death of the circus as the nineteenth century knew it – there were more permanent *chapiteaux* at the beginning of the century than at its end – is the increasing prominence given to the circus as a literary theme. There are numerous examples: Huysmans's Miss Urania in *A Rebours*, Catulle Mendès's 1879 novel, *La Vie et la mort d'un clown*, Félicien Champsaur's *Lulu, roman clownesque* (1901), all confirm that the *fête foraine* was a subject of predilection to authors of diverse literary tendencies. The circus was equally cherished by a certain kind of author who looked to the past and lost worlds for inspiration. By the end of the century, popular theatrical arts were a dying breed, but lived on, as Starobinski makes clear, in the hands of 'écrivains "cultivés"'.[28]

This is not to say that what the 'cultivated' author made of the circus theme met with universal approval. One particularly hostile critic, the *Gazette de France*'s Armand de Pontmartin, rather harshly judged Goncourt's novel to be worthless on account of its plot:

> Un ouvrage qui s'intitule roman, et qui, à travers des prodiges d'intempérance descriptive et un luxe inouï de détails techniques et spécialistes, arrive à la 249e page, sans qu'il soit possible d'apercevoir ombre ou lueur d'action, d'intrigue ou d'intérêt romanesque.

Pontmartin, perhaps unwittingly admitting the fundamental shift towards Decadence in the novel, boldly goes on to equate deficit of intrigue with the decline of western civilisation and 'l'effondrement de la vraie France', for which even the most vitriolic critic must admit Edmond de Goncourt is not solely responsible. The main basis for his claim is the profession of the main characters:

> Mais les personnages de M. Edmond de Goncourt, dans ce roman *des Frères Zemganno*! ces gymnastes, ces acrobates, ces hercules, ces prêtres, ces

---

[28] *Portrait de l'artiste en saltimbanque* (Paris: Flammarion, 1970), p. 22.

clowns, qui ne sont, à vrai dire, que les parasites, les objets de luxe, les branches gourmandes de la démocratie ou plutôt de la classe populaire![29]

Not only are they parasites and proponents of luxury for its own sake, they are rootless, without homeland, and therefore, for Pontmartin, mongrels who are impossible to understand. He criticises from an anti-democratic viewpoint that, ironically, Edmond de Goncourt (and many Decadents) would have shared. Pontmartin recognises that Goncourt has rid his text of intrigue in order to worship what hitherto had been an indulgence no artist could afford: the artistic quest for its own sake.

Conclusion

In the context of this 1879 novel of the circus, what appears as low culture or low art – taking place as it does in a popular environment and being performed by 'common' artists – is in fact a refined representation of an ideal of pure art. It pairs base environment, which fascinated both Naturalists and Decadents for different reasons, with cultivated artists, and upsets the boundaries between the two. As such, it fits with Lyn Pykett's assessment of the *fin de siècle* as 'a period of fierce cultural contest and a defining moment for observing the processes by which the boundaries between high culture and popular culture are established and policed'.[30] Due to the autobiographical instability of the text, the quest of the Zemgannos is inextricably linked to the quest of the Goncourts. As such, *Les Frères Zemganno* is easily interpreted as a *document humain* of Edmond de Goncourt's life. Yet, the documentary realism of *Les Frères Zemganno* exposes many of the issues at stake in novels that vacillate between representation of this world and fantasies of others, and between fact and fiction. Details are drawn from different realities and contribute to the *vraisemblance* of the portrayal of the circus environment, but also destabilise it by foregrounding themes increasingly redolent of un-

---

[29] 'Semaines littéraires DLXXIII, M. Edmond de Goncourt, *Les Frères Zemganno*', *La Gazette de France*, 11 May 1879.
[30] *Reading Fin de Siècle Fictions*, ed. by Lyn Pykett (London and New York: Longman, 1996), p. 4.

reality and Decadence. The implications of depicting the circus – which is the domain of illusion, disguise and deception – within a realist framework are interesting, for the choice of environment seems to carry with it an implicit rejection of mimetic representation. As such, the novel is a document of literary and aesthetic change.

LA FAUSTIN: ORIGINS AND HEREDITY

> Les paons blancs qu'on a vus errer dans mes jardins
> N'aimaient que l'aube pâle et la lune voilée
> Et plus blancs que le marbre pur des blancs gradins
> Etalaient largement leur roue immaculée.
>
> Ils aimaient mon visage et mes longs cils blancs
> Mais leur cri détesté brouillait le doux silence
> Et mes mains ont rougi les plumes de leurs flancs
> J'ai tué les oiseaux de joie et d'innocence.
>
> – Marie de Régnier, 'Les Paons'[1]

In *La Faustin*, research is deployed towards painting a specific thematic end that focuses on the neuroses of the *fin de siècle*. The novel is replete with ambiguous genealogies that complicate notions of 'historical reality' and 'accuracy' and diminish its claim to documentary realism. As such, the text is far from the (fundamentally unachievable) aims of the Goncourt brothers as expounded in *Germinie Lacerteux*. *La Faustin* is neither 'real' nor 'realistic', it is not a 'study' based on a particular empirical case, it does not 'come from the street', and it is scientific in neither content nor approach.

La Faustin*'s Multiple Origins*

Numerous articles and letters by, amongst others, Henry Céard, Gustave Geffroy and Guy de Maupassant, testify that one fictional actress dominated *fin de siècle* French literature: La Faustin.[2] Pierre-Jean Dufief concurs: 'La Faustin, elle, recueille l'assentiment unanime

---

[1] Bibliothèque de l'Arsenal, M.S.S. 14363, fols 68-69.
[2] Henry Céard, '*La Faustin*, par Edmond de Goncourt', *La Vie moderne*, 28 January 1882; Gustave Geffroy, 'Les livres: *La Faustin*', *La Justice*, 21 March 1882; Guy de Maupassant, 'Les Femmes de théâtre' *Le Gaulois*, 1 February 1882.

des écrivains fin de siècle et devient le livre-culte d'une génération'.[3] By contrast, nineteenth-century French theatre was dominated by two actresses, Rachel Félix (1820-58) and, later, Sarah Bernhardt (1844-1923), though others, including Réjane (1857-1920) were also influential.[4] It has been speculated that Juliette Faustin is based on Félix and/or Bernhardt, but in actual fact, there is precious little hard documentary evidence to support this view. Nevertheless, comparisons between the fictional thespian and accounts of the historical actresses do provide important insights into the role of empirical reality in the novel.

The theatre and its female representatives long interested both Goncourt brothers and Edmond alone wrote several biographical histories of eighteenth-century actresses, including *La Saint-Huberty* (1882), *Mademoiselle Clairon* (1890), and *La Guimard* (1893). Most of these illustrious figures were earlier introduced in some form in the joint writings of the Goncourt brothers (*La Femme au dix-huitième siècle*, for instance, or *Portraits intimes du dix-huitième siècle*). A novel dealing with the theatre was projected early in the brothers' career, only to resurface in 1871 as a novel 'sur la vie de théâtre' (*Journal*, 14 May 1871). All the same, a significant transformation of the original idea took place between 1871 and 1882, for *La Faustin* deals more with a particular actress than with the theatre in general.

To this history can be added the fact that in 1856 the slim volume *Les Actrices*, telling the story of the actress Armande, was published. Mireille Dottin-Orsini, modern editor of *Les Actrices*, has argued that the youthful 1856 work is based partly on Rachel and declares that with *Les Actrices* 'nous en sommes encore... aux féeries, aux vaudevilles, aux mélodrames, à la Fantaisie'.[5] Furthermore, she claims that the reason Juliette Faustin's past is not explored and explained in *La Faustin* is that her past is, in fact, *Les Actrices*.[6] The earlier work might in this respect function as a companion volume to the longer

---

[3] 'Les Goncourt précurseurs de la décadence', *Les Cahiers Edmond et Jules de Goncourt*, 3 (1994), 13-22 (p. 17).
[4] Rachel's full name was Elisabeth Rachel Félix and in her youth she was called Elisa, recalling another of Goncourt's novels. See Nicole Toussaint du Wast, *Rachel, amours et tragédie* (Paris: Stock, 1980), pp. 18 and 96.
[5] Edmond and Jules de Goncourt, *Les Actrices (Armande)*, p. 17.
[6] Edmond and Jules de Goncourt, *Les Actrices (Armande)*, p. 80.

novel. If Armande and Juliette share the same past, then there is a corresponding link between Rachel and Juliette. Consequently, *La Faustin* looks to the past work of the Goncourt brothers – *Les Actrices* – as well as to a historical and biographical life – Rachel's – and testifies to a continuity of thematic interests over the course of Goncourt's pre- and post-1870 career. Together, these factors point to creative continuance between mid- and late-nineteenth-century works. On a more general level, the link between the two texts suggests how the Romanticism of mid- nineteenth-century literature was re-elaborated during the *fin de siècle*. Themes dealing with drama and introduced in the joint works of the Goncourts are updated and given a new twist in Edmond's solo novel.

The return to pre-Naturalist sources (or documents) in *La Faustin* diminishes the aesthetic obligation to document the novel and to make it a historical document in and of itself. An explanation for the lack of documentation relating to actresses for *La Faustin* is Goncourt's mistrust of actors, expressed clearly on 2 October 1881 in the *Journal*. In response to a discussion with the actor Got about preparing a role, he comments:

> Les comédiens, quand vous les interrogez sur leur métier, vous racontent un tas de blagues. Got, aujourd'hui, ne voulait-il pas me persuader que l'intonation d'un vers, d'une phrase, un comédien ne la cherchait pas avec le bruit de sa bouche, que c'était une opération cérébrale et que le premier coup, l'acteur y arrivait, quand il l'avait cherchée avec sa cervelle. Alors, pourquoi Rachel, cette intonation, la cherchait-elle avec ses lèvres et sa langue, pendant une heure, une heure et demie?

The word of an actor need not be taken as writ. Implicit in this comment is that Goncourt had enough resources as a historian of actresses not to have recourse to further documentation in order to write a fictional account. This undermines the need to incorporate documents if they do not correspond to a pre-established vision and recalls Colin Burns's conception of Zolian truth as the author's truth, rather than an external *a priori* truth.[7] The novel's claims to documentary accuracy are jeopardised. Got's account, which prioritises rational cerebral reflection, is dismissed in favour of Goncourt's

---

[7] 'Documentation et imagination chez Emile Zola', *Les Cahiers naturalistes*, 24-25 (1963), 69-78 (p. 69).

interpretation of Rachel's more physical, bodily and sensual approach to the stage.

The author's familiarity with actresses is further evidenced by the fact that he had seen both Rachel and Sarah Bernhardt perform. Goncourt was an acquaintance of Bernhardt, to whom he offered the lead in a theatrical adaptation of the 1882 novel (she declined: *Journal*, 22 Feb. 1894), and she also portrayed Phèdre in an 1875 production of the play. Both Goncourt brothers dined with Rachel at their relative Nephtalie de Courmont's (*Journal*, 30 Aug. 1892) and, according to one critic, attended the sale of Rachel's effects after her death.[8] Juliette does something similar. After quitting the theatre, the last event she attends before forsaking Paris is an auction of the effects of an unnamed actress (chapter 41). A further similarity between Rachel and La Faustin is that the former abruptly abandoned the theatre for several months after an ominous thirteen stagings of *Cleopatra* and retired to the countryside.[9] This same course of action is taken by Juliette, who walks out on *Phèdre* for her lover after few performances and flees with him into reclusion at Lake Constance. Juliette's deficient genealogy could therefore be due to the author's over-familiarity with the theatrical environment. Goncourt, if anything, borrows incidents and details from the historical actress' life in order to create his own actress who is plagued by duality, by the inability to escape the theatre without escaping it physically, and by an inability to love that is contingent upon the former in the novel, but not necessarily in life.

Théophile Gautier, author, poet and intimate friend of the Goncourt brothers – Edmond wrote a preface to an early biography in 1878 –[10] wrote of both Rachel and her interpretation of Phèdre in 1843 in *Histoire de l'art dramatique en France depuis vingt-cinq ans*, proving to what extent the literary world was captivated by the world of theatre and performance. In chapter three of the *La Faustin*, Juliette hears a reading of Euripides' version of *Phèdre*, *Hippolytus*, while preparing her role. Sainte-Beuve, who has the literary equivalent of a cinematic cameo, alerts her to this version of the play (p. 34).

---

[8] Toussaint du Wast, p. 307.
[9] Toussaint du Wast, p. 129.
[10] Emile Bergerat, *Théophile Gautier: entretiens, souvenirs et correspondance* (Paris: Charpentier, 1879).

Hippolytus ties Juliette to Rachel, as a remark from Gautier illustrates: '[Rachel] vous rapportait tout de suite à l'antiquité la plus pure. C'était la Phèdre d'Euridipe, non plus celle de Racine'.[11] The interpretation of La Faustin as Rachel is further strengthened, for Juliette herself searches for antique inspiration in order to renew Racine's play. On top of this, a critic named Théo, who finds no appeal in Racine, is present on the opening night in the novel. In this manner, the historical Gautier is written into the fiction. A result of this name-dropping is that the novel is situated in time and its link to external reality is established. There are, therefore, parallels between fictional and historical characters.

The meeting of teacher and student in chapter 20 raises different questions. In this instance, Juliette visits the Marquis de Fontebise, where she states that 'il y a positivement deux femmes qui ne se tiennent pas dans ce rôle' (p. 165). Not only is Juliette caught between being a woman and being an actress, but her theatrical character is divided, as well. Phèdre belongs to both Euripides and Racine and is torn between her roles as lover, wife and mother. But Phèdre's dilemma does not set Juliette thinking about her origins, as it does Renée Saccard in *La Curée* (1871), where the presentation of debased incestuous love also verges on the Decadent.[12] In Goncourt's text, the only way for an actress to portray Phèdre's duality is to abandon bourgeois existence and to live art to the full. Juliette's senses must, according to Fontebise, be excited, she must feel Phèdre's passion and pain. A true misogynist, Fontebise suggests this solution: 'Trouve vite un mécréant d'amant qui te batte... et que tu aimes... ça te donnera peut-être le *la* du rôle' (p. 168). There is a tension between two competing visions of Phèdre. Juliette herself does not know from whence her character stems. Given the novel's premise that actresses are divided between their status as women and their status as performers who assume fictional identities, this imbalance in Phèdre, who is described as the 'grande hystérique légendaire' (p. 99), inevitably has a destabilising effect on Juliette.

---

[11] *Histoire de l'art dramatique en France depuis vingt-cinq ans, deuxième série* [1858-59] (Geneva: Slatkine, 1968), p. 424.
[12] On this, see Sara Via, 'Une Phèdre décadente chez les naturalistes', *La Revue des sciences humaines*, 153 (1974), 29-38.

The novel itself mentions several historical actresses by name and even compares La Faustin to Rachel: 'les uns mettant la nouvelle tragédienne au-dessus de Rachel' (p. 175). Accordingly, certain critics posit Sarah Bernhardt as a possible model for the novel. Certainly, this is the opinion of Catherine Simon Bacchi, Arthur Gold and Robert Fizdale. Their studies maintain that Bernhardt was the muse and model of many authors, including Goncourt: Simon Bacchi writes that 'c'est Sarah Bernhardt qui servit de modèle à Edmond de Goncourt pour son roman *Faustin*', while Gold and Fizdale assert that 'several *romans-à-clef* about Sarah's life, almost as lubricious as *Barnum*, were to be published, among them Edmond de Goncourt's *La Faustin*, Félicien Champsaur's *Dinah Samuel*, and Jean Lorrain's *Le Tréteau*'.[13] Nowhere, however, does Goncourt reveal explicitly who his models were, nor does he reveal Juliette's origins, even though research went into the proper transcription of other aspects of the novel.[14] Documentary evidence points to a different, yet complementary, conclusion to that proposed by Simon Bacchi *et al*, one that considers the process of creation and inspiration as not nearly so absolute and straightforward.

Goncourt was the godfather of Lia Félix's child,[15] but it was Rachel's other sister, Dinah, who wrote two revealing letters to him during the genesis of the text. Both letters deal with visiting the Comédie Française for research purposes. The *Journal* describes one of these visits on 15 June 1881. This is the only evidence in the *Journal* and in the Goncourt correspondence of research 'pris sur le vif' for *La Faustin* between 1879 and 1882. Other references to documentation 'sur le vif' predate both the novel and Edmond's solo career, and confirm continuity between pre- and post-1870 works.[16] Contemporary dressing rooms and plays serve as a backdrop for a

---

[13] Catherine Simon-Bacchi, *Sarah Bernhardt: mythe et réalité* (Paris: Presses universitaires de la S.E.D.A.G., 1984), p. 76; Arthur Gold and Robert Fizdale, *The Divine Sarah: A Life of Sarah Berhardt* (New York: Alfred A. Knopf, 1991), p. 27. See also Noëlle Guibert, *Portrait(s) de Sarah Bernhardt* (Paris: Bibliothèque nationale de France, 2000).
[14] See particularly the following letters from Claudius Popelin and Heredia on the Greek used in the text: B.N.F. M.S.S. N.A.F. , 22473 fol. 53 and 22465 fol. 248.
[15] Ricatte, *La Genèse de 'La Fille Elisa'*, p. 171, n. 2.
[16] Dottin-Orsini gives a comprehensive account of pre-1870 research in 'Les Frères Goncourt et le "roman des actrices"'.

drama that could take place in either the late nineteenth century if based on Sarah Bernhardt, the mid-nineteenth century if based on Rachel, or the eighteenth century if based on any number of actresses who caught Goncourt's attention as a biographer and a historian. Alternatively, the novel can be interpreted as atemporal due to the fact that it is an amalgamation of all of these details and eras, due to the fact that few specific references to time are made, or due to the iconic name of the heroine.

Juliette's Enigmatic Origins

The lack of specific genealogy for Juliette Faustin, compared to Goncourt's other characters, – even Chérie's parents are discussed – is undoubtedly related to, though by no means necessarily caused by, the lack of documentary sources pertaining to her. Of the protagonists of the three final novels, Juliette is the one with the least information relating to her in the Goncourt correspondence. In this sense, she is disconnected from any documentary process of creation and from family history and stands alone among Goncourtian characters.

In addition, *La Faustin* is free from the hereditary prerogatives upon which the Naturalist novel, and many of the Goncourts' novels, were built: the eponymous heroine's origins are never described, there is no weighty family history of dementia, or acting, that contributes to her downfall. Rather, her downfall is a product of her double identity as actress – a very Decadent theme in its depiction of the duplicity, duality and artifice of women – and has much more to do with her profession than her background. In terms of literary creation, the documentary origins of the novel reinforce the ambiguous genealogy of the characters and the move away from scientific explanations based in Naturalist cause and effect. Goncourt does not study the downfall of an actress and her lover. The lack of specific genealogy of the main character is a reflection of both the sources that contribute to the text and a wider aesthetic shift away from causes but towards effects.

Juliette announces that as far as her costume is concerned, 'je m'en fiche pas mal d'être bien historiquement' (p. 106), and, interestingly for a man who is also a historian, Goncourt seems to adopt the same position relative to his protagonist. As Nordau once observed:

> M. Edmond de Goncourt professes to depict a contemporary Englishman, an actress also of our own times, events in Parisian life – *i.e.*, all of them mattershe [sic] might have observed, and with which he ought to be familiar; but what he does relate is so incredible, so impossible, unprecedented, that one can only shrug one's shoulders over the childish fable.[17]

The enigmatic origins of the main character – both in terms of the process of literary creation and in terms of plot – make it difficult to situate the novel historically, and this deviates dramatically from earlier works by the Goncourt brothers. Previous works are situated quite expressly in specific environments at specific historical moments, much as Zola's *Rougon-Macquart* series takes place during the Second Empire. In *Germinie Lacerteux*, for instance, a precise date is provided for Mlle Varendeuil's birth – 1782 – and her childhood during the Revolution has a direct effect on her circumstances as an adult. In *La Faustin*, the absence of a root in a historical moment displaces attention from the 'reality' and referentiality of the story to its 'unreality', to its status as fiction. What can be traced of Juliette's genealogy relates to her name, which is flagrantly drawn from fictional and legendary sources, as Thorel-Cailleteau makes clear:

> Mais [Juliette Faustin] entretient avec son rôle, en tant que rôle, un rapport ambigu, qui s'inscrit jusque dans son nom: Faustin peut en effet rappeler Fausta, l'épouse de Constantin dont la légende veut qu'ayant entretenu avec son beau-fils Crispus des relations coupables [not unlike Phèdre], elle ait entraîné la mort de celui-ci, avant d'être elle-même étouffée dans un bain chaud. De plus l'actrice se prénomme Juliette, ce qui rappelle évidemment Shakespeare et un personnage bien incompatible avec celui de Phèdre... mais aussi la descendance de Vénus, s'il faut croire Jules César, qui, via Iule, se prétendait issu de la déesse. En La Faustin s'additionnent ainsi des rôles qui vont en permanence la piéger, lui interdisant tout accès direct à la réalité, qu'elle s'emploie toujours à désincarner.[18]

The precise nature of *La Faustin* as fiction, as opposed to a 'true' story, as the Goncourts so valiantly attempt to claim with regard to

---

[17] *Degeneration*, p. 481.
[18] *La Tentation du livre sur rien*, pp 205-06.

Germinie, is underscored. The atemporal framework in *La Faustin* makes Juliette almost emblematic; but, even without this genetic framework, the protagonist is alienated from heredity by virtue of the fact that her origins are never discussed in the text.

The link between the actress and heredity is further weakened by the fact that she is unlikely to produce any progeny because her biological instincts are taken over by theatrical instincts: she is not a woman, she is an actress. Juliette is an example of 'insexualité' (p. 60). She is sterile and androgynous, and the notion of actors as 'insexuel' is reiterated in *Chérie* where reference is made to 'la mimique insexuelle' (p. 65). Juliette's womanly qualities are buried under 'l'espèce de masculinité de l'artiste' (p. 102). Her main limitation, therefore, is that she is an actress. As her lover, Lord Annandale, screams from the deathbed: 'Une artiste... vous n'êtes que cela... la femme incapable d'aimer' (p. 307). Whether this suppression of biology and femininity is voluntary or not, it fits into a very pessimistic, almost Schopenhauerian, view of reproduction and women, where procreation is the ultimate sin (a view that is also on display in *Chérie*). This theme itself verges on the Decadent, and, to be sure, in Decadent literature such as Rachilde's *La Marquise de Sade*, the theme of female sterility is taken to extremes.

Annandale: Lover and Place

The imprecise history applies just as much to other characters, notably Lord Annandale and Georges Selwyn, as it does to Juliette, but contributes to different thematic issues, including the corruption and perversion of aristocrats (rather than artists) who inhabit artificial paradises and hells of their own creation.

Lord Annandale's genealogy – or more precisely the origins of his name – has been traced from the India of Kipling, to a love story and, finally, to Dumfriesshire, location of the Scottish Annandale.[19] Theodore Child (1855-92), an English author who brought Irish

---

[19] Pierre Bourdat, 'A propos d'Annandale, hypothèse d'une source indienne de *La Faustin*', *Les Cahiers Edmond et Jules de Goncourt*, 4 (1995-96), 245-48 (p. 247).

Naturalist George Moore to Edmond de Goncourt's 'Grenier',[20] wrote to Goncourt on the subject of the British aristocracy on 4 March 1881 and proposed Annandale as a possible name.[21] Goncourt borrowed and combined Child's information in order to christen his actress' lover, William Rayne, Lord Annandale. *La Faustin* itself discards much of the genealogy put forward by Child: the details of Annandale's family are few and far between and are detached from a cause and effect formula – his mother is French, his aunt is mad, and his father would have disowned him for having a relationship with an actress ('prenant peur de son amour pour elle', p. 184). Nowhere is it suggested that Annandale's illness arises out of any particular hereditary predispositions other than nobility. Yet, his nobility, as well as his past impious behaviour, are intimately connected to the Decadent theme of the decay of aristocratic races at the end of the nineteenth century. Indeed, his downfall could be attributable to what Minhar and Valette, in *A l'écart* (1891), describe as 'le sang pourri par les péchés de [ses] ancêtres'.[22]

The name William Rayne, Lord Annandale, contributes to an aura of mystery and has strong evocative powers. Against the background of Annandale in India, Juliette Faustin's romance gains exotic and idyllic connotations. While the two lovers are never together in India, it is specified that Juliette is the lover of a man who has been attacked by a tiger while there in an official capacity. This attack triggers dreams: 'une chasse au tigre donnée par le vice-roi des Indes, une chasse dans laquelle il y avait un blessé qu'elle voyait tantôt avec la figure de William Rayne, tantôt avec la figure d'un homme inconnu' (p. 87).

The Byronic nature of her love is intensified still more by the Scottish element in the history of the courtship, both in the setting of the lovers' first encounter and in the symbolism of the names. Child specified that the names he provided are either no longer in use by the British nobility or are purely fictitious, but history itself points to a different conclusion. The similarities between the historical name Annandale and Goncourt's character are too marked to be mere coin-

---

[20] Not much is known of Child. Julia Daudet mentions him as a visitor to Goncourt's 'Grenier' in *Souvenirs autour d'un groupe littéraire*, p. 149.
[21] B.N.F. M.S.S. N.A.F., 22457 fol. 132.
[22] Ed. by Sophie Spandonis (Paris: Champion, 2004), p. 71.

cidence. The historical symbolism of William Rayne's title is consummated by the fact that the most famous Lord Annandale was Robert the Bruce, thereby associating the fictional Lord to an ancient line.

The fictional Annandale's family seat is a 'château en Ecosse' (p. 5). There are, into the bargain, white peacocks at the castle. These spectral birds are likened to 'de blanches âmes de trépassées, habillées du satin d'une robe de mariée' (p. 6). Decadent writers like Robert de Montesquiou, Jules Laforgue, Jean Lorrain, Marie de Régnier and Oscar Wilde adopted Goncourt's extraordinary birds, as Mireille Dottin-Orsini has shown.[23] Peacocks themselves are naturally Decadent animals insofar as they are both outrageously decorated and degenerate, by virtue of the fact that they are unable to fully fulfil the role normally assigned to birds in nature: flight. White peacocks are even more unnatural (or anti-natural) as they lack the distinctive flamboyant colourings of most of their species. These birds are drained of colour and are ethereal, ghostly.

Annandale's castle is a moss-covered heap surrounded by 'verdures [...] des limbes' (p. 6). An ever-encroaching mist and an overgrown forest intrude on the grounds. These are all familiar topoï used to establish a gothic atmosphere in Romantic literature, and were all modernised in *fin de siècle* literature. This is stressed by Jean Pierrot who conceives of the link between Romanticism and Decadence as follows: 'In the context of the history of the imagination, the decadent esthetic... constitutes a major stage in the continuous development that had its source in Romantic 'fancy' and led eventually to the equivocal wonderland of surrealism'.[24] In *La Faustin*, 'fancy' is present on the level of escape and Lorrain praises the novel for its 'modernité si fantastique'.[25] All three main characters seek to escape

---

[23] In '*La Faustin*, les paons blancs et l'agonie sardonique' (pp. 253-55) she lists occurrences of white peacocks in later literature. Notable are Robert de Montesquiou's poem 'Offrande à Edmond de Goncourt' read to the dedicatee by Sarah Bernhardt (3 March 1895) and published in *Les Hortensias bleus*, as well as Jean Lorrain's poem 'Les paons blancs'. The birds apear in Laforgue's *L'Imitation de Notre-Dame la Lune* (1886) and *Moralités légendaires* (1887), as well as in Wilde's *Salomé*. In July 1881, as the novel was being completed, the author visited relatives at Jean d'Heurs in Lorraine and saw peacocks on their property (*Journal*, 20 July 1881).
[24] *The Decadent Imagination 1880-1900*, trans. by Derek Coltman (Chicago and London: University of Chicago Press, 1981), p. 9.
[25] *Corres. Lorr-Gonc*, 25 Aug. 1893, p. 88.

from their realities. Selwyn escapes nature through perversion; Annandale escapes the restrictions of his class through ceaseless travel and love with an actress; Juliette attempts to suppress her duality by escaping the theatre for faraway wonderlands, and, tellingly, by reading de Quincey's *Confessions of an English Opium Eater* and listening to Beethoven.

The otherworldly theme, or the theme of escape to artificial paradises, is also carried to the retreat at Lake Constance, which is remarkable for the 'Moyen Age artificiel de certaines parties des constructions' (p. 289). Here, Annadale sleeps amidst the 'mobilier des drames du passé' (p. 302) in a modern Gothic bed replete with red sheets. The name Annandale, while being accurate and chosen after research, belongs to both a documentary and a Decadent aesthetic. It demonstrates to what extent the idea that the novel should be based on factual documentation can contribute to an end result that is far from referential and far from the prerogatives of Realist-Naturalist literature. Georges Peylet corroborates this view, holding that the novel leaves behind the aesthetic of the *document humain*, even though it appears to be a typical Goncourtian study of individual pathology:

> En apparence donc, [Goncourt] continue à suivre le modèle naturaliste. Dans *La Faustin* comme dans *Germinie Lacerteux*, il semble se pencher sur un cas pathologique en étudiant un système nerveux d'actrice. En réalité le romancier met en place un art maniériste qui se détache du réel qu'il prétend étudier, au point que l'objet initial d'étude semble se vider de son contenu... Le contenu de *La Faustin* cesse d'être réaliste à partir du moment où l'art de Goncourt ne se situe pas directement sur le plan de la *mimesis* mais se place sur celui du fantasme.[26]

Everything contrives to make the romance between Lord Annandale and La Faustin seem unreal: the setting, which is linked to Annandale's name, is a backdrop to the performance that is La Faustin's love. In an early review of the novel called 'Les Femmes de théâtre', Maupassant focused on the performance-like aspect of romance when discussing the accuracy of Goncourt's representation of actresses in love:

---

[26] 'L'Art maniériste d'Edmond de Goncourt dans *La Faustin* ou la déviation du modèle naturaliste', in Cabanès, pp. 261-74 (p. 264).

> Quelque captée que soit leur étreinte, n'y a-t-il pas toujours un peu de mise en scène dans leurs manifestations, un peu de déclamation dans leurs ardeurs? Ne jouent-elles pas, malgré elles, une comédie ou un drame d'amour avec des réminiscences des pièces, des intonations apprises?

This opinion is supported in a passage from the novel. Juliette's second performance of Phèdre is triumphant and the narrator warns that the actress and the character are in the process of becoming inextricably united: 'Et les paroles de Racine ne racontaient plus au public l'amour de la femme de Thésée, mais racontaient à William l'amour de Juliette, et, avec l'ombre des forêts de la Grèce, elle lui parlait de l'ombre des bois de l'Ecosse' (p. 177). Her identity has been subsumed by her part.

Duality, ambiguity, and artifice plague the novel. Nothing is as it seems. Phèdre is divided between Greece and France; Annandale – also known as William Rayne – is divided between Scotland, India, and France; the main character, finally, is referred to as both Juliette and La Faustin. The play is confused with La Faustin's own life, and her own love is plagued by the presence of performance and the theatre. As she states in relation to time spent with Annandale in the Hôtel de Flandres in Brussels, where their room reverberates with organ music from the church next door, 'N'aimons-nous pas quelquefois un homme pour les circonstances dans lesquelles nous l'avons aimé?' (p. 4). The roots of the lovers' relationship can only be traced to environments that are romantic, mysterious and gothic – India, Scotland and Belgium – where their romance contributes to a storybook version of love in which they act out roles. Everything contributes to an aesthetic of performance. Nothing is as it seems because Juliette and Annandale each belong to two realms, the one immediate, the one distant in time and space. The documentary precision of Annandale's name contributes to this theme whose *vraisemblance* is far from verifiable.

The noble's name allows the character to evoke the two equally distant and fantastic worlds of India and Scotland without fear of realist inaccuracy. However, it also ties the character to two legendary worlds, at least one of which – the realm of Scottish legend and history – was popular in the nineteenth century. Walter Scott's broody castles permeated the early half of the century (Edmond was familiar with Scott)[27] and Stevenson's *Jekyll and Hyde* (1886) the latter. Huysmans praised the settings of the novel and commented on the 'surprenants et quasi-paradisiaques paysages Ecossais et Allemands'.[28] The origins of the name Annandale, therefore, provide a clear illustration of the use of documentation to provide grounding in both myth and reality. They show how specific facts can be adapted to contribute to a certain imaginary tradition that resonates far beyond the mimetic. The name has much to do with an imaginary tradition popular in Romantic and Decadent novels, but not rigidly placed in a specific temporal framework in the fiction.

Past Lives: Georges Selwyn, Degenerate

Theodore Child, it seems, uncannily suggested a name that had thematic significance beyond what he could have expected. Nor was Annandale his sole surprisingly appropriate suggestion – in the same letter he also helped create Annandale's debauched nemesis (or possibly his alter ego), Georges Selwyn. 'Georges Selwyn... c'est un *sadique*' (p. 285), the Englishman is an 'apôtre satanique du mal' (p. 287). The word 'satanique' is also used to describe Annandale and, in fact, it binds the two men together. In his final agony, Juliette's lover's face is dilated in 'une sorte d'épouvantable caricature satanique' (p. 306). The reappearance of the degraded and corrupt Englishman, the reforging of his childhood 'amitiés funestes, impies' (p. 287) with William Rayne, precipitates the demise of Lord Annandale. Degenerate and evil love links the men.

On first presentation, the sadistic Englishman is repeatedly called 'l'honorable' Georges Selwyn and the context of this presentation detracts from his dignity and nobility while adding to his eccentricity. The irony of the punctuation is reinforced by a description that is not particularly flattering:

---

[27] Donizetti's *Lucia di Lammermoor*, based on Scott's *The Bride of Lammermoor*, is the opera that Chérie attends immediately before dying and the opera that Emma Bovary listens to before embarking on her disastrous affair with Léon.

[28] *Corres. Huys-Gonc*, letter 11, 19 Jan. 1882, pp. 71-72.

> On dîna – et tout en buvant tout le temps de l'eau-de-vie au lieu du vin, et ne mangeant que d'un potage à la queue de boeuf à faire venir des ampoules sur la langue, et d'une salade de concombres dont il vida le ravier –, 'l'honorable' Georges Selwyn fit les [sic] frais d'une conversation sur la situation politique de l'Allemagne, les diplomates anglais du continent, les salons de Vienne, le théâtre de Racine et de Corneille, formulant des jugements d'homme d'Etat, racontant des anecdotes, laissant échapper des mots profonds, tirant de sa mémoire des citations interminables, montrant une connaissance extraordinaire de toutes les littératures de l'Europe, et cela sans un symptôme d'ivresse, et dans une langue française se débrouillant d'heure en heure, et devenant incisive, méchante, et parfois atrocement gouailleuse (pp. 272-73).

Selwyn is presented as an unappetising dilettante man of the world and this description may well be drawn from empirical reality. As Mario Praz explains: 'George Augustus Selwyn (1719-91), [was] one of the most conspicuous figures of society under George III'.[29]

Whether Theodore Child, who was so conscious of British titles, was aware of this coincidence of names is a matter for speculation. That Edmond de Goncourt should be familiar with Selwyn is, as Praz rightly argues, almost unquestionable: 'The name of the eighteenth-century sadist must have been well known to the Goncourts, who were keen students of that particular period' (p. 416). That the real Selwyn was remarkable in the eighteenth century due to his strange habits, particularly his obsession with public executions,[30] offers fitting parallels for the Goncourtian protagonist, who is decidedly depraved. The fictional Selwyn is the owner of a 'petite maison sur les côtes de Bretagne' called the *'Chaumière de Dolmancé'* (p. 292). Appropriately, Selwyn's behaviour conforms to the image of the chevalier de Dolmancé created by the Marquis de Sade in *La Philosophie dans le boudoir* (1795): he has theories on love 'où il y [a] de l'assassin' (p. 287).

---

[29] *The Romantic Agony*, trans. by Angus Davidson (London: OUP, 1970), p. 415. Praz's insights are powerful, yet his study furnishes a fine example of the way in which Edmond's novels are subsumed under the novels of the Goncourts: he refers repeatedly to the Goncourt brothers' *La Faustin*.

[30] John Heneage Jesse, *Memoirs of Celebrated Etonians: including Henry Fielding, the Earl of Chatham, Horne Tooke, Horace Walpole, George Grenville, Thomas Gray, George Selwyn, Lord North, Earl of Bute, Earl Temple, etc.*, 2 vols (London: R. Bentley, 1875), I, p. 104.

While Selwyn's genesis can be reconstructed using letters, the themes attached to his character and his character's genealogy remain the same with or without reference to his documentary origins. Regardless of what is known of the real man, the fictional Selwyn's past is only vaguely hinted at in the text, and this through physical appearances: his features are 'vieux comme le monde' (p. 273) and connect him to a declining civilisation. Physical degeneracy and general social decline were powerfully felt forces at the end of the nineteenth century, when European civilisations underwent revolutionary transformations following industrialisation and democracy. The aristocracy, of which Selwyn is a member, was perceived as being in an unstoppable state of decline. Although the fictional Selwyn suffers from nervous disorders that are a result of his physiology, his maladies are not linked to any extensive family history, but to a more general history of the decline of civilisation. His personal heritage is alluded to only once, by reference to a distinctive and uncanny physical trait:

> L'homme prenait encore un caractère étrange, de ce qu'au milieu de ses cheveux, très noirs, une mèche blanche – la mèche, disait-il, qu'avaient tous les membres de sa famille – était arrangée et mise en évidence avec une certaine affectation (p. 274).

Like his nervous disorders, the overemphasised postiche-like strand of white hair is significant because of the dandyesque aspect it lends Selwyn's appearance, rather than because of the medical condition that causes it. That his family all have this characteristic is as important as the manner in which Selwyn grooms himself with affectation. Heredity is thus of equal consequence as the effects it can lead to. But it is the result that is important: there is no attempt to study the causes of Selwyn's appearance, affectation, or depravity.

Selwyn's genealogy is further obscured by Praz's observation that a description by Maupassant of the poet Algernon Charles Swinburne (1837-1909) – who crops up time and again in Decadent lore – bears resemblance to Goncourt's character (pp. 418-19). Goncourt's art-collector friend, Philippe Burty, remarks on 'ce lord que vous avez fait si compliqué, chevalier, et swinburnien'.[31] Praz also identifies other

---

[31] B.N.F. M.S.S. N.A.F., 22455, fols 442-43.

possible models for Selwyn, thanks to clues found in the *Journal*. These include Baudelaire, because of his hands (Oct. 1857), and Barbey d'Aurevilly (9 May 1875). Michel Caffier, on the other hand, proposes Frédéric Henkey as a model (p. 243).[32] Themes such as sadism, dandyism, and affectation in fashion were all-permeating in literary circles of the Romantic and Decadent periods, but were exploited to different ends. Habits or proclivities that seem idiosyncratic may in fact be representative of the archetypal 'Decadent' man or the archetypal 'dandy'. On the other hand, the depraved characteristics of Selwyn are emphasised in the text, and it would be difficult, possibly unjust, to ascribe these characteristics to all dandies.

The force of place given to Selwyn's disquieting habits fits into a Decadent aesthetic of degeneracy and decay. Depravity is a means of confounding nature: Selwyn takes pleasure in his conditions, one of which is the urge to destroy objects of aesthetic and monetary value. Elisa, oddly, suffers from a similar disorder: 'il lui venait aux doigts une maladresse qui lui faisait tomber fréquemment les objets des mains' (p. 170), and this is also, of course, famously the case in *Nana*. Juliette, on the other hand, merely lives amongst 'des choses d'un grand prix, mêlées à des objets de deux sous' (p. 8). A doctor, the reader is told, is studying Selwyn's curious condition for a book on '*Troubles nerveux*' (p. 275). As to Praz's dismissal of Edmond de Goncourt's belief that a new school would be born of *La Faustin* (*Journal*, 8 Feb. 1882) as megalomania, it is too perfunctory by half. This is especially true given that he himself goes on to explore the links between Goncourt's Selwyn and other fictional sadists of the *fin de siècle*, as well as between Goncourt's novel and the novels of Huysmans and D'Annunzio. Moreover, he concludes that of the three models for *fin de siècle* sadists identified by him, one is Swinburne, one is Goncourt's Selwyn, and one is the Englishman described in the Goncourt *Journal*. The influence of the novel at the time is thus considerable, as Praz proves almost in spite of himself.

---

[32] See also *Journal*, 7 April 1862.

Documenting Depravity and Decay

While there is no Naturalist scientific or medical explanation of Juliette's split personality, nor of Selwyn's degradation, there is evidence that Goncourt researched Annandale's malady. The general condition that plagues Juliette, and by extension all actresses, is not defined in medical terms and has little basis in nineteenth-century (much less twenty-first-century) science. The so-called 'agonie sardonique' (p. 304) that eats away at William Rayne, on the other hand, was researched by a correspondent from the 'Ecole des hautes-études, laboratoire d'anatomie comparée et d'histoire zoologique'.[33] The writer, Ponchet (the same man who helped research monkeys for *Manette Salomon*, see p. 86 above), provides ample information on the conditions 'le rire sardonique', 'le grand zygomatique' and 'le Risorius', but reports that there are no traces of 'agonie sardonique' in the four medical dictionaries consulted.[34] This does not prevent the term from being used in the novel, however, which demonstrates that documentation is only useful in as much as it corroborates a preconceived idea and fits into a given aesthetic. A clue as to where the term 'agonie sardonique' comes from is given in the novel itself, when a doctor explains the rarity of Annandale's disease:

> Voyez-vous, madame, les jeux bizarres du muscle risorius et du grand zygomatique?... un cas qui n'a jamais été observé scientifiquement... Les livres de médecine allemands, anglais, français, la nomment cette agonie... et vraiment la nomment-ils?... mais aucun livre d'aucun pays ne la décrit... et nous n'avions la certitude de son existence que par la mention qu'en fait, d'après le récit de Tronchin, Mme d'Epinay, une de vos compatriotes qui a laissé des Mémoires dans le siècle dernier (p. 304).

Once again the novel reaches into the eighteenth century for inspiration, with the added fact that here it makes reference to its own sources and possibly to Goncourt's historical writings.

Ponchet describes the physical manifestations of both 'le grand zygomatique' and 'le Risorius' and there are affinities between his text and the description of Annandale in the final chapter of *La*

---

[33] B.N.F. M.S.S. N.A.F., 22473 fol. 176, fols 178-79.
[34] The 'rire sardonique' is first mentioned in the *Journal* on 14 May 1871, in a passage relating an encounter between Rachel and Paul de Saint-Victor.

Faustin. Lips are slightly curved and 'exprime complètement la joie... depuis le simple sourire jusqu'en rire le plus fou. Il ne rend aucune autre expression...' ; 'la joie exprimée par le grand zygomatique paraît fausse'.[35] Goncourt's account of the sinister laugh, however, is different in tone and focuses more closely on death and morbidity:

> Car ce n'était plus le sourire informulé et contestable du commencement. C'était, cette fois, bien le rire, oui un rire montant et descendant en même temps que le râle dans une gorge, un rire retroussant d'une manière atrocement ironique des lèvres violacées, un rire courant dans le sinistre *rictus* des dernières convulsions de la vie sur une face humaine, un rire – le rire, cette si douce enseigne, sur un visage, du bonheur et de la joie –, devenu une sorte d'épouvantable caricature satanique... (pp. 305-06).

Whereas in the letter the 'joie' is false, in *La Faustin* this falseness is so extreme as to be a satanic caricature. This satanic laugh also makes an appearance earlier in the century: Baudelaire discusses the condition with regard to the Irish novel, *Melmoth the Wanderer*. Of Melmoth, he writes: 'Il est [...] la résultante nécessaire de sa double nature contradictoire, qui est infiniment grande relativement à l'homme, infiniment vile et basse relativement au Vrai et au Juste absolus... ses organes ne supportent plus sa pensée'.[36] More important is the comparison with Madame Bovary's laugh in her last moments, when 'Emma se mit à rire, d'un rire atroce, frénétique, désespéré'.[37] It could also be a reference to *Lucia di Lammermoor*: Lucia goes mad thinking she has been spurned by her Scottish baronial lover; in *La Faustin*, however, the spurning is presented from the lover's perspective.

The information available concerning the genesis of the three protagonists poses problems of dating and setting. It is also much more ambiguous than the information pertaining to secondary characters: details relating to several minor characters can be found in the *Journal*. On 3 February 1881, Goncourt reveals the source of La

---

[35] B.N.F. M.S.S. N.A.F., 22473 fols 178-79.
[36] 'De l'essence du rire et généralement du rire dans les arts plastiques' [1855], in Charles Baudelaire, *Critique d'art, suivi de critique musicale*, ed. by Claude Pichois (Paris: Gallimard, 1992), pp. 185-203 (p. 191).
[37] Gustave Flaubert, *Œuvres*, Ed. by A. Thibaudet and R. Dumesnil, Pléiade, 2 vols (Paris: Gallimard, 1951), I, p. 589.

Faustin's lover Blancheron, stating that the name was drawn from an eighteenth-century source (an 'agent de change' tells him that there is a nineteenth-century Blancheron, as well). The philosopher who sits beside the actress at dinner on the night of her première is mentioned on 26 April and other inspirations are revealed on 28 October of the same year.[38] This creative process is also encountered in *Chérie*, where secondary characters are born out of scraps from the *Journal*, whereas the main character has much more elaborate and convoluted origins that draw on Naturalist creative processes but play on Decadent themes.

Conclusion

In conclusion, *La Faustin* draws extensively on Goncourt's prior knowledge of the world of both eighteenth- and nineteenth-century theatre. This is especially true insofar as Juliette Faustin herself has been compared to Rachel Félix and Sarah Bernhardt, insofar as Félix Braquemond designs part of her apartment and Jules Janin (1804-74), Saint-Victor (1825-81), and the editor of *Le Figaro*, Villemessant (1812-79), all figures from the nineteenth century, are present at the premiere of her *Phèdre* (pp. 125-26). This confusion of temporal issues means that the novel transcends any particular historical boundaries and is instead timeless and distant from the everyday reality of the Second Empire. Empirical documents, together with the author's own memories and anecdotes about his friends, contribute to a blurring of the meaning of research 'pris sur le vif' and attest to the association between literature and history that is brought to the forefront in the role of documents in *Chérie*. More importantly, in the use of documentation, the drift toward Decadence is conspicuous. The overlap between Naturalist and Decadent themes is all-pervasive. Decadence borrows from Naturalism its obsession with heredity – this can be seen in *La Faustin* just as it can in *A Rebours* – but Naturalism uses heredity as a starting point, a factor in the general decline of individuals and of civilisation, rather than as an end to be celebrated in its own right.

---

[38] For additional sources see Caffier, pp. 241-43.

CHÉRIE: FEMALE DOCUMENTS

> Et je m'adresse à mes lectrices de tous les pays, réclamant d'elles, en ces heures vides de désœuvrement, où le passé remonte en elles, dans la tristesse ou le bonheur de mettre sur du papier un peu de leur pensée en train de se ressouvenir, et cela fait, de la jeter anonymement à l'adresse de mon éditeur.
> – Edmond de Goncourt, Auteuil, le 15 octobre 1881.[1]

The role of documentation in Edmond de Goncourt's novels is nowhere as interesting as in his final novel, the composition of which mirrors historical writing. *Chérie* has been said by one critic to be a 'juxtaposition de documents réels'[2] and by another to be fabricated 'par simple "collage" des documents fournis par les lectrices'.[3] Marcel Sauvage calls *Chérie* 'une suite de confidences féminines, transposées pour une monographie' (p. 135). All of these appraisals emphasise the place of empirical documents in the text, documents allegedly furnished by readers, but it is not in and of itself remarkable that a courtship between author and reader should take place. In the nineteenth century, many authors, including Flaubert and Balzac – who reportedly received over 12,000 letters from the public – benefited from correspondence-based relationships with their readers.[4] It has even been suggested that epistolary exchanges are a theme in nineteenth-century literature.[5] What is remarkable here is that by going directly to his readers, by urging them to send him their childhood confessions so that he might use them in his next project, a novel about the 'jeune fille moderne', Goncourt undermines traditional conceptions of authorship: he establishes that his text is what in modern critical terms is called a 'hypertext', a text derived from

---

[1] *La Faustin*, ed. by Jean-Pierre Bertrand, p. 8.
[2] Marie-Claude Bayle, *'Chérie' d'Edmond de Goncourt* (Naples: Edizioni scientifiche italiane, 1983), p. 6.
[3] Philippe Hamon, 'Autour de *Chérie*', in Cabanès, pp. 275-85 (p. 281).
[4] Christiane Mounoud-Anglès, *Balzac et ses lectrices: l'affaire du courier des lectrices de Balzac. Auteur/lecteur: l'invention réciproque* (Paris: Indigo & Côté-Femmes, 1994), p. 21.
[5] Hamon, p. 281.

anterior texts.[6] The question of which anterior texts (or 'hypotexts') were used remains, to some extent, a mystery.[7]

Goncourt's call-to-pens was designed to solicit anonymous contributions – perhaps as a means of guaranteeing objectivity – but the documents that eventually made their way to the author and into the novel all emanate from readers who were in some way connected to him. The information provided by these women – as noted down by Goncourt and by the women themselves – will be the focus of this chapter, which will seek to analyse the intertextual process that leads from the confessions to the final text and to explore the link between fact and fiction in this *fin de siècle* novel.

History and the Journal

While the method of acquiring documentation for *Chérie* may well be novel, the use of documents to write fiction conforms to Realist and Naturalist patterns of literary creation. As was made clear in the opening chapter on documentary processes, the Goncourt brothers likened the role of the novelist to the role of the historian and famously branded the novel 'history that could have been'. Useful parallels can be drawn between the documentary formula described in the preface to *La Faustin* and the exposition of the ideal technique for historical research outlined in the prefaces to several of the brothers' historical studies, notably *Portraits intimes du dix-huitième siècle* (1856), *Sophie Arnould* (1857), *La Duchesse de Châteauroux* (1860), and *Madame de Saint-Huberty* (1880). The prefaces to each of these works emphasise the central role of private documents, such as the 'lettre autographe', in bringing to life historical figures. *Portraits intimes du dix-huitième siècle* is a good example of this:

> [...] L'histoire intime; c'est ce roman vrai que la postérité appellera peut-être un jour l'histoire humaine. Mais où chercher les sources nouvelles d'une telle

---

[6] Gérard Genette, *Palimpsestes: la littérature au second degré* (Paris: Seuil, 1982), p. 13.
[7] Neither the carnet nor the manuscript, held in a private collection (Gimpel), are available for consultation. See the introduction and first chapter of Bayle. For more information on the manuscripts see 'Miscellanées', *Les Cahiers Edmond et Jules de Goncourt*, 6 (1998), 296-97.

> histoire? Où la surprendre, où l'écouter, où la confesser? Où découvrir les images privées? Où reprendre la vie psychique, où retrouver le for intérieur, où ressaisir l'humanité de ces morts? Dans ce rien méprisé par l'histoire des temps passés, dans ce rien, chiffon, poussière, jouet du vent! – la lettre autographe. Qui révélera mieux que la lettre autographe la tête et le cœur de l'individu?[8]

Methodology similar to that expounded and employed in relation to historical works is put to use in *Chérie*, and this raises questions regarding the handling and treatment of empirical reality in the novel. *Chérie* is composed as though the main character were a historical, rather than an imaginary, figure. When searching for 'facts', Goncourt often turned to his *Journal*, as if what it contained were somehow authoritative, as if the *Journal* itself were a giant 'lettre autographe'.

Documents that are, essentially, impressions and memories of conversations and events that are inscribed or noted down in the Goncourt *Journal* are used primarily in the portrayal of secondary characters in *Chérie*. Those based on notes in the *Journal* are caricatures, akin to La Bruyère's characters,[9] or images of a world that floats around Chérie (to make reference to another of Goncourt's passions, *japonaiseries*). In this respect, secondary characters fulfil a purely decorative function. The absence of a bond between the girl and the other characters is accentuated by the differences in their genesis: few of the secondary characters are based on written documents provided by women readers. Put differently, historical antecedents or likenesses of characters such as Malvezin, the Maréchal Haudancourt, and his secretary, are found in the *Journal*. In contrast, details contributing to the main protagonist are drawn from the *Journal* as well as from reader contributions.

Secondary characters are as two-dimensional as the heroine is multi-faceted, and rarely do the two meet. This is reinforced by the fact that there is very little interaction between secondary characters and Chérie. Her entourage has little bearing on her behaviour; they are rarely presented in action. The one person who does greatly influence the girl is 'la possédée, la détraquée, la toquée' (p. 221), Suzanne

---

[8] *Œuvres complètes*, XXXVIII-XXXIX, pp. 9-10.
[9] Jeremy Wallace has analysed the Goncourt-La Bruyère parallel in 'Les Goncourt, La Bruyère et l'art du portrait', *Les Cahiers Edmond et Jules de Goncourt*, 6 (1998), 74-94.

Malvezin. Malvezin is pushed toward 'l'excentrique, l'étrange, le malsain' (p. 221). She is never introduced directly to the reader, but she is interesting in her own right as her debased nature springs from her belief, which echoes Taine, that there is 'ni bien ni mal, ni vice ni vertu' (pp. 221-22). She wears 'toilettes spectrales' and 'maquillages horrifiques' and practices a 'religion *nevrosée*' (p. 222).

Private Confessions and Authorship

The novel makes use of documents that are furnished by readers, told in their own voices and recorded in their own hand. According to Bayle's analysis there are four main contributors to *Chérie*. One of these is Mademoiselle Abbatucci, daughter of the French Minister of Finance; Chérie, by contrast, is granddaughter of the Minister of Justice. In the Goncourt *Journal*, there is frequent reference to stories of Mademoiselle Abbatucci's childhood (most importantly, that which is recounted on 30 Sept. 1878). Abbatucci does not, however, appear to have provided any written sources herself.

The second contributor is Julia Allard.[10] Early in their friendship, Goncourt suspected her of being a talented author in her own right, insinuating that she wrote for her husband: 'La femme [d'Alphonse Daudet] écrit et je la soupçonne d'être l'artiste du ménage' (*Journal*, 5 June 1874). Julia Daudet furnished her friend with details of her childhood and also published her own memoirs, *L'Enfance d'une Parisienne*, which, as its title suggests, deals with much the same subject matter as *Chérie*. This coincidence of subject matter – it is similar to Zola's *Joie de vivre* (1884), as well – is all-important. Such were the similarities between certain themes of *La Joie de vivre* and *Chérie* that Edmond de Goncourt requested that passages of his novel be suppressed from serialisation.[11] More generally, it shows the interest in the subject of young girls in *fin de siècle* novels.

---

[10] Henceforth, Allard will be referred to as Julia Daudet. Unless otherwise stated, references to Daudet will refer to the author of *L'Enfance d'une Parisienne* and not her more prolific husband, Alphonse, nor her more political son, Léon.

[11] See *Journal* 18 Feb. 1884 and *Corres. Huys-Gonc*, letter 12, 21 April 1884, pp. 76-78, n. 2.

The third contributor is Catherine Junges, Nikolai Tolstoy's niece, who wrote to Goncourt in response to the preface to *La Faustin*, although she had previously met him in 1878. The Russian aristocrat translated part of her childhood diary dealing with her first love so that Goncourt might use it as a *document humain*. It describes the environment in which she was raised. Finally, Pauline Zeller, lady-in-waiting to Princess Mathilde Bonaparte, who allegedly hoped to marry Goncourt – Ricatte refers to her as the 'tendre soupirante d'Edmond' – sent the author her 'cahier rouge' detailing her First Communion preparations.[12] Noticeably absent from this roster of contributors are anonymous letter writers. In effect, it is unclear how many responses from 'ordinary' readers Goncourt received.

Chapter 33 is an example of how a diary and letters are incorporated into the text. Details of Chérie's First Communion preparations and her juvenile religious fervour are given in the so-called 'règlement de vie' (p. 114), which, according to two critics, is drawn directly from Pauline Zeller's text.[13] Zeller herself clarified the term when she explained in a letter to Goncourt that 'le règlement de vie se fait pendant la semaine de la Première Communion et l'on s'inspire des avis qui ont le plus vivement frappé pendant la retraite et les plus propres à aider à se corriger ses défauts'.[14] Although the novel as a whole charts the moral and physical growth of a child through to virtual adulthood, there are remarkably few passages that approach the subject using the voice of the protagonist herself. Chapter 33, however, does precisely this: it is here that Chérie states how she will act, as though she is giving instructions and rules of conduct not only

---

[12] *La Création romanesque chez les Goncourt 1851-1870* (Paris: Armand Colin, 1953), p. 164, n. 35. To these names could be added several others: Line de Nittis and Léonide Leblanc, Marie Bashkirtseff, Valtesse de la Bigne, and Léonine Véri. See Fosca, pp. 336-37; Peter Collister, 'Marie Bashkirtseff in Fiction: Edmond de Goncourt and Mrs Humphrey Ward', *Modern Philology*, 82 (1984-85), 53-69; Ricatte, *La Création romanesque chez les Goncourt*, p. 164, n. 35; Yolaine de la Bigne, *Valtesse de la Bigne ou Le Pouvoir de la volupté* (Paris: Librairie académique Perrin, 1999), p. 166; B.N.F. M.S.S. N.A.F., 22477 fols 252-53. Anna Kroeker of Wiesbaden and Marie Durand of Vienna both wrote too late to be of any use to Goncourt, in May 1884 and 1885 respectively. B.N.F. M.S.S. N.A.F., 22466 fol. 391 and B.N.F. M.S.S. N.A.F., 22461 fols 138-39.

[13] Bayle, pp. 2 and 58; Ricatte, *La Création romanesque*, pp. 166-67.

[14] B.N.F. M.S.S. N.A.F., 22478 fol. 41.

to herself but to her director, not God but Goncourt, the narrator and author.[15] She writes: 'Je ferai toujours' (p. 114), 'Je me mettrai au travail' (p. 116), 'J'honorerai la sainte Vierge d'une manière toute particulière' (p. 117), 'Ce que je crois' (p. 119). The heroine is heard in what is the longest chapter, giving an impression of intellectual lucidity not evidenced in the rest of the novel. Chérie quickly breaks the rules she sets out, however, undermining the authority of the 'règlement' as well as the intellectual honesty of her statements: they are shown to be fiction.

One facet of Chérie's personality, the influence of religion, is explored in what Zeller and Goncourt term the 'règlement de vie'. The second example of private confessions potentially used in the novel comes in the form of a letter from Catherine Junges that focuses on matters of the heart rather than matters of the soul. As in the case of Zeller's 'règlement', part of Junges's diary is reproduced in *Chérie* and is further recycled in *La Revue indépendante* on 1 May 1884 as 'Une passionnette de petite fille'. Junges's diary becomes Chérie's 'cahier de problèmes' and is another of the few occasions where the reader gains entry to the main character's mind.[16] It is stipulated by the narrator that Chérie's diary is not only a palimpsest, but it is written in a school notebook 'à contresens de l'écriture des devoirs' (p. 186), making it quite subversive. She is writing against the grain, subverting her 'devoirs', both her homework and her duties. The explanatory letter provided by Junges is condensed and details are used in the novel to describe Chérie's 'amourette', or what Junges calls 'l'histoire du premier amour d'une fillette'.[17] Junges's 'amourette' is for only one man, whereas in the course of her journal Chérie mentions at least five possible suitors by name. She goes so far as to declare herself 'amoureuse de trois cents jeunes gens' (p. 189),

---

[15] References such as 'des lettres de mères qui me sont adressées' (p. 136) implicate the narrator in the process of creation first alluded to in the call-to-pens issued in *La Faustin*. The reader is thereby led to identify the narrator with the author.

[16] Bayle (pp. 24 and 58) believes that the 'cahier' is based on Zeller's text: 'Le chap. LVI [...] est en grande partie la reproduction du *Journal intime* de Pauline Zeller'; 'Le chap. LVI qui contient la copie presque intégrale du *Journal intime* de Pauline Zeller'. B.N.F. M.S.S. N.A.F., 22478 fol. 41.

[17] B.N.F. M.S.S. N.A.F., 22466 fol. 332.

which is to say that she is enamoured of an entire society and the idea of love.

An example of Goncourt's reworking of Junges's diary occurs in chapter 56. In this chapter, the protagonist is fifteen years old to Junges's sixteen. Although the styles of the source diary and the fictional diary contrast, certain phrases are almost identical. If this were the sole similarity, it could be ascribed to coincidence, but the passage from Junges is also used elsewhere. Junges wrote on 6 June: 'je suis si heureuse, si heureuse, je n'ai besoin de rien, de rien que de savoir qu'il est là, près de moi…'. While Chérie uses a similar formula, she is less certain of her emotions: 'Je suis heureuse! De quoi? je n'en sais rien; je crois que c'est d'être jeune et jolie' (p. 186). Chérie's happiness stems from the external world of appearances, while Junges's sentiment springs from private emotions. Junges writes on 12 April that her feelings are so powerful that 'tantôt j'ai comme une douleur, tantôt je suis gaie'. In contrast, the reader is led to believe that Chérie's fluctuating emotional state is caused by her desire to love, not by a love that exists, and this belies a conception of a woman driven to love, and driven by a force that if left unheeded can be nothing if not malignant. She confesses:

> Samedi, 21. - Mon cœur déborde d'une affection que je voudrais répandre au dehors. J'éprouve un besoin d'aimer. Je voudrais un ami… Tantôt je suis triste à en pleurer, alors je me fourre dans un roman; tantôt je suis gaie et je bouscule tout le monde… (pp. 195-96).

This situation changes. By the end of the novel it transpires that the protagonist has been withholding her feelings from her diary. What Junges states in her journal, Chérie hides from hers: revealed confessions become fictional secrets. What the male author learns from women becomes something that the female protagonist cannot reveal directly to a man. Following the protagonist's premature death, the Maréchal Haudancourt, her grandfather, finds a note in which Chérie's intimate thoughts are revealed:

> Je suis heureuse, bien heureuse; je n'ai besoin de rien… que de savoir qu'il est là, où je suis. J'avais tant de choses à lui dire… mais je n'ai rien su lui dire de ce que j'aurais voulu… Ça n'a été ni gai, ni agréable, ce moment de causerie avec lui… C'était comme si je ne sentais plus rien, comme si je ne me rappelais plus rien!' (p. 308).

These words are almost exactly those written by Junges on 6 June and show a heroine not nearly as ordered and controlled as the 'règlement de vie' would have us believe. The cause of Chérie's mental decline into madness and physical decline to death pivots on the contents of this note which, chronologically, is discovered too late to shape the course of events that result in her death. By noting these feelings outside her 'cahier de problèmes', and by not addressing them in her 'règlement de vie', the protagonist leaves them untainted by the petty concerns of the young society girl. The bubbling, spontaneous girl of the 'cahier', based on a document, is not the 'real' Chérie, but a persona, and the same is true of the pious girl of the 'règlement'. Chérie hides under the layers (sections may be more apt, as layers implies depth) of her personality. Although she is based on external sources, none of them is definitive.

On a more general level, the division (or separation) of Junges's journal into two parts – one of which forms the fictional journal, the other of which is a scrap of paper – shows clearly that source documents can be manipulated and fictionalised to the detriment of documentary and historical accuracy. Not even the main character acts as though diaries or the 'lettre autographe' can, should or do contain all the truth. This being the case, Chérie's concealment calls into question the very foundations of the novel, by calling into question the notion that the documents that contributed to the novel are worthy as objective data. This jeopardises the historical truth of the novel – can novels really be written as history can? – in addition to jeopardising the mimetic impulse and the worthiness of historical projects. It leads to the conclusion that the interpretation of childhood expressed in *Chérie* is not based on the documentary evidence; rather, the sources are used to support a predetermined vision of females. The documents are manipulated to fit Goncourt's ends – although the letter writers do not decline into madness, Chérie does – that posit that the female of the species will hide her true self even in private documents that might be used to reconstruct 'le cœur de l'individu'. Etymologically, 'cœur' is related to core, something that is pessimistically shown to be absent in *Chérie*. The only person who can see beneath the surface is the author, for the story is the author's creation. Thus, even though he professes to want to give a voice to young women, very little of the story is told from the perspective of the heroine.

The 'règlement de vie' and the 'cahier de problèmes' are both supposedly written by the protagonist. In reality, evidence suggests that the documents come from at least two different sources. Chérie is presented as having several authors, none of whom is related to her creator. The construction of the novel implies that if there is no one definitive author, there can be no unified character. Emptiness lies at the centre of the novel. As a consequence, the *je* of the diaries is revealed as highly problematic. The author, Goncourt, is transformed into a 'bricoleur' (as Lévi-Strauss in *La Pensée sauvage*, and later Genette and Foucault, posit the term): someone who constructs novels – not unthinkingly – out of the pieces of material available to him. The material used may not have been written with a novel in mind. Genette writes:

> Le propre du bricoleur est en effet d'exercer son activité à partir d'ensembles instrumentaux qui n'ont pas été, comme ceux de l'ingénieur, par exemple, constitués en vue de cette activité. La règle du bricolage est 'de toujours s'arranger avec les moyens du bord' et d'investir dans une structure nouvelle des résidus désaffectés de structures anciennes […].[18]

Whereas Lévi-Strauss compares the task of the 'bricoleur' to a process of myth creation (and Goncourt's use of documents feeds into a myth of femininity), Genette applies the idea of 'bricolage' to the literary critic; but, it also applies to the present novel in as much as neither the letters nor Julia Daudet's volume of 'souvenirs' would have been intended to be included in a work of fiction. It is less clear whether the novel of 'pure analysis' – that is to say the plot-free psychological novel – can be likened to literary criticism and called a metalanguage, for *Chérie* is not about the documents it incorporates, but is instead the result of the fusion of these documents. That the author is in one way or another a 'bricoleur' is all the more true given that the reading public knows that the author/prefacer asked his female readers to contribute to the text. By proceeding in this fashion, Goncourt undermines his own authority. Whether he would accept this interpretation or whether he was aware of his own preconceptions is open to debate. Nevertheless, the issue of 'bricolage' can be linked to

---

[18] 'Structuralisme et critique littéraire', in Gérard Genette, *Figures I* (Paris: Seuil, 1966), pp. 145-70 (p. 145). See also Claude Lévi-Strauss, *La Pensée sauvage* (Paris: Plon, 1962), pp. 26-33.

the argument that antecedents and causality seem to have weakened roles in these novels. In this case, though, narratives fall together, things fall into place, rather than being explained by straightforward filiation; the text presents itself as a collage because there is too much detail.

There is not a complete abdication of authorial responsibility and authority, however, as the source texts are not used unthinkingly in *Chérie*. All of this means that the novel contributes, wittingly or unwittingly, to the demise of a notion of authorship that posits authors as authorities or masters of their own texts. The play between hypertext and hypotext, between source and product, unity and diversity, between a dominant Naturalist discourse and the discordant voices of the protagonist, and the lack of traditional plot (there are very few events in *Chérie*, much less a climax) is remarkably avant-garde. Indeed, it goes some way to announcing the emergence of the disjointed narratives of the modern era.

While Zeller and Junges are quoted in the novel, their discourses are not harmoniously blended. Jean Levallois, a contemporary of Goncourt's, addressed the problem posed by sources in his 1884 review of *Chérie*:

> D'après son propre témoignage, [Goncourt] a réuni sur ce sujet une foule d'observations, une vaste collection de documents humains. Mais évidemment, lorsqu'il s'est agi de fondre tous ces documents, d'harmoniser toutes ces observations, l'artiste n'a plus su qu'en faire ni comment s'y prendre.[19]

Has the author lost the ability to work from documents? Certainly, Levallois presents this lack of harmony – or the obvious presence of other voices that are neither the narrator's nor the protagonist's – as a failure on Goncourt's part. Another perspective, which acknowledges Levallois's diagnosis, would contend that the multiple documents and consequent division of the main character shows the extreme modernity of both the subject matter of the novel and its composition and narration. Documents are solicited from readers with the explicit intention of using them in a novel. Rather than being reduced to a single discourse (the narrator's), these documents coexist in the text as

---

[19] 'Causerie littéraire', *Le Télégraphe*, 28 April 1884.

fragments of womens' voices. At the same time, the interventions of the narrator (coupled with references to the creative process such as 'des lettres de mères qui me sont adressées', p. 133),[20] combined with the now somewhat dated and misogynistic conception of the female and the feminine, restricts the plurality of voices from fulfilling their expression. In this sense, outright Modernism is not achieved.

Types and Illness

In terms of the contemporary literary field, the way that the documents are managed suggests that the dominant Naturalist discourse of types is disintegrating because the female contributors cannot be reduced to a type. The paradox is that the documents buttress a not impartial substitute discourse based on Chérie's eccentricity, virginity, and malignant biology. Chérie dies for want of a husband; love, for her, is an instinct she does not want to satisfy. The malevolence of the female body is itself a terribly Decadent supposition, intimately linked to the physiological need to reproduce. Jean Pierrot, clearly alluding to Schopenhauer's philosophy, speaks of the 'pitiless necessities of a physical, physiological and social determinism that holds man in thrall to the laws of heredity' and sees love in the Decadent imagination as 'merely an unconscious subjection to an instinct aimed solely at the survival of the species'.[21] Fittingly, Chérie rejects the prerogatives of the survival of the species when she announces to her grandfather, like Renée Mauperin before her, that she will not marry: 'Je ne veux pas me marier' (p. 235).

The protagonist's nervous condition is based on a process of documentation that indicates that Chérie is not a 'typical' adolescent; indeed, she suffers from the so-called 'grandes perturbations' that arise in extreme circumstances in Goncourt's novel when biological instincts are not obeyed.[22] There is also an autotextual link to *Renée Mauperin* (1864). Virginal heroines normally die of consumption, but

---

[20] The only mother to write in that capacity and whose letters are in the Goncourt correspondence is Daudet.
[21] *The Decadent Imagination 1880-1900*, p. 10.
[22] See the following letters: B.N.F. M.S.S. N.A.F., 22471 fols 293-94 (26 May [1882?]) and B.N.F. M.S.S. N.A.F., 22471 fol. 292.

Chérie morbidly relishes and aestheticises her decline. There is one other character in the novel who flaunts sickliness, and she too is unmarried and highly eccentric. Chérie's childhood acquaintances, as married adults, distance themselves from their friend because of her pathological illness. Although the documentation offers some justification for Chérie's illness, it is nonetheless based on a conception of the female of the species as ruled by her reproductive system. As Bayle points out, there are countless reasons for Chérie to die that have nothing to do with a biological or scientific framework: 'la question des tares héréditaires, bien que certainement importante, nous semble, ici, seulement un prétexte' (p. 30).

The multiple documentary sources suggest that the novel intends to present a hereditary type by seeking common ground between the women's contributions; however, in the text, type is opposed to individual. This is made explicit when Chérie's uniqueness *and* universality are affirmed in two contradictory statements: firstly, in chapter 60, 'Chérie était la femme qui n'est jamais tout le monde, Chérie était l'être rare' (p. 204); secondly, in the very next chapter, 'Chérie était semblable à toutes les jeunes filles de seize ans' (p. 206). Chérie is both type and individual, or more precisely, individual turned type. The 'individual' source texts are appropriated to fit with Goncourt's general and rather extreme vision of women as fatal. This generalising vision is based on a conception of stereotypes, but the examples used to present it are remarkably specific. All in all, considered as a history of the 'jeune fille', Chérie is highly contentious. The documentary process cannot be pinpointed: there is no one model for the main character – it is not a true Goncourtian *roman-à-clef* – and there is no way of authenticating assertions. This destabilises the text and calls into question the role of the *document humain* as both source for, and product of, a certain type of literary creation based on mimetic representation and historical methodology. The disjointed nature of *Chérie* as a history means that external sources no longer need to be referred to in order to demonstrate the heteroclite nature of the text. Indeed, the disjunction of the text is both internal and external. Whereas before the identification of documents and models could contribute to the interpretation of a text, *Chérie* illustrates that a text based on empirical documents is a place of disunity – as in Decadence, all that matters is internal life, which can never be fully apprehended. Moreover, the disjunction between the parts becomes an internal matter, foreshadowing the modernism of Apollinaire and, later, Cubists, who made extensive use of collage techniques.

Julia Daudet's Childhood

The unpublished letters and diaries submitted by Zeller and Junges are used to give the protagonist her voice. The voices they provide are only expressed in the novel through the private writing of the heroine. Insofar as this is the case, the documents keep their original function: female confessions remain female confessions, although they are spread across the novel and lose the cohesion given them by their original authors. There is also, however, a published work exploited in *Chérie*, and this document is deployed in a very different fashion to Zeller's and Junges's diaries and letters. As was mentioned earlier, Julia Daudet's main contribution to the novel – though she may not have been aware of it – was *L'Enfance d'une Parisienne* (1883), part of which is dedicated to Goncourt.[23] Fragments of *L'Enfance d'une Parisienne* were published in the magazine *La Vie Moderne* in 1883,[24] the year before *Chérie* was published, and the Alphonse Daudet-Edmond de Goncourt correspondence makes it quite clear that the latter had read these passages. In fact, not only did Goncourt read the passages, he praised them in a letter to Julia Daudet: 'Chère Madame, Il faut en faire beaucoup comme cela de morceaux à *L'Enfance d'une Parisienne*, il faut en faire un gros, gros volume. Tout à fait charmant le morceau publié par *La Vie moderne* aujourd'hui'.[25]

Daudet's themes are appropriated in such a manner as to make Goncourt's character an expression of *fin de siècle* malaise. Chapter

---

[23] The section comprising 'L'arbre de Judée', 'Les rondes', 'Vigneux', 'Saint-Pierre', and 'Départ' is dedicated to Goncourt. *Œuvres de Madame A. Daudet 1878-1889: L'Enfance d'une Parisienne; Enfants et mères* (Paris: Lemerre, 1892). See also *Corres. Gonc-Daud*, letter 186, 18 August 1883, p. 127.
[24] 'La leçon de lecture', *La Vie moderne*, 17 June 1882; 'Le Mensonge', *La Vie moderne*, 24 March 1883; 'Départ', *La Vie moderne*, 7 April 1883; 'L'Enfance d'une Parisienne – fragments III', *La Vie moderne*, 19 May 1883.
[25] *Corres. Gonc-Daud*, letter 171, 7 April 1883, p. 119.

10 of *Chérie* describes the protagonist's love of dolls, and this same fondness is the focus of a chapter in Daudet's work. In the original account, Daudet explains that should dolls get wet, their paint runs, leaving a tear-like stain on their faces:

> Après j'en eus beaucoup d'autres, des poupées peintes qui perdaient leurs joues roses à la moindre goutte d'eau. Quels désespoirs! La poupée lavée, déteinte, et mes doigts rouges de ses fraîches couleurs... Une tâche blanche qui ressemblait à une larme mal essuyée la défigurait d'un côté; j'avais le cœur gros pour longtemps (p. 14).

The effect of water on dolls is taken up by Goncourt in a discussion of Chérie's passion for her second doll, Mlle Mastoc. That Mlle Mastoc is the second doll is highly relevant: her first lifeless companion was left, literally, to rot:

> Malheureusement, un jour de distraction, [Chérie] l'oublia sur un banc du parc, il survint un orage dans la nuit et, quand elle la retrouva le matin, c'était une bouillie, ses doigts enfonçaient dedans. Je n'ai pas besoin de vous dire l'épouvantable désespoir qui suivit (p. 53).

This scene provides a material example of decomposition and differs significantly in focus from Daudet's treatment of the meeting of water and dolls. In the original account, sadness is expressed through first person narrative; Goncourt's heroine, on the other hand, does not directly express any feelings about the disintegration of her doll. Whereas Daudet reports her sentiments directly, in Goncourt's novel this task falls to the narrator rather than the character. Again, contrary to Julia Daudet's young Parisian, Goncourt's fictional character has no voice and is unable to speak for herself except in private forums. Madame Daudet's knowledge and biography are needed to build the 1884 novel, but her voice is not. This might explain the shift in emphasis from fingers reddened by the 'fraîches couleurs' of disfigured dolls to the image of hands penetrating putrefied ones. The intertextual network also illustrates how one document, in this case a published memoir, can be transposed into another whose premise is vastly different. The effect of water on dolls is a sufficiently specific subject as to preclude any mere coincidence between the two versions.

A 'thematic transposition'[26] of the source text has taken place. By altering Daudet's version of events, the author is able to make it coincide with his more troubling conception of female childhood.

The doll episode, though remarkably specific, is related to larger thematic issues. While the demise of the first doll allows Goncourt to introduce a replacement, who comes with a 'trousseau complet' (p. 54) dating from 1830, dolls are also linked to the imagination and to the female's supposed need to reproduce. The novel dwells on the role of the imagination in young girls and on the manner in which a girl is a 'victime volontaire d'une illusion tout à fait extraordinaire, et dans laquelle l'inanimé et la mort de ce qu'on touche [une poupée] n'a pas même le pouvoir de l'enlever à son hallucination maternelle' (p. 52). To say that a doll is inanimate is accurate; to state that it is dead is not merely overstating the case, it is also a means of suggesting that the doll is a morbid object (and that playing with dolls is also morbid). This sentiment is also expressed in *La Fille Elisa*, where the heroine becomes stupidly absorbed looking at 'deux poupées macabres' (p. 68) in a shop window. The young Chérie is unable to differentiate between make-believe and reality: because she does not distinguish between the imaginary and the real, seeing her doll rot is the equivalent of seeing a human decay. This fascination with decay is carried through to adulthood: Chérie progressively transforms herself into a doll, withdraws from society, and leaves herself to rot.

Chérie's heightened emotional awareness and her propensity to fictionalise herself are evidenced in the final events of the novel. Aware that her very presence scares the other members of the audience, she listens rapturously to *Lucia di Lammermoor* 'comme tirée hors d'elle-même par la musique d'amour avec ses grands yeux extasiés' (p. 329), and, much like La Faustin, escapes into the drama by placing herself in it.[27] Through the melting together of dream and reality, a Decadent imprint is left on the story. Dufief writes that 'les Décadents feront de l'activité onirique la principale occupation de personnages qui confondent souvent rêve et réalité' and Chérie here approaches this state.[28] The resonance between documentary sources

---

[26] See Genette, *Palimpsestes*, p. 293.
[27] Lucien Faucou provided Goncourt with information about productions of *Lucia di Lammermoor* in Italy and Paris: B.N.F. M.S.S. N.A.F., 22462 fol. 52.
[28] 'Les Goncourt précurseurs de la décadence', p. 18.

and fiction exhibits this tension: documents of 'reality' (Daudet's non-fiction account) are subtly transformed to become part of an aesthetic of eccentricity and pessimism.

Although *L'Enfance d'une Parisienne* and *Chérie* share a common subject, Goncourt's interpretation of the bond between girls and dolls has a very different emphasis than Daudet's. The maternal instinct – which neither author questions – is presented as natural in *L'Enfance d'une Parisienne*. Goncourt's interpretation transforms maternity based in 'nature' into a conception of maternity as a natural yet malevolent instinct that tampers with both her judgement and her ability to discern reality from fantasy. Chérie, for instance, falls prey to an 'ardente maternité' (p. 54) for Mlle Mastoc. The biological is, under Goncourt's pen, grotesque; Chérie is an example of sexual enslavement. This particular *fin de siècle* discourse posits women as undeniably (perhaps irretrievably) disturbed, something that is suggested in none of the female documents amassed during the process of creation.

In another episode, Julia Daudet fondly recalls the property, called Vigneux, where much of her childhood was spent. In this many-roomed abode, children get lost amidst closed doors and endless corridors, and only enter certain rooms in their nightmares. It is clear from an 1882 letter that Daudet broached this subject with Goncourt. It is also clear from this note that the two authors had been discussing, if not the subject of both of their texts, then at least the subject of Goncourt's. She reflects: 'Je pensais à ce que vous me disiez des peurs des enfants, avez[-]vous remarqué la terreur que leur laisse un rêve, et leur facilité à retomber dans le même rêve effrayant.'[29] She goes on to cite her son Lucien as an example of this. Daudet's own fearful and pseudo-Gothic dreams are recalled in her memoirs, where it is written:

> Nous n'entrions pas, mais, la nuit, l'impression ressentie revenait avec toutes sortes de terreurs; nous étions enfermés là, sans trouver d'issue, criant de détresse et livrés à cet inconnu que recèlent les vieilles pierres. [...] Nos rêves à nous, erraient par cette maison trop grande qui donnait de l'espace à nos imaginations enfantines, les surexcitait, à toute heure, de recherche et de mystère (p. 102-03).

---

[29] B.N.F. M.S.S. N.A.F., 22459 fol. 40.

Environment exerts enormous influence on mental states according to this interpretation of fear, and that the imaginary takes precedence in girls' minds is something that Goncourt would not refute. In *Chérie*, a group of young girls fall prey to their own acute imaginations. In Daudet's scenario, the victims call for help; in Goncourt's, the timorous, virtually mute children are scared of their own voices. The episode, which begins quite dramatically, takes place as Chérie and her playmates explore the uninhabited upper rooms of 'le Muguet', the family home in Lorraine:

> Un coup de vent fermait la porte de la chambre où le petit monde venait de se faufiler, et pas une des petites filles, même en se haussant sur la pointe des pieds, n'était assez grande pour atteindre la serrure. Un premier moment de stupéfaction suivi d'une angoisse inexprimable, dans laquelle ces enfants avaient la terreur qu'on ne découvrit [sic] pas où elles se trouvaient, et qu'elles restassent indéfiniment enfermées. Elles se voyaient, les pauvres petites, […] coucher au milieu de ces vieilles choses commençant à leur faire peur, si peur qu'aucune ne se sentait assez brave pour appeler: parlant tout bas, comme si elles redoutaient le bruit de leurs paroles (p. 74-75).

There is no question that the episodes are comparable, but what was in Daudet's account a dream is in Goncourt's account a frightening reality.

Another scene merges the memories of two women. Julia Daudet recalls with affection a childhood friend and neighbour: 'ce voisin de notre âge habitant une maison de garde au bout du mur de la propriété. (p. 110) Chérie also has a country companion, Mascaro, who is much more remarkable than Daudet's friend who appropriates 'la nature et se distr[ait] des saisons' (p. 109):

> Ce bizarre amoureux de la nature [Mascaro] avait refusé de prendre une chambre aux communs du château, et s'était établi au fond du parc dans une ancienne loge de portier en ruine, près d'une porte abandonnée, où il vivait dans la société de toutes sortes d'animaux difformes, infirmes, éclopés, d'animaux phénomènes, réunis dans une fraternité sans exemple (p. 61).

This passage is interesting for two reasons. Firstly, it evokes an eccentric living in the midst of a Lorraine equivalent to Brocéliande, and Mascaro's liberty is in contrast to females in the novel who are prisoners of their worlds: Chérie's mother is guarded within a walled compound in the park of Le Muguet; Chérie is a prisoner of her society and, to escape, imprisons herself in her own mind. The second point of interest arises from the description of the animals. While they are based on documentation – the *Journal* attributes them to Mlle Abbatucci – the outlandish animals strike curious poses and are diseased.[30] Evidently, only eccentrics and the genetically-challenged need apply for inclusion in this novel. The 'documents' that are drawn from female sources and included in *Chérie* are chosen because they are unusual, not because they are typical.

Conclusion

In 1889, Alidor Delzant, one of the earliest critics to study the Goncourt brothers, offered the following insight into reader contributions to *Chérie*:

> Peu de femmes, à la vérité, répondirent utilement à l'appel qui leur était adressé. Les lettres envoyées contenaient surtout le récit d'aventures bizarres ou romanesques dont l'auteur avait pris soin qu'il n'avait que faire. Avait-il beaucoup compté, du reste, sur des confidences lumineuses?[31]

Whether or not Goncourt counted on receiving many useful letters, it is certain that the documents from Zeller, Junges and Daudet served him well, precisely because they were 'aventures bizarres [et] romanesques'. What is less clear is whether these confessions actually enlightened him. Based on the comparisons made here, it seems more accurate to conclude that the documents were used to confirm a pre-established vision of woman as doomed by biology and unable to

---

[30] The *Journal* describes the animals in the following fashion: 'il y avait un mouflon qui, après s'être consulté un moment des yeux avec deux chiens, partait à la chasse en leur compagnie. A cette chasse, quelquefois, un de ces deux emportait par la peau du cou, dans sa gueule, un certain chat de la maison qui, après s'être rebiffé et avoir juré comme le diable, faisait gaiement sa partie. Il existait aussi un canard qui avait des accès d'épilepsie, pendant lesquels il tombait sur le dos sans pouvoir se relever. Il poussait alors des cacardements féroces, jusqu'à ce qu'un des chiens le remît sur ses pattes d'un coup de nez' (15 Sept. 1882). The description in the novel reads: 'un mouflon borgne, deux chiens galeux, un chat porteur d'une corne entre les oreilles, un canard attaqué d'une maladie qui, de temps en temps, le faisait tomber sur le dos sans pouvoir se relever sur ses pattes' and so on (pp. 61-62).
[31] *Les Goncourt* (Paris: Charpentier, 1889), p. 239.

come to terms with her own passions, instincts and voices. As such, Goncourt's vision of the female has much in common with the emerging Decadent movement of the 1880s.

Yet, his very Decadent theme contrasts with the very modern literary techniques that contributed to the novel. Ultimately, the contextual change in documents establishes an aura of decay that manifests itself in the main character's non-homogeneous identity, in her relation to biological instincts, and in her deteriorating health. On a more general level, because no one voice is definitive, the incorporation of so-called objective and factual documents into the text challenges both notions of textual authority and the validity of the pseudo-scientific bases of the Naturalist novel, as well as the pseudo-historical aims expounded in the preface to *La Faustin*. For his historical writings, Goncourt collected multiple documents relating to one person; in this work of fiction, documents relating to several people feed the creation of a single sickly character. *Chérie* is a fictional subversion of the historical process in which the *document humain* becomes a way to decorate the text. While his historical writings bring to life celebrated women, *Chérie* silences female voices. In the end, it is a male, rather than a female, document.

LANGUAGE AND FORMS

PLOT DEVELOPMENT

> Let us define a plot. We have defined a story as a narrative of events arranged in their time-sequence. A plot is also a narrative of events, the emphasis falling on causality.
> – E.M. Forster, *Aspects of the Novel*[1]

Plot development is one of the areas where Edmond de Goncourt's novels deviate most dramatically from typical conceptions of the Naturalist novel. This difference can be appreciated on a structural level as well as in the extent to which the texts rely on physiological paradigms less as a means of explaining events than as a means of decorating the narrative. There are overarching structural or compositional similarities between the four novels, but, paradoxically, it is their structural instability that attests to their common parentage. All four feature brisk transitions between chapters of enormously different lengths and focus. In each novel, chapters leap from subject to unconnected subject; chapter length can have little to do with the significance of the chapter content. In each novel, time is extremely malleable. Emile Hennequin commented in 1884 that chapter follows chapter 'sans lien presque qui les aligne, sans transition qui les assemble et les dénature par une relation logique'.[2] As a consequence of this structure, the logical progression of the narratives is seldom immediately apparent.

Structures

La Fille Elisa is unique from the perspective of plot development as it has a relatively tight structure for a Goncourtian novel: a prologue, two halves of similar length, the first having 34 chapters, the second 30. Yet, its chapters are unevenly balanced. One of the shortest introduces the crucial love affair between Elisa and the soldier,

---

[1] Ed. by Oliver Stallybrass (Harmondsworth: Penguin, 1974), p. 87.
[2] 'Les Romans de M. Edm. de Goncourt', *La Revue indépendante*, 1 May 1884.

Tanchon; some of the longest describe people who have minimal importance in the narrative (random prostitutes in chapters 37 and 38, a musician in chapter 12). One chapter (3) accounts for six years in one sentence, while others lurch from travelling furiously around France to being settled at a brothel near the Ecole militaire (chapters 18 and 19). Chapter 42 makes reference to 'deux années en prison', while chapter 43 begins 'la nuit'. Although the shape of the novel is by all accounts quite rigid, the violent variations and contrasts within the two parts are extreme.

Regardless of the mischievously misleading framework of *La Fille Elisa*, none of the subsequent novels has so formal a structure. *Les Frères Zemganno*, which has 86 chapters, also advances through time by leaps and bounds. The first 60 chapters describe Gianni's and Nello's life from childhood to present. The remaining chapters focus, for the most part, on the discovery of the jump, and the few weeks surrounding it, thereby displaying how temporal aspects of plot development are organised, condensed and expanded. Within the first half of the 1879 novel, which unlike *La Fille Elisa* is not formally divided into halves, huge spans of time are accounted for in very few words. In contrast, *La Faustin* has 64 chapters that recount at most a year in the main character's life, the central event of which is William Rayne's return in chapter 21. *Chérie*, on the other hand, has a remarkable 105 chapters that cover almost two decades and range in length from tens of pages to a few inchoate and impressionistic sentences. In the 1884 novel, it would be well nigh impossible to identify one chapter as most important, or to identify one chapter as a definitive turning point in the story. The novel could be said to hinge on Chérie's non-marriage, but her announcement regarding this is buried deep inside a chapter dealing with, for the most part, a visit to a horticulturalist.

There is nothing on a presentational or structural level to suggest an orderly or systematic advance or progression in these texts. In spite of this, Emile Zola, in what seems a rare moment of critical blindness, praised *Les Frères Zemganno* for 'la largeur et l'unité du livre', calling it 'le plus serré' of Goncourt's novels.[3] In comparison, Zola's own novels, and indeed many Decadent texts, tend to contain chapters

---

[3] B.N.F. M.S.S. N.A.F. 22478 fols 189-90.

of similar length and are fairly evenly balanced. Such is the case with *L'Assommoir* (1877), *Nana* (1880) and *Au Bonheur des Dames* (1883), which have between twelve and fourteen chapters with an average number of pages. Indeed, *L'Assommoir*'s thirteen chapter structure has a symbolic function, charting as it does the ascent and downfall of Gervaise Macquart. *Germinal* (1885) and *La Terre* (1887) are even more rigidly structured, the first comprising seven parts that are further subdivided, the second five constituent parts. Moreover, in Zola's novels, chapters tend to focus on a particular subject and can be usefully identified by their theme. Even quintessentially Decadent novels like *A Rebours* (1884), *La Marquise de Sade* (1887) and *Monsieur de Phocas* (1900) retain balanced structures, and Péladan's fourteen volume series *La Décadence latine* (1884-1908) is divided into two symbolic 'septénaires'. Edmond de Goncourt's lack of structure, which was imitated by mercifully few authors save perhaps Francis Poictevin, appears to be a somewhat primitive means of destroying narrative, a pre-emptive strike against the novelistic form.

Some of Goncourt's chapters are so short that they are like parts of a whole; others so long that their relation to the narrative is not immediately clear. This is a feature that can also be found in the Goncourts' early novel (used in the loosest possible sense), *En 18...* (1851), as well as in novels like Poictevin's *Ludine* (1883). Structural imbalance is also generated by the so-called documentary focus of the texts: *La Fille Elisa* contains a letter and reproduces a prison menu; *Les Frères Zemganno* describes at length a past pantomime performance; *Chérie* includes a list of balls, a diary, a rule of conduct, and an obituary notice. This method of confusing genres can be found in many *fin de siècle* texts. Daniel Sangsue cites Paul Adam's *Chair molle* (1885) and Félicien Champsaur's *Dinah Samuel* (1882) as examples of this phenomenon and relates the practice to a Sternian tradition stemming from *Tristram Shandy*.[4] The chapters of Goncourt's novels that include these 'documents' (which may or may not be drawn from reality) are among some of the longest, but nevertheless have very little bearing on events. Indeed, the deployment of documents often aggravates narrative continuity. On

---

[4] 'L'Excentricité fin-de-siècle', in *Dieu, la chair et les livres*, ed. by Sylvie Thorel-Cailleteau, pp. 459-82 (p. 463).

the whole, in the three later works, while the stories themselves become less intricate, the accumulation of fragments of varying length and content substitutes for temporal advancement. Moves through space become moves through time by virtue of the fact that – to borrow Freudian terminology, if not psychology – events and states are condensed and stretched to fit the narrative.[5]

Family History

In keeping with Naturalist desires to base plot on analysing how people with specific hereditary dispositions are affected by Taine's three determinants – *race, milieu, moment* – two of Goncourt's novels, *La Fille Elisa* and *Chérie*, both of which start *in medias res*, provide biographical information about the characters and the milieux from which they spring early in the text. Biographical information is provided in *Les Frères Zemganno* as well, but in *La Faustin* it is largely absent and what little there is is not used to explain Juliette's behaviour. Positivist scientific models provide a backbone for *La Fille Elisa*, but in later texts are present only on a superficial level: they no longer inform plot development.

The relatively rigid nature of *La Fille Elisa*'s structure, which Baldick has somewhat extravagantly described as being 'the most ambitious and successful essay in composition in any Goncourt novel',[6] is reflected in its plot, which is the most conventionally Naturalist of the four post-1870 works. The main character has several hurdles to overcome, all of which test her psychological and physiological constitution. The narrative proper begins by providing years' worth of biographical and background information that is, for all intents and purposes, unnecessary to the unfolding of the story, although Elisa's violent temperament plagues her throughout the novel until she altogether loses the desire and ability to act in any way. Childhood illness leaves her with residual traces of 'hébétement' (p. 15); she is pushed into violent action by 'impulsions mystérieuses' (p. 154); she loses control of her body 'à l'improviste' due to 'sensations

---

[5] Sigmund Freud, 'On Dreams', in *The Freud Reader*, ed. by Peter Gay (London: Vintage, 1995), pp. 142-72 (p. 153).
[6] *The Goncourts* (London: Bowes and Bowes, 1960), p. 55.

[...] fugaces' (p. 104), and suffers from an 'indigestion avec des espèces de convulsions' (p. 105) that leads to 'phénomènes hystériques' (pp. 106). 'Il y avait chez elle,' it is specified, 'cette distension de la fibre, cette mollasserie des chairs' (p. 73). The theme of silence is introduced when Elisa is still a child, as she endures a 'resserrement douloureux du gosier' (p. 104) and 'des maladies de la gorge et du larynx' (p. 131). By the end of the novel, which plots Elisa's physical and mental deterioration, these physical manifestations of animality are reflected in her moral life: 'bientôt l'indifférence de son corps pour tout, Elisa la retrouvait dans les mouvements de son âme' (p. 169). In this sense, the role of physiology and medical explanation in the 1877 novel is not to be underrated – the body may well be related to the soul. Nevertheless, the details provided in Book One are not central to plot development, for even if Elisa were not psychologically and physiologically touched, she would still be forbidden from speaking in prison in the second part of the novel.

At the beginning of *Chérie*, the reader is presented with a tea party in progress (narrated in the present) only for the novel to lurch to an uncharacteristically long chapter that attempts to explain the protagonist's aristocratic genealogy. This includes copious (and tedious) detail on grandparents and great-grandparents. By 1884, however, heredity is largely incidental to Goncourt's story, as Chérie's behaviour is not influenced by any genetic traits specific to her. It is female biology in general that is malignant, not Chérie's specific biological or genetic make-up. It is the female's link to reproduction that is both distasteful and harmful. Nature is insidious and inescapable, a fact that is finally acknowledged in Chérie's embracing death. There are no events that test her composition. Subsequent to the initial presentation of her family, there is little mention of anyone other than the girl's grandfather. Her dead father (whose career resembles that of the Goncourts' father) is said to be notable for his 'force physique' (p. 19). There is a 'ressemblance extraordinaire de la petite avec le jeune officier' (p. 42), but she nonetheless dies through a lack of force, through a lack of will to survive, and is thus the opposite of her father. Her Spanish mother flees into the woods of the family property, Nonains-les-Muguet, renouncing speech, after her husband's death. She is then locked in a walled compound on the grounds of the family home. Despite possible similarities between mother and daughter, her mother is mentioned only in passing and plays a negligible role in the novel, despite the fact that, much like her relatively silent daughter, she wilfully refuses to speak. It is never specified whether Chérie inherits this trait from her mother. The only indications of inherited characteristics are references to her mother's Spanish blood – blood that makes Chérie a 'mongrel' who matures more quickly than her purely French peers. All in all, little attempt is made to tie Chérie's deteriorating mental and physical state to that of her parents. She is, on the other hand, the last in her line and her desire to abandon life can be read in part as a wilful and conscious extenuation of her family that would please even the most hardened Schopenhauerian.

In *Les Frères Zemganno*, family history is initially tied to the story of the Zemgannos' acrobatic feat. In the opening chapter of the 1879 novel, the Bescapé family circus ride from the distance into the foreground, slowly coming into focus as the chapter progresses, and subsequent chapters all deal with Gianni's and Nello's childhood and parentage. The most prominent inherited trait that the brothers share, their fatal flaw of sorts, is their dreamy nature that makes them yearn for beautiful artistic achievement. This craving is attributed to their 'sang bohémien' (p. 73). Their 'virtuosité' or 'ascendance bohémienne' (pp. 159 and 134) in things musical and artistic stems from their bohemian Russian mother who is repeatedly described with reference to her wild primitiveness. She is a 'fille de ces primitives populations vagabondantes' (p. 21) and acts 'ainsi qu'une bête' (p. 65). Nello is more like her, sharing as he does her 'conformation physique' (p. 117). This physical resemblance prompts Gianni into action when he realises that mother and son share the same constant cough. Nello's cough 'réveillait dans la mémoire de Gianni un souvenir, le souvenir que leur mère était morte d'une phtisie' (p. 117) caused by an unnamed malady ('on ne le savait!', p. 66). The fear of illness is related to the fact that the brothers depend on their bodies for their art, and their art is not only their livelihood, but provides their life with meaning. Yet, no matter: in the end, it is unimportant that Stepanida Bescapé dies of a 'phtisie' because the brothers' downfall is independent of their hereditary characteristics and has precious little to do with health. Moreover, it is stated that all circus performers live with the thought that 'cette force adroite dont ils vivent, peut être tout à coup supprimée par une maladie, un rhumatisme, un rien de dérangé dans la machine physique' (p. 148). By all accounts, Gianni's worry stems from two sources: it is the worry of all gymnasts as much as a particular fear of a hereditary curse.

Physiological details are used to a lesser extent in causal relationships in *La Faustin*. With respect to Juliette's performances, attention is on the transformation of the woman into the actress, with descriptions pertaining to 'développements des organes vocaux' (p. 102) and the 'muscles de la face' (p. 81). Otherwise, physiological information is used to different ends than in previous novels, and paints a picture of voluntary as much as biologically or genetically imposed corruption. *La Faustin* is the only one of Goncourt's four novels that does not provide elaborate background information regarding the main characters. In truth, little is revealed about Juliette's upbringing and parentage other than that she and her sister were late and impoverished orphans. There is, on the other hand, much detail relating to Bonne-Ame, Juliette's incorrigibly libertine sister. Bonne-Ame, on whom 'crispations nerveuses coururent ondulantes' (p. 68), is propelled towards ever more diabolically debauched action so that she is at last astonishingly described as having 'la farouche grandeur de la prostituée de l'Apocalypse' (p. 242). The encounter between Juliette and the fencing instructor likens them to animals, such is their desire to copulate (in the end, though, Juliette flees before she succumbs to her malevolent animal instincts). Elsewhere, in what can be construed as a metatextual comment on the mechanisms governing Naturalism, a character laments the fact that his lover has failed to have a child. As Lord Henry in *The Picture of Dorian Gray* believes that Dorian would make an interesting study, so Goncourt's character thinks the mating experiment would result in a 'produit très particulier... très curieux... très extraordinaire'. 'L'expérience,' he states, '[n'a] pas réussi' (p. 227). To say this reveals nothing, if not a certain scepticism or playfulness with regard to faith in science and belief in the validity of studying evolutionary principles in the novel.

A conspicuous shift away from Naturalism is visible in the diminishing importance assigned to medical and sociological cause and effect in Edmond de Goncourt's novels. This ties into David Weir's contention that 'the difference between naturalistic determinism and decadence is the difference between a mechanism for malaise and the malaise itself' (p. 45). These four novels are examples of the growing distinction between the two. They present alternative approaches to the connection between causality and aesthetic values, and a distrust of scientific explanation that attests to the mediation between Naturalism and Decadence, as neither the mechanism for malaise nor the malaise itself is, at this stage, fully developed.

Events and Suspense

As scientific doctrine loses its dominant position in providing explanations for characters' motivations and evolution, so the mechanisms governing how events unfold become less reliant on traditional storytelling tools such as suspense, which is surprising given that two of the novels were serialised. Tadié's observation about the joint works is equally true of the solo novels: 'l'intrigue, donc le combat, joue un rôle modeste' (p. 31).

La Fille Elisa can be summarised very briefly, such is the relative dearth of action and event in its pages. In short, the main character runs away from her Parisian home to become a prostitute in Alsace-Lorraine. After a rural idyll of a few years, she leaves her provincial brothel to follow her lover across France, tormented, much like the wandering Zemgannos, by a 'besoin inquiet de changement', 'en quête d'un mieux' (p. 70). She eventually returns to Paris where her ideal lover, a soldier with whom she refuses to sleep, attempts to rape her. She kills him and is sentenced to spend the rest of her days in prison. There she is condemned to perpetual silence and dies, several years later, of madness. In terms of intricacy, the plot is, to say the least, not very involved.

Where there are signs of suspense in Goncourt's 1877 text, it is produced by telling the tale from a position of completion, by making story (what events have happened chronologically) and plot (the way they are presented textually) diverge. The jumps between present and past, and the jumps within the past, allow the narrator to manipulate what details are revealed, and when. The novel builds up, slowly, to a murderous climax, but this climax, presented in chapter 48, after one of its results (the trial) has been presented, has little do with the theme of the second section of the novel, that of silence. In other words, the central concern that is the prison, according to the author's stated intentions in the preface (for what they are worth), has little to do with the main incident that occurs in the novel: the murder. As such, Elisa's actions are disconnected from the focus of the novel, and are secondary to their outcome: how Elisa gets to prison is of little consequence, so long as she gets there. Her life as a prostitute is kept separate from the account of her descent into hysteria due to the fact that the novel is divided into two halves. Although Ricatte argues that 'dans le roman l'hystérie d'Elisa est une conséquence de sa vie de prostituée',[7] the two states seem to be fairly distinct in terms of structure and the manner and order in which events are revealed to the reader. Indeed, they could be two independent stories: the story of a prostitute and the story of a prisoner.

Notwithstanding the fact that there are few events in *La Fille Elisa*, they are all introduced through textual clues so that a modicum of suspense is created within the story through carefully timed revelations. This is first exemplified in the prologue, which plunges the reader directly into a trial that is not mentioned again until the final chapter of Book One. Opening and closing the first book with trial-related details establishes symmetry. The first chapter of the second book maintains the legal thread of the preceding chapters, focusing on the transfer of the criminal to the prison, symbolically called 'Noirlieu'. These details occasion a certain amount of puzzlement about the trial: what has Elisa done? Why is she on trial? How does Book Two relate to Book One?

In Book Two, the mystery is resolved, but not before the prison is described. Prior to her arrival at Noirlieu, Elisa had hidden a letter in her hair. No further explanation of this gesture is offered. It can only be assumed that it is pertinent:

> Avec le brusque mouvement d'une mémoire qui se rappelle une chose oubliée, subitement, elle tirait du milieu du linge, qui remplissait un petit panier de paille noir, un morceau de papier graisseux qu'elle glissait dans ses cheveux, le dissimulant sous l'épaisseur de son chignon (p. 115).

---

[7] *La Genèse de 'La Fille Elisa'*, p. 60.

When it is eventually revealed that this letter was improbably and somewhat vampirically written in blood, 'la vision de la terrible journée lui revenait' (p. 143). At this point the narrative moves a further step into the past, until the events of Elisa's and the soldier's courtship converge with the principal story of her imprisonment. Regardless of these loose threads, clues are few and far between. On the other hand, the few strands of mystery that are left in place, together with the pseudo-medical framework deployed to justify Elisa's violent disposition, illustrate the mechanisms governing plot development, mechanisms that are less conspicuous in the later novels.

Les Frères Zemganno is presented in a much more straightforward manner than its predecessor. It begins with the brothers' childhood and finishes with the end of their circus career. In opposition to *La Fille Elisa*, *Les Frères Zemganno*, like the two later novels, advances chronologically. No mystery is presented in its initial pages and prolepse surrounds but one issue: the success or failure of the gymnastic routine that Gianni and Nello have spent years trying to perfect. The abstract possibility of failure is first raised in chapter 20, where the difficulty for gymnasts of coordinating bodily movements is emphasised: 'où, une seconde seulement, le manque d'entente de leurs deux corps, l'inintelligence de leur contact, pouvait amener pour l'un et pour l'autre, et quelquefois pour tous les deux, le plus grave accident' (p. 86). This comment is followed by the assurance that the brothers' lithe bodies will always operate in unison, that two will always be one. The subject of failure is only temporarily put aside, though, for chapter 29 specifies that the money from the sale of the family's travelling show is being safeguarded in case of unforeseen circumstances, 'pour un cas imprévu, pour un de ces accidents arrivant si souvent dans leur profession' (p. 108). It is later explained in general terms that all it takes for a stunt to fail is a 'grain de sable inconnu' (p. 154). None of these negative remarks are made specifically with Gianni and Nello in mind, but in subsequent chapters this changes.

The selfless Nello will do anything his brother asks of him, no matter how dangerous: 'tout ce que tu trouveras, au risque de me casser le cou, je le ferai' (p. 169). The foolishness of the new stunt is underlined by Nello who exclaims to his brother, not without humour, and using a strange expression itself redolent of Decadence or Symbolism: 'Bon merci! Le saut tout seul ne te paraît pas suffisant... et il y a une sauce à ton saut d'équilibre, je parie... et du violon vertigineux..., et de tout le diable et son travail... et peut-être de la casse' (pp. 187-88). The final article of the Zemgannos' contract stipulates that the circus management is not responsible for any work-related accident. The seeds of doubt are sown through these seemingly banal comments. Nevertheless, there is no reason that the two acrobats should fail, as the textual hints of failure and danger are not immediately connected to any action that produces a negative (or positive) effect on the situation: action is deferred. There is no suggestion that a hereditary trait or medical condition will lead to failure or that the characters are being influenced by their environment. Indeed, biology and physiology – apart from the manner in which gymnasts and acrobats manipulate their bodies – have little active role in the narrative.

In order to overcome the problem of what will cause the brothers' downfall – as no hereditary fault or condition more sinister than an over-involvement in their art plagues them – an agent of change is introduced into the story, in a fine illustration of *deus ex machina*: it is at this point in the narrative that the American equestrian, Tompkins, surfaces. Tompkins, who has a 'physionomie fauve, animale' (p. 185), is described in terms of her eccentricity and impetuousness, her wealth and luxury, and her exotic and self-indulgent extra-curricular activities. She is, in other words, the quintessential *fin de siècle femme fatale*. It is Tompkins who brings about Nello's downfall, possibly in retribution for his having spurned her amorous advances, possibly as a result of her fetish for disaster. What should have been the cause of the accident according to more Romantic logic – the artist's ambition to go too far – is not, in fact, the cause in *Les Frères Zemganno*. Perhaps because of the biographical undercurrents of the novel, the connection between artistic ambition and life is left ambiguously open.

From the moment Tompkins is presented, the text focuses more and more closely on the details leading up to the first public performance of the Zemganno brothers. Accordingly, time closes in on the main characters. The night of the performance is spread over five chapters, one of which – 66 – is the longest in the novel. Some of the happenings in these five chapters are meant to occur simultaneously. As a consequence, the night of the performance has dream-like qualities. The leap itself is akin to a daydream and each of the constituent chapters contributes to the overall drama by painting different impressions and points of view.

As *Les Frères Zemganno* centres more closely on specific events (rather than, for example, general states or extended periods of time), the possibility of failure supplants the possibility of success that until this point had been advanced by the narrator. No longer are negative suggestions rebutted by assertions affirming the skill and superiority of the brothers. Nello is told to stop harassing the equestrian and to be fearful of her, but instead, satisfaction with his artistic progress encourages him in his actions. The director of the *Cirque d'été* believes that the audacity of the brothers' stunt must be publicised widely. Drawing attention to the fact that their art comes before their lives, he tells them: 'Le danger, le péril de la mort, qu'il y a dans votre exercice… il est besoin que la presse développe, mâche cela au public' (p. 204).

On the night of the première, Gianni perceives that his brother is racked by doubt, 'un doute du succès' (p. 210). The public is hungry for excitement because 'la fortune d'un avenir, ou la vie d'une talent est en jeu' (p. 211). They want to 'voir manger de l'homme' (p. 211). There is an added worry: Tompkins, who is not normally present at the circus when she is not working, is present on the night of the première. To add to the sense of unease, in a passage similar to the third chapter of *Monsieur de Phocas*, the remarks of the audience regarding the success-rate of the gymnasts are reproduced: 'et ils ne l'ont jamais manqué' (p. 216). This statement is not met with any reply, but with ellipses that forcibly change the subject. Ellipses and absences abound in this section and contribute to a growing sense of nothingness, absence, and danger. The same treatment is given to two other statements: 'le moindre contact…' (p. 216); 'Je ne voudrais pas faire l'échange de mes membres contre les leurs dans une heure d'ici…' (p. 217). As Jacques Noiray observes, 'c'est seulement comme *blanc*, comme indicible pur, que la chute de Nello peut être montrée dans le récit'.[8] Given the association between the Zemgannos

---

[8] 'Tristesse de l'acrobate', p. 107.

and the Goncourts, this aesthetic of emptiness operates as a pessimistic mirror to the Goncourts' own aesthetic struggles. All of these doubts – the audience's and Nello's – undermine the possibility of the Zemgannos discovering a 'pure' art and successfully performing a new stunt. The doubts are condensed into a few chapters, even though in actual fact they underpin the entire narrative and are the dark foundation upon which it is built.

The concentrated build up of action in *Les Frères Zemganno* is in stark contrast to *La Faustin* and *Chérie*. In these two novels there is precious little plot and limited use of techniques such as foreshadow or suspense. In addition, cause and effect is detached from a Naturalist framework. Plot, or narrative interest, is almost completely absent from the 1882 and 1884 novels – particularly *Chérie* – and replaced by analyses of intimate psychoses. Juliette's illness, if indeed it can be called an illness, is entirely internalised. Like a female Henry Jekyll, she admits 'je suis *deux*' (p. 46) and refers to her 'maladie du théâtre' (p. 254). Her problems are related to her profession, not her constitution.

La Faustin is an actress whose aristocratic British lover reappears just as she embarks on the performance of a lifetime as Phèdre. Her keeper, Blancheron, commits suicide (not seen in the novel, but announced by a suicide note), enabling her to pursue her affair with Lord Annandale. Annandale, however, in a bid to strip her of the power she draws from artifice, does not wish to share her with the public, so she eventually forsakes her career. Once distanced from the theatrical environment, acting, fairly predictably, obsesses her. In the climax, her lover throws Juliette out of the room when she mimics his illness. Otherwise, very little happens, a fact that is doubly apparent when it is compared to Zola's *Nana*, which, like Goncourt's novel, involves a kept woman and the theatre. *Nana*, however, also involves prostitution, lesbianism, physically abusive relationships, arrest and abandonment, hereditary alcoholism, in addition to themes dealing with the theatre. Likewise, whereas there are logical stages to Nana's mother Gervaise's deterioration (told in *L'Assommoir*), there are no stages to Juliette's and Annandale's individual downfalls. Juliette is presented as divided from the outset of the novel, because she is an actress and not because of her heritage. Annandale's illness is only analysed in the closing chapter, during his agony. How he arrived at this drastic state is incidental to the story. The comparison between *La Faustin* and *Nana* is telling as it demonstrates how two authors, allegedly of the same literary persuasion, approach a similar subject and achieve different end results.

The Zola-Goncourt comparison is also enlightening with respect to both authors' literary output in 1884. *Chérie* and *La Joie de vivre* both portray the development of young girls and, as mentioned with reference to the *document humain*, reproductive issues are present in each. Both contain scenes relating to menstruation. In *Chérie*, three chapters describe the transformation from girl to woman – the 'métamorphose morale' (p. 140), occasioned by the onset of puberty – but the issue is not referred to again, even though it is briefly specified (as in *Ludine*)[9] that it leaves Chérie with a 'sensibilité maladive tout à fait anormal[e]' (p. 140). In *La Joie de vivre*, Pauline's menstruation is a structuring device: she bleeds on the night of Lazare's marriage to another, and when their child is born. Chérie has everything she wants except a husband (yet she refuses marriage) and she eventually goes mad and dies as a consequence. She faces no challenges other than those posed by her own reproductive organs.

La Joie de vivre, on the other hand, is a Cinderella story gone wrong, where the hard-done-by Pauline is orphaned and impoverished by her extended family who take advantage of her while thwarting her romantic intentions. Nonetheless, the saintly Pauline cares for them and saves them in times of crisis (saving the child of the man she loves, Lazare). In Goncourt's novel, Chérie announces in passing to her grandfather that she does not wish to marry. The rest of the novel portrays the girl doing progressively more degenerate things, including eating maggoty cheese. The unquestioned scientific link between reproduction and degeneration is, of course, tenuous, and does not seem to adequately account for the turn of events. She becomes ill and deranged until she is ecstatically overwhelmed by an opera in the penultimate chapter. While at the theatre, Chérie says 'Adieu' to a friend and the following, final chapter consists solely of an obituary notice. Goncourt's 1884 novel seems positively devoid of narrative

---

[9] The comparison was first made by Jean de Palacio in Francis Poictevin, *Ludine* [1883], ed. by Jean de Palacio (Paris: Séguier, 1996), pp. 21-22.

interest when compared to Zola's. As Maupassant, who admired the book, said laconically: 'Point d'intrigue. Ce n'est pas un roman'.[10]

The absence of cause and effect and, indeed, plot, is intensely unorthodox in terms of nineteenth-century fiction (as Flaubert would no doubt agree). In 'J.-K. Huysmans', for instance, Arthur Symons observes that 'with Zola, there is at all events a beginning and an end, a chain of events, a play of character upon environment'.[11] In *Chérie*, a metatextual hint is given as to why Goncourt adopts a different method. In a discussion of childhood memories, it is stated that 'l'enfance, en la mémoire de celui ou de celle qui se souvient, ressemble à un grand espace vide, dans lequel quatre ou cinq petits événements se lèvent, surgissent dans une espèce de netteté photographique' (p. 72). This remark applies as much to the last Goncourtian novel, where events are either absent or detached from each other, as it does to Chérie's recollections, and functions as a screen that suggests a depth of character that is not really present.

By 1884, Goncourt's novels describe much more than they recount any linear tale. This highlights a fundamental distinction between two of the primary modes of literary representation that dominate late-nineteenth-century French literature. The changing presentation of physiological and psychological analysis at work here announces the emergence of Decadent discourse, which is more closely aligned to the emerging fields of psychology and psychoanalysis than with the sociological trappings of Naturalism. Not only do Goncourt's works progressively rely less on Naturalist causality, but they rely less on event, or cause and effect, of any kind, preferring to concentrate on fragmented moments in characters' lives, interspersed with reflections of a very general nature.

Tense and Time

The challenges posed to the hereditary and causal framework of the novels are compounded by practices associated with *écriture artiste*. One of the principal means by which the linear progression of the

---

[10] 'La Jeune fille', *Le Gaulois*, 27 April 1884.
[11] 'Les influences d'un sentiment'.

novels is hindered is in the juxtaposition of specific time markers and narration in the imperfect tense, resulting in a false sense of progress that petrifies the text. In addition, sentences are denied verbs altogether, in an ultimate act of plot assassination.

In *La Fille Elisa*, there are textual clues that create minor intrigues within the past story (that is to say, within the story of the misadventures that lead to Tanchon's death). Most of Book One is descriptive in nature, telling of changes in Elisa's circumstances and then describing the environment and people who surround her. A break in this monotony comes when chapter 20 opens with 'le moment était venu' (p. 65). This statement implies that suspense had been building up to this climatic moment, but the verb tenses in the succeeding description cast doubt on this. In truth, the chapter merely offers more description. All that occurs is Elisa's nightly hour of soliciting. False suspense is at work. An impression of temporal progress is given when a 'typical' situation is being described: one paragraph begins 'soudain' (p. 68), another 'enfin' (p. 68). Time indications show not an unlikely or atypical event, but a repetitive, monotonous and normal occurrence in the life of the (or a) prostitute. Monotony is intensified by repeating the phrase 'elle allait, revenait' (pp. 65-66) four times in one paragraph. In this way, the chapter paints both a given night and any given night, and produces an immobilising flow between general and specific, between precise moments in time and timelessness.

The polarisation of general and specific is carried through to *Les Frères Zemganno*, where certain textual structures prevent any sense of progression through time. Chapter 12 is an example of the manner in which the linear impetus of the novel is thwarted through lack of action. It unfolds with the sweeping assertion that 'les années se succédaient et perpétuellement ils [les frères] couraient la France' (p. 61). The examples of the clown brothers' peregrinations are all prefixed with 'un jour ils étaient' – an instance of the meeting of the imperfect tense and the singular event. This is used no less than nine times in one (rather repetitive) paragraph. The next paragraph links events with the conjunctions 'un jour' and 'un autre' (used five times); 'et de' joins actions in the final paragraph. All of these conjunctions freeze the narrative by presenting lists of places. These lists inform the reader of physical displacements through over-elaborate precision.

The distinctiveness of each place is negated, however, due to the fact that each movement is presented in a similar fashion. All movement is presented as equally important insofar as each place name occupies the same place in the syntagm: a succession of names replaces actions. The ensuing chapter, by contrast, only emphasises the malleability of time. It begins 'certains jours' and deals, paradoxically it would seem, with the particular behaviour of the gymnast clowns' mother, Stépanida Roudak.

In other instances, verbs are conjugated in such a way as to make it difficult to identify the central action of a sentence. This makes it difficult to establish any cause and effect relationships in the texts, and renders it potentially impossible for the narratives to advance. In *Les Frères Zemganno*, for example, the following sentence begins by signalling an unexpected event, only to conceal the actual incident within a complex maze of subordinate clauses: 'Soudainement, la lune se dégageant des arbres, tombait en plein sur l'enfant dormant, qui comme chatouillé par sa blanche clarté, se mettait à remuer la grâce de son corps nu dans des mouvements indolents' (p. 13). The movement across time suggested by 'soudainement' is negated by the paralysing structure of the sentence. There is a contradiction between time markers and verb tense. Any sense of anticipation introduced by 'soudainement' is cancelled out by the use of present participles that camouflage the main clause, and, therefore, the action. The sentence would have been unproblematic, however, if the more active past historic had taken the place of the imperfect, or, as it is called in the novel, 'ce cruel imparfait' (p. 255). Instead, false suspense is created by the use of this tense to designate events that are not typical, but specific. The imperfect confers a somewhat despairing sense of timelessness, of inability to progress, on a scene that is supposed to be unique. It is also, in many ways, the impressionist tense *par excellence*, as it gives the lasting point-of-view of an observer, rather than telling the story as a series of self-sufficient events. The imperfect reigns in *Les Frères Zemganno*, and in *écriture artiste* in general, and its use has prompted Jacques Noiray to write that it 'indique [...] une perte d'être, une négativité, une abolition dans le temps. Il est le signe de l'irrémédiable'.[12] Lack of active verbs creates

---

[12] 'Tristesse de l'acrobate', p. 94.

fixity, and this fixity transforms individual moments into ones more universal and timeless.

In terms of the meeting of time and tense in Goncourt's novel, the obvious comparison to be drawn is with the novels of Flaubert, where the phenomenon of description paralysing action arises first and perhaps most distinctly in the nineteenth century. This is especially true of the continual use of time-related words in conjunction with the imperfect. Jean-Pierre Duquette has identified precise time markers as one of the factors that contributes to the temporal paralysis that plagues *L'Education sentimentale*. 'Grâce à ces marques', he writes, 'on voit s'établir tout un réseau de moments indépendants les uns des autres, qu'il n'y a plus alors qu'à relier entre eux (par la lecture même, linéaire).' He continues: 'le fait que ces indications soient pour la plupart très vagues, contribue à créer l'impression de temps dépassé, d'éternel présent un peu opaque, de temps du rêve'.[13] There is little movement across time in the Flaubertian novel according to this assessment; descriptions are isolated from an active temporal framework and 'au lieu de faire avancer le récit', one critic argues, 'elles le retardent, le suspendent'.[14] A well-known essay by Proust, 'A propos du style de Flaubert', also comes to a similar conclusion.[15] In Edmond de Goncourt's novels, nothingness and emptiness prevail as a result of both the tension between time and tense that disrupts the linear flow of the narratives, and the extremely loose structuring of the novels which fragments them. While this stylistic trait may be encountered in the Goncourts' joint novels, its inertia is doubled in the later texts due to their thematic focus.

In *La Faustin* and *Chérie*, tense is equally problematic. The closing scene of the 1882 work confusingly deploys both past historic and imperfect in an account of a conversation. When Annandale erupts at Juliette the first time, the verb used is 'dit'. Juliette's response, and Annandale's second outburst, are both in the imperfect: 'Annandale jetait, une seconde fois' (p. 307). Because of this imperfect, the lover's words will ring forever. *Chérie* opens with an event that,

---

[13] *Flaubert, ou l'architecture du vide* (Montréal: Presses de l'université de Montréal, 1972), p. 100.
[14] Jean Levaillant, 'Flaubert et la matière', *Europe*, 485-487 (1969), 202-09 (p. 207).
[15] In Marcel Proust, *Contre Sainte-Beuve, Pastiches et mélanges, Essais et articles*, ed. by Pierre Clarac, Pléiade (Paris: Gallimard, 1971), pp. 586-600.

unlike others in the novels, is narrated in the present. There are several other manners in which *écriture artiste* contributes to a growing sense of paralysis in these novels: paragraphs are formed of a single sentence that spans pages; paragraphs start 'et', continuing a list begun in the previous one; and, in a shining example of Bourget's definition of Decadent style, words are separated from action as parts are detached from the whole and act independently of any human impetus or will: 'la silhouette rouge de l'avocat se promenait', 'des phrases commencées se taisaient' (*FE*, p. 4). No one is responsible for these actions and events because no person is attached to them.

An equally effective means of immobilising the novels is the use of verbless sentences. These convey a feeling rather than an action, a state rather than an event, and are deterrents to narrative continuity. As there is no activity in these sentences, textually and linguistically they are non-events. Several examples can be found in *La Fille Elisa*: 'Et aussitôt debout, devant la petite porte d'introduction de l'accusée, qu'il tient fermée derrière lui, un capitaine de gendarmerie' (p. 6) ; 'au dehors, aucun bruit, la paix d'un quartier mort, le silence d'une rue où l'on ne passe plus, la nuit tombée' (p. 29), 'aussitôt sur leurs sièges les juges' (p. 6). The poetry is definitely not in motion. Verbless sentences, or sentences without principal clauses, feature in the other novels as well and fulfil the same function.[16] They are similar to the verbless sentences of Rimbaud's and Mallarmé's prose poems and correspond to the Goncourts' desire to write a novel that is a 'poème en prose des sensations' (*Journal*, 7 Feb. 1869), or what in *Les Frères Zemganno* is called 'petits poèmes gymnastiques' (p. 128). There is no linear movement across time allowed in these scenes because there is no active verb to propel the plot.

Narrators

Progression through time is also prevented by narratorial intrusions. This interference fulfils several functions, most of which diverge from typical Naturalist practices whereby the narrator does not overtly

---

[16] An example from *Chérie*: 'Des futaies de soixante ans descendant à pic autour de la propriété et l'enfermant dans un rideau aux dessous de bois tout fleuris, lors du printemps, de pervenche et de muguet' (p. 39).

insinuate himself into the text. On the one hand, they delay the moment when textual information is revealed; on the other, narrator interventions are much more insidious. This is particularly the case when they yield a barrage of so-called evidence or proof, or make oblique reference to the creative process, to sources external to the text, and, in the process of doing so, shatter the illusion of fiction. These interventions frequently destabilise the type/individual correlation that the texts rely on to retain their scientific authority.

Perhaps the most striking example of a narrator intervention transpires in *Les Frères Zemganno*, where the manipulation of time contributes to the inevitability of failure from the moment Tompkins appears on the scene. Once the brothers' stunt is underway, the narrator halts time: the gymnasts are left in mid-air as the action is stopped. Ironically, this is the only moment that their supreme desire to consummate a 'suspension dans le vide' (p. 119) is realised, though, crucially, it can only be accomplished artificially through the intervention of the narrator, through the act of reading rather than through the act itself. While the spectators stare 'visages soulevés vers le haut du tonneau' (p. 220), the narrator interrupts with a question, delaying the moment that the outcome of the feat is revealed: 'Mais que se passait-il dans cette seconde anxieuse où la foule cherchait, voyait déjà le jeune gymnaste sur les épaules de son frère?' (p. 220).

What is remarkable is that it is not events, or the revelation of hereditary weaknesses, that foreshadow and signal disaster, but rhetorical pauses in narration. In the end, the cause of the failure of the leap is external to the brothers. It is not something they have control over, it is not something to which they are genetically predisposed, nor is it something the reader witnesses: the reader does not see the prop barrels being switched by Tompkins (the implied cause of the accident). Narration (the moves through time) and description (the painting of the scene) interrupt and delay the moment when the success or failure of the act is revealed. As a consequence, the brothers are artificially paralysed in their fantasy before they come crashing to their terrible fate the instant the narrator's intervention is over.

The description of the Zemgannos' leap furnishes one example of how the narrator's position can lead to paralysis, literally in the case of the paralysed Nello, and figuratively in the case of the novel. A paralysis similar to that created by the temporal instabilities involving tense and time and the concentration of all the action into concise blocks is occasioned by the narrator's intrusions into the text and the manner in which information passing as evidence is presented to the reader. One tactic that is often used by the narrator in these novels is to announce an event and then describe the place and people who are influenced or introduced by the change. In this manner, general remarks are backed up by examples taken from the protagonists' lives. In *La Fille Elisa*, this gives the impression that the novel is not so much a work of fiction, but a study where hypotheses are backed up by the appropriate evidence. After asserting that 'elle avait de tranquilles soirées de paresse pareilles à celle-ci' (p. 29), a description of what could be any night follows in a separate chapter. *La Faustin* uses this structure as well: 'semblables à celui-ci' (p. 8). It is done repeatedly in *Chérie*: 'en voici un exemple' (p. 48), 'là-dessus un détail' (p. 92), 'voici la scène qui s'était passée la veille entre le grand-père et la petite fille' (p. 228).

Such a procedure does much to draw attention away from the fictionality of the novel, towards its so-called 'reality'. It disrupts the flow of the narratives by isolating examples from the thrust of the story, often placing them in their own chapters. The 'reality' of the texts is also established by using a process of exemplification that refers to documents. In *Chérie*, the procedure is used in relation to the 'règlement de vie': 'Voici le règlement de vie, tel qu'il était écrit sur un petit cahier de papier blanc' (p. 114). Another example, from *Les Frères Zemganno*, shows the same narrative technique: 'Voici le libretto d'une de ces fantaisies dont le Cirque conserve encore la mémoire' (p. 128). This remark closes a chapter; the following chapter describes, in depth, the said routine. This method of exemplification does not contribute to the development of plot. It splits descriptions into two units, suggesting that there is a difference or a change. It even offers little insight into the characters. It does, however, convey the narrator's grasp of the circus environment and substitute descriptions for plot progressions.

Another way that the narrator's dominance of the text is established is the manner in which the reader is often either directly or implicitly addressed in the narratives. In *La Fille Elisa*, the narrator approaches the reader thus: 'vous les voyez' (p. 33), 'disons-le' (p.

58). In *Les Frères Zemganno*, the statements 'vous le connaissez' (p. 166), 'vous auriez dit' (p. 25) and 'là était le coup de théâtre' (p. 46) fulfil the same function, as does 'vous vous la rappelez' (p. 97) in *Chérie*. More importantly, in chapter 15 of *La Fille Elisa*, the narrator includes himself and the reader in the same social and intellectual category, educated and male. This is accomplished by moving from the first person singular 'ai-je dit' to the first person plural 'nous' in a discussion of the working-class woman as reader of fiction (this can also be compared to the portrayal of Juliette and Chérie as readers): 'Nous donnons notre intérêt, notre émotion, notre attendrissement, une larme parfois à de l'histoire humaine que nous savons ne pas avoir été. Si nous sommes ainsi trompés, nous! comment l'inculte et candide femme du peuple ne le serait-elle pas?' (p. 50). A diatribe on 'le silence continu' consolidates the narrator's position in chapter 40 of *La Fille Elisa*, but the observation on the power of books can just as easily be considered in metatextual terms. Colette Becker construes chapter 15 as a commentary on the development of the novelistic form. She views *La Fille Elisa* as a fine example of the questioning of the Novel, traditionally held together by an alternance of descriptive pauses and intrigue:

> Si l'on définit le modèle canonique du genre [roman] comme un récit de fiction avec personnages, fait d'une alternance de scènes [...] et de pauses (résumés ou descriptions), et marchant à travers péripéties et rebondissements vers un dénoument, *La Fille Elisa* paraît être un exemple privilégié de cette mise en question.[17]

The narrator's superior status is further reinforced in the final chapter, in which his own past is related: it is revealed that Edmond de Goncourt is the narrator of the novel as well as its author. Framing devices of this sort are conventional in nineteenth-century literature; Goncourt, however, goes beyond normal conventions with his revelation. In its closing pages, *La Fille Elisa* divulges its own history and offers insights into how it came into existence: 'Il y a des années, je passais quelques semaines dans un château des environs de Noirlieu. Un jour de désœuvrement, la société avait la curiosité d'aller visiter la Maison de détention des femmes' (p. 196; cf. *Journal* 28

---

[17] '*La Fille Elisa*, ou comment tuer le romanesque: "une stupide absence d'elle-même"', *Les Cahiers Edmond et Jules de Goncourt*, 7 (1999-2000), 194-204 (p. 195).

October 1862).[18] Julia Daudet – and she is probably not alone – believed that this revelation spoiled the text.[19] The link between fiction and reality at the end of the novel is highly complicated. Noirlieu is an over-motivated name that connotes fictionality and is virtually the opposite of the actual prison that was visited by the Goncourts, Clermont. Both appear to be nothing more than stereotypical literary devices.

The blurred distinction between author and narrator adds to the moral and textual authority of the latter, by insisting that he is not a purely fictional being. This conforms closely with the Naturalist notion of the author as sage, scientist, and critic who explains rather than invents. Authorial interventions also bolster the legitimacy of the view of the novels as documentary studies based on observed reality – a Naturalist preoccupation – and occur in all four novels. In *La Faustin*, they are particularly meaningful as the interventions come to carry the entire narrative insofar as they legitimise the authority and veracity of the text. Two examples of how the narrator cites empirical sources draw attention to this fact:

> Ecoutez, sur ce premier moment de défaillance, la confidence faite à un de mes amis par une de nos plus vaillantes actrices (p. 44).

> Et ici, je ne puis résister à la tentation de donner, sur cette vie en partie double, un autre morceau de la lettre citée plus haut (p. 45).

Interrupting these two digressions is a statement pertaining solely to Juliette. Moreover, the recipient of this letter is not specified – a lacuna that calls into question the reliability of the statements. Even if the source were known, difficulty would arise because one specific case, no matter how valid the source, cannot be extrapolated to apply to all cases. A similar interjection in *Chérie* fulfils the same function: when the narrator states 'à ce propos, je me rappelle dans une représentation de Philémon et Baucis, à l'Opéra Comique, avoir entendu une fillette de treize ans…' (p. 236), it signals his presence in both fiction and in some external reality. Nonetheless, one of the primary functions – if not the primary function – of these passages is

---

[18] This strategy is repeated in *Chérie*, where the narrator makes reference to 'mon frère et moi' (p. 44), clearly alluding to Jules and Edmond.

[19] *Corres. Gonc-Daud*, letter 43, 5 Nov. 1876, p. 42.

to insert the narrator into the text and to authenticate his assertions. This, in turn, implicates the reader in the narrator's belief system. Strangely enough, these tactics fulfil an almost anti-Naturalist function as they detract from the scientific authority of the novel, by drawing the narrator and author – whose views dominate the story at hand – into the realm of the fictitious and by drawing the reader out.

This textual strategy diverges from accepted Naturalist practices where the author/narrator is expected to hide behind the text. In *La Fille Elisa*, due to the often didactic tone of the novel, the narrator's point-of-view rather than the heroine's relation to, and experience of, the outside world carries the story. Becker declares that 'loin de s'effacer derrière le personnage, (comme le demande Zola dans sa définition du roman naturaliste et comme il tend à le faire), Goncourt multiplie les intrusions d'auteur, les commentaires'.[20] In *La Faustin* and *Chérie*, the narrator's perspective and biases dominate because the characters themselves are fragmented and torn between several competing voices.

One effect of accentuating the narrator's omniscience is that Goncourt's texts vacillate between general and specific. This to-ing and fro-ing has implications as far as the mediation between Naturalism and Decadence is concerned. In chapter 4 of *La Faustin*, the doings of Juliette are largely eclipsed by the arguments of a narrator who discusses histories of actresses and the transformation of actresses into stage roles. Interestingly, instead of recounting Juliette's personal heritage and genealogy, the history of actresses as a type (or stereotype) is told. Underlying the novel is the premise that all actresses, regardless of their personal circumstances, share common characteristics that force them into acting careers. There is a clear shift away from Naturalism, where biology, physiology and heredity contribute to a diagnosis of the type, towards a much more coloured view of characters.

Although the idea of the type is present in both Naturalist and Decadent literatures according to this analysis, its role has been transformed. No longer contributing to a social-Darwinian model of humanity, in this case types instead serve to reinforce the narrator's misogynist beliefs, no matter how biased. In this manner, the

---

[20] '*La Fille Elisa*, ou comment tuer le romanesque', p. 196.

Plot Development

narrator's preconceptions are transformed into (pseudo)scientific fact, even though the 'science' and the scientific analysis, most obvious in the form of inductive logic that identifies repeated patterns of behaviour, are missing. Edmond de Goncourt replaces Naturalist scientific justifications with simply stated ideas. The 'type' becomes a malady in itself, as specific cases are studied through the lens of preconceived ideas – often mere clichés or *fin de siècle* fantasies – rather than vice versa. Nowhere is this truer than in chapter ten of *La Faustin*, where Juliette is presented as a representative example of 'the actress':

> Mais la phrase obséquieuse était dite [by Juliette] de la voix la plus rêche, et comme par une femme qui va égratigner. Il y a encore une particularité à noter chez les actrices, dans cette période de l'incubation d'un rôle, et surtout dans le labeur agaçant et contrariant des répétitions, elles sont comme enveloppées d'austérité, de froideur, d'*insexualité* (p. 60).

It is implied that because all actresses are plagued by duality – another being takes over as the role takes root in the actress – it follows that Juliette should be. Individual identity becomes hazy: Juliette is referred to as both 'l'Actrice' and 'La Faustin'. In the 1882 novel, narrator interventions, digressions and explanations come to replace plot. Furthermore, insofar as plot is spurned, and replaced by sensation in terms of both stylistics and thematics – the hyper-sensitive, nerve-wracked artist is a recurrent theme in the literature of the nineteenth century – the Decadent aesthetic emerges in Edmond de Goncourt's novels. All in all, narrator interventions divide and paralyse the text by offering, sometimes over several chapters, examples better suited to non-fiction than fiction, or ill thought through preconceptions based on no analysis at all.

Conclusion

The immobilising force of verb tense is a centrepiece of Edmond de Goncourt's novels. Oppositions between time and tense result in stasis, as does the elimination of the pseudo-scientific apparatus that organises Naturalist conceptions of literature. The presence of a Naturalist theoretical framework against which the novels could be contextualised diminishes. Where once there was positivist scientific doctrine, in later novels this is substituted on a thematic level with the narrator's fantasies. This presents a clear challenge to Michel Raimond's assertion that these sorts of modifications at the end of the nineteenth century did not apply to the Goncourts' novels: 'le lecteur était tiraillé entre deux registres différents: il entrait dans un agencement de circonstances particulières et de personnages singuliers; mais d'autre part, il s'en évadait au profit de la généralité des considérations ou de la subjectivité de l'auteur'.[21]

The unravelling of the Naturalist framework, visible in terms of narration through the diminishing significance, and subsequent dispersion, of events, as well as in the changing organisation of time and the authority that is placed in the narrator's voice, is a sign of the decomposition of a literary model. In this respect, *La Fille Elisa*, *Les Frères Zemganno*, *La Faustin* and *Chérie* move towards the environment-less novels of psychological subjectivity and distraction, where outside events are of little to no relevance to the life of the character and, by extrapolation, to the narrative as a whole. This is as perceptible in another founding Decadent text, *A Rebours*, where the protagonist has only extremely limited contact with the world outside the one he fabricates for himself ('visiting' London while in a Parisian pub), as it is in *La Faustin* and *Chérie*. The demotion of cause and effect driven plot leads eventually to novels that are pieced together from external sources, or made to appear as such, and whose cohesion stems from the very fact that they are fragmentary; to novels where progression through time is more a function of the reading process than plot development.

---

[21] *La Crise du roman des lendemains du Naturalisme aux années vingt* (Paris: José Corti, 1966), pp. 179-80.

Textual Voices

> Ecrire ou parler c'est user d'une faculté nécessairement commune à tous les hommes.
> – Remy de Gourmont, 'Du style ou de l'écriture'[1]

In Edmond de Goncourt's four novels, speech is important both on a thematic level and from the point of view of disruptive textual practices. Just as a shedding of Naturalist apparatuses is apparent in the diminishing intricacy of plot in his work, so it is apparent on a thematic level in the textual representations of speech. In *La Fille Elisa*, *Les Frères Zemganno*, *La Faustin* and *Chérie*, direct discourse fails to unite characters with their environment. This has several consequences, the most notable of which is the sense of isolation and alienation that leads to the mental and physical decline of characters. Representations of speech also affect plot development by creating a semblance of non-action that immobilises the flow of the narratives. This immobility undermines transactional conceptions of language that posit it as an effective means of communication; instead, representations of speech play on the confusion of genres.

Less Talk

Jean de Palacio maintains that 'la communication entre les êtres demeure [...] le principal enjeu de l'œuvre des Goncourt'.[2] Direct discourse has a central function in Goncourt's post-1870 novels, but not for the same reason that it does pre-1870. Ricatte calls the 1867 novel *Manette Salomon* a 'roman des idées' and speaks of its 'esthétique parlée', by which he means that the Goncourt brothers' personal beliefs are expressed in the numerous tirades of the

---

[1] In Remy de Gourmont, *La Culture des idées* (Paris: 10/18, 1983), pp. 15-52 (p. 22).
[2] 'Le Silence des Goncourt', *La Revue des sciences humaines*, 259 (2000), 27-39 (p. 35).

characters.³ Characters are perceived by him as being the mouthpieces of the authors and, as a result, he is more interested in what is being discussed than in who is engaged in discussion. In addition, he argues that the Goncourts' preferred method of presenting dialogue in *Germinie Lacerteux* is in massive blocks, and he implies that this style is tried and true: 'Pour l'agencement du dialogue, les deux frères restaient d'ailleurs fidèles dans *Germinie* à la technique des blocs monolithiques'.⁴

With respect to the brothers' joint literary creations, critics are drawn by the prominence of dialogue. Eric Bordas affirms that 'on parle beaucoup dans les romans des Goncourt',⁵ but this does not appear to be the case as far as Edmond's solo works are concerned, or at least not as far as his protagonists are concerned. Marie-Thérèse Mathet has argued the opposite: she believes that there is no evolution as far as dialogue in the Goncourt novels is concerned, and that there is always an abundance of speech.⁶ Yet, it seems impossible not to talk in terms of difference when it comes to the solo novels. From the point of view of dialogue, these texts are virtually silent. *La Faustin* is an exception – direct discourse dominates its first forty chapters (there are 64 in total) – accounted for by the fact that its subject, the theatre, is itself vocal. Some have argued that the reason for this apparent metamorphosis from spoken prolixity to relative silence stems from the fact that Jules, rather than Edmond, excelled at dialogue.⁷ Such evaluations are unverifiable. There is, however, a case for arguing that the repositioning is indicative of a move towards a conception of literature that places less faith in mimetic representation and the ability of language to convey an external reality. This would correspond with Vivienne Mylne's assertion regarding the changing complexion of literary dialogue in the nineteenth century, namely that

---

³ *La Création romanesque chez les Goncourt*, pp. 353, 355 and 356.
⁴ *La Création romanesque chez les Goncourt*, p. 293.
⁵ 'Interactions énonciatives dans *Charles Demailly*', in Cabanès, pp. 209-23 (p. 209).
⁶ 'La Parole des personnages dans l'œuvre romanesque des frères Goncourt', in Cabanès, pp. 237-45 (pp. 237-38).
⁷ See Ricatte, *La Création romanesque chez les Goncourt*, p. 293; Bayle, p. 61; and Michael Youngs, 'The Style of the Goncourts in their Novels: Vocabulary and Imagery' (unpublished doctoral thesis, University of Leeds, 1964), p. 265.

a marked confidence in verbal communication lasted only until the *fin de siècle*.[8]

Direct discourse is present to a different degree and function in each of Goncourt's novels, though there are similarities in its implementation, both on thematic and stylistic levels. Although *La Fille Elisa*'s follow-up, *Les Frères Zemganno*, is not as silent as its predecessor, which portrays a woman condemned to silence, there are still only two passages of dialogue that involve neither of the two main characters. In chapter 53, Tompkins and the circus director converse; in chapter 66, various members of the public discuss the performers' impending jump. The majority of conversations involve only the two brothers. Gianni and Nello communicate little with peripheral characters, but they do communicate with each other. There are eleven exchanges between them, in addition to seven conversations involving Gianni and third parties. Nello participates in no dialogues other than when speaking with his older brother, despite the fact that he is described as being 'loquace' while Gianni is said to 'parl[er] peu' (p. 53). Additionally, the dispersion of dialogue changes as the brothers' search for artistic innovation is furthered. There is no extended dialogue in the first quarter of the novel and the amount of dialogue increases once Nello is no longer able to perform.

A similar phenomenon occurs in *La Faustin*. In this case, the percentage of direct discourse drops dramatically once the protagonist is reunited with her lover, even though the opening scene of the novel features Juliette waxing lyrical about her time spent with Lord Annandale, and craving his return. The novel relies less and less on dialogue as the story advances. In this text, there are lots of isolated lines, lots of short dialogues, and few extended conversations. This reduces the capacity of the lovers to interact verbally. To begin with, there are many dialogues. In chapter 1, Juliette, her sister and two men converse (there are interesting similarities between this scene and Lorrain's 'Chez l'une d'elles' in *Histoires de masques*). Many more characters are involved in the conversations in chapters 2 and 3. Juliette's and Annandale's final discussions, on the other hand, are monosyllabic and laconic on her part. In chapter 56, she responds

---

[8] *Le Dialogue dans le roman français de Sorel à Sarraute*, ed. by Françoise Tilkin (Paris: Universitas, 1994), p. 117.

firstly by silence and then by a simple refusal: 'non'. In many respects, this portrayal of speech is marked with mimetic ambition. It is only realistic that the world of Parisian theatre should be verbal, just as it is only right that remote chateaux in Europe should be silent. In other ways, though, the representation of speech contributes to a fragmentation of the novel and is associated with the themes of hysteria and ruin.

It is in *Chérie* where segmentation on a structural level is perhaps most apparent, and where the differences in spoken aesthetic pre- and post-1870 are felt most fully. In marked contrast to *La Faustin*, where the majority of chapters are dialogic (although the concentration of dialogue lessens as the *dénouement* nears), few of *Chérie*'s 105 chapters are devoted to the large monolithic chunks of dialogue that mark the pre-1870 output. In those chapters that do contain high proportions of dialogue, more often than not it is secondary characters – namely Mme Tony-Fréneuse, Chérie's chaperone; the Maréchal, her grandfather; or her friends – rather than the eponymous heroine, who speak.[9] Her angry words in chapter 7 finish as nothing more than 'une menace des lèvres dans une bouche aphone' (p. 46). Chapter 62, which depicts gossiping children, is two-thirds spoken, but the heroine herself is far from verbose, uttering one sentence. Chapter 79 is also largely spoken, but much more space is given to descriptions of speech. The longest passages of dialogue in which the protagonist partakes can be qualified for the most part as gossip, conversations that focus primarily on third parties and are not essential to the unveiling of plot. Elsewhere, Chérie is like a wind-up doll: her voice is 'chantonnante et mécanique' (p. 94) and she displays a downright disaffection with communication and speech.

Writing Silence

In these novels, silence contributes to the isolation, alienation, and madness of characters, but it also participates in the disruption of traditional narrative due to the implications of reproducing it textually.

---

[9] Youngs (p. 122) estimates that the Chérie has 172 lines of dialogue in the novel, which has upwards of 3000 lines of text.

More often than not, speech is presented as an ineffective means of communication and contributes to some form of decline.

La Fille Elisa is plagued by quiet, which is largely accounted for by its subject matter: silence and incarceration. This theme is itself revealing, dealing as it does with emptiness and the unsayable. The vital role of silence here has been summed up in the following way: 'Tout aboutit dans la première partie a une conséquence unique; tout dans la seconde, part d'une cause unique, le silence. Tous les aspects de l'avilissement d'Elisa en prison se ramènent à ce seul facteur'.[10] This raises a key point regarding direct discourse and dialogue in these novels. In the works dealing with women, although there is very little common ground between the characters' lives and backgrounds, by the end of the novels the verbal is in one way or another associated with mental disorder – even death.

Speech is a tool used to accentuate the psychological disorders of female characters. Elisa speaks in 'phrases courtes et saccadées' (p. 21). The first dialogue in the novel results in 'une violente attaque de nerfs' (p. 54). Upon leaving the quiet, rural brothel she displays a compulsive need to 's'étourdir de bruit, de tapage, de loquacité' (p. 72). While working in the prison's *Cordonnerie*, her final working-place, 'souvent, dans un coin, montait subitement à une bouche un flot de mots désordonnés' (p. 188). From this moment on, Elisa, who is surrounded by people who are forced into silence and whose words long to erupt to the surface, 'commença à descendre, peu à peu, tous les échelons de l'humanité qui mènent insensiblement une créature intelligente à l'animalité' (p. 190). Elisa, 'la bête' (p. 163), entertains no life with those around her, and instead lives in the dream world of her memory. On her death bed, the only part of her body that looks alive are her lips: 'la bouche seule encore vivante dans sa figure tendait vers la garde des lèvres enflées de paroles qui avaient à la fois envie et peur de sortir' (p. 199). She dies before she finds the power to say anything. While *La Fille Elisa* may appear to be a quintessential Naturalist novel that studies cause and effect in the life of a prostitute, a sub-category of literature at the time, the silence of the main character is a means of introducing a revolt against crude positivism and faith in language as a means of communication. There is a parallel

---

[10] Ricatte, *La Création romanesque chez les Goncourts*, p. 127.

with *La Faustin*: there, too, the demise of the main characters is a function of the loss of ability to operate through verbal communication.

The silence that is encountered openly in the 1877 novel is elaborated more subtly in Goncourt's ensuing works. Chérie's mother, who is peculiarly deranged, wilfully turns mute after her husband's death. The end of this text is diametrically opposed to the end of *La Fille Elisa*: in chapters 103 and 104, Chérie speaks more than she does in the rest of the novel, yet she terrifies her interlocutor. This outburst, like the one that tempts Elisa on her deathbed, consolidates Chérie's physical decline into decadence and announces her imminent death. In these closing pages, Chérie's speech is nothing but the babble of a woman appearing in society for the last time. Her babble is restricted to gossip about extra-marital affairs and her appearance (she wants to appear 'vivant… ce soir encore', p. 328). In an aside, she states that 'la maladie, la mort il faut […] cacher cela, lorsque l'on est une femme à la mode' (p. 332), something that she appears to lament.

Although women are the primary interest in all but one of these novels, men are not entirely immune to troubles with speech. By the end of *Les Frères Zemganno*, speech is unrestrained due to the emotion that it must convey: 'les pensées de [Gianni] se mettaient à parler tout haut, et devenaient en quelque sorte ces espèces de cris entrecoupés, par lesquels ont besoin de jaillir d'une poitrine les grands et profonds chagrins' (p. 230). Interestingly, the character does not talk, his thoughts do, and not in words, but in cries. Speech is linked to the physical destruction of Gianni's brother and the failure to revolutionise acrobatics, but not to hysteria or lunacy.

In *La Faustin*, on the other hand, Lord Annandale suffers the same impulses as Elisa. 'Par moments,' it is written, 'seulement sa bouche devenait bruissante de la sonorité de paroles avortées et brisées, qui commençaient à s'échapper dans de confus éclats de voix' (p. 298). For him, too, the inability to communicate is the sign of an ultimate mental degeneration, caused by a mysterious disease whose signs appear overnight (but which is not hysteria like Elisa's). In every case, the characteristic symptom is that words are presented as issuing not from the character as a subject, but from fragments of the body or from the fragmented soul of the character. Words exist and say something, but they do not express a person; instead, they signify division within the person and an inability to control language.

Whereas in the final pages of *Les Frères Zemganno* and *Chérie* unbridled speech is a mark of decline, in *La Faustin*, as in *La Fille Elisa*, it is silence that marks the heroine's demise. Juliette is uncharacteristically silent in the final chapters of *La Faustin*. Her instability – expressed through an excessive and overbearing artistic drive attributed to her profession – is illustrated by her silent mimicry: 'la Faustin était despotiquement amenée à une imitation étudiée' (p. 306). In a normal acting situation, the actress would be verbal; here, she relies on gestures. Meanwhile, the doctor who tries to explain her lover's illness speaks in broken sentences that convey his shock and excitement at finding a case of so-called 'agonie sardonique'. Juliette is transformed from a quintessentially verbal character – the actress who declaims other people's invented words in front of an audience nightly – to a semi-mute character when isolated in the countryside far from any potential spectator. The ivory tower scenario allows her only to act and mimic what is around her. Voice, here, has little to do with interaction and everything to do with expression. When withdrawn from the theatre, she loses the ability to communicate and the only language left to her is drama, which in her case is as much a matter of voice as it is of gesture.

Juliette's reliance on drama is further compounded by her bouts of somnambulism in which she acts out a Racinian role. When dreaming or interpreting invented lives, La Faustin speaks. Otherwise, she is predominantly silent. Even in her dreams Juliette is other; even when she sleepwalks, she is haunted by others' words; even her unconscious is permeated by her theatrical voice. As the text progresses, she loses control of her identity. The focus on acting and artifice is central to the emerging doctrines of the modern era, where language could be transformed into a virtuoso performance. One interpretation of Decadence is as the moment when the exchange value of language is repudiated in favour of the secret, hidden powers of words and other art forms. 'Le décadentisme', writes Pierre van Bever, 'c'est aussi le moment où, menacé dans son verbe même, le poète répudie la valeur d'échange du langage pour s'intéresser exclusivement à ses pouvoirs secrets'.[11] In this manner, Juliette abandons communication altogether by the end of the novel and instead silently mimics her dying lover, from whom she is forever alienated.

Isolation is all-pervasive in Goncourt's novels and raises discursive problems, particularly in the representation of silence. In chapter 8 of *Chérie*, as in the example of the supposedly garrulous Nello, the reader encounters a curious passage that proclaims the protagonist to be verbose: 'parlant comme un beau diable, et disant force choses déraisonnables' (p. 48). As there is no example of this devilish babble, the impression is given that there is a private realm of thought that is, and will remain, inaccessible. The absence of, or failure to represent, direct discourse replaces the girl's loquacity. The reverse is true of *La Fille Elisa*, where the prostitute's voice is silenced as much by the narrator as by the legal system. Again, the heroine's inner thoughts remain largely hidden. The 1877 novel is, in this respect, a very accurate representation of both the dangers and the aesthetic necessity of reducing people to silence: the author/narrator himself silences his characters in the same way that the law silences prisoners. This 'poetics of silence', as Jean de Palacio, theorist of Decadence, christens it, is encountered in all four novels. It is an example of 'la recherche, flaubertienne en effet, du "livre sur rien", la constitution d'une poétique du silence, y compris dans des œuvres apparemment naturalistes'.[12]

One-Sided Structures

The reign of silence in Goncourt's novels is attested to by monologues masquerading as dialogues. On several occasions in *Chérie*, a one-sided structure prevents communication between characters. When her governess, Lizadie, tells Chérie a story, the passage is more akin to soliloquy or monologue than exchange. In chapters 41 and 49, characters refuse to engage in conversation. In chapter 41, Chérie rejects the role of interlocutor outright by opting to remain silent. Textually, silence is reproduced through the intervention of the

---

[11] 'Signification du "décadentisme"', *La Revue des langues vivantes*, 34 (1968), 366-72 (p. 367).
[12] 'Le Silence des Goncourt', p. 33.

narrator and is gleaned from the words of the sole speaker. The chapter outlines in general terms the changes that take place in a girl's relationships with men. It posits that, from one moment to the next, young females become embarrassed by the presence of the male. In this episode, the voice of the typical male, through the voice of the narrator, is heard, but is not answered directly:

> - Eh bien, qu'est-ce que tu as? Tu ne me dis rien?
> On ne vous répond pas, on ne s'approche pas, on reste lointaine et tout embarrassée (p. 138).

This one-sided structure opposes a precise discourse with a general one. The male discourse dominates an unexpressed female discourse by reducing it to silence, by making the female an 'on' and not an 'elle'. A charitable critic would perhaps account for this by invoking the diverse female voices that contributed to construction of the character; nonetheless, there is a clash between specific and general and, as a result, the passage can be classified as neither dialogue nor monologue.

Meanwhile, the same elocutionary structure is repeated in chapter 49, though this time a specific, attempted, conversation between grandfather and granddaughter takes place. Twice the Maréchal addresses his granddaughter; twice his questions go unanswered. What is significant, in both cases, is that oral responses are replaced by descriptions in the guise of responses, and this silences the transactional function of direct discourse in the text. At the same time, the Maréchal's secretary attempts to engage the silent adolescent in conversation, but is forced to rely on the visual rather than the oral for answers to his questions: 'Chérie ne répondait pas, écoutait ironique, regardant son interlocuteur avec ce regard de sphinx de la femme, ce regard tout plein, à certaines heures, de choses énigmatiques qui ne se laissent pas lire' (p. 156). Her refusal to either act or speak is qualified by the narrator's reasoning. This thinking valorises *fin de siècle* clichés and echoes Baudelairian formulations of woman as a form of beauty to be avoided at all costs. To protect oneself from the temptations of woman was to silence her. Rather than explaining what the protagonist is thinking in her silence, the narrator languorously states what she looks like. The secretary himself then takes up this point of view:

> - Quels yeux!... Dites donc, il doit y avoir de drôles de pensées derrière ces yeux-là.
> - Oh! Je ne les dirai à personne! s'écria la jeune fille dans un mouvement de refermement de tout son être (pp. 156-57).

The visual, rather than the oral, is a means of communication in this scene – the secretary gets a response only when he deciphers her eyes. Curiously, the visual is also a barrier concealing the truth from both character and narrator. It is not until later the same evening, protected by a long descriptive paragraph, that Chérie's undeniably *fin de siècle* sadness is revealed by the use of one simple verb, 'je m'ennuie' (p. 157), a verb whose noun is often cited as one of the principal factors motivating Decadent creation: 'reality is boredom, as only superior writers know, and the superior being is the decadent'.[13]

Because there is no exchange of information between characters in these situations, the passages of direct discourse are not transactional; rather, they disclose the gulf separating the narrator's perspective and his heroine's silence. As in *Madame Bovary*, the conversations are not active, to borrow Gothot-Mersch's formulation, 'elles n'ont rien d'actif. Elles ne constituent pas un véritable échange, une discussion menant à une décision (c'est-à-dire l'action)'.[14] Where the view of interpersonal contact as expressed in *Chérie*, *La Faustin*, and to a certain extent *Les Frères Zemganno*, differs from Flaubert's is that Goncourt's protagonists are driven by a willingness to destroy communication and to speak instead through a more artistic and refined visual language. Emma Bovary, by contrast, fails because she attempts to replace reality with a romanticised fiction, as the well-known description of her as 'étant de tempérament plus sentimentale qu'artiste, cherchant des émotions et non des paysages' so fittingly indicates.[15] Emma never ceases to believe in talk. This is precisely what Chérie and Goncourt's other hypersensitive and nervous artists want to avoid. The distance separating the two conceptions of escapism is the distance between bourgeois and aristocratic aesthetics.

Isolating the heroine's voice within a descriptive framework – an oft-used tactic in Goncourt's novels – fragments the narrative: it is

---

[13] Williams, p. 74.
[14] 'Le Dialogue dans l'œuvre de Flaubert', *Europe*, 485-87 (1969), 112-21 (p. 115).
[15] Flaubert, *Œuvres*, I, p. 324.

used here to show the girl's lassitude and isolation; it is used in *La Faustin* to show the breakdown of the lovers' relationship; it is used in *La Fille Elisa* to show how distanced the prisoners are from their keepers. This strategy has been commented upon in general terms by Sylvie Durrer, who sees it as part of a wider move toward a fracturing of narrative:

> Parmi les différentes formes de cisellement de l'interaction figure l'isolement d'une réplique au discours direct. La pratique de la réplique isolée s'inscrit dans le travail de fragmentation, dont elle constitue une des manifestations les plus extrêmes, et semble se développer dès le XIXe siècle; auparavant, les écrivains ne procédaient pas à un tel fractionnement du dialogue.[16]

The rejection, or collapse, of interactive discourse between characters is a central trait of Goncourt's novels. His characters' disinclination and inability to communicate isolates them from their environment and sequesters them within their silent surroundings. The dearth of linguistic exchange means that the text cannot advance in a conventional manner. Nor should it be forgotten that the fragmentation of discourse also reflects the divided nature of the characters.

Voices of Authority

The representation of silence coincides with the characters' downfall and isolation and thwarts the advance of the narrative, but there are also additional constraints on discourse. One of the principal areas exploited by dialogue and direct discourse is the conflict that opposes individual voice with the voice of authority, be it legal, artistic, linguistic or textual.

The first direct discourse in *La Fille Elisa* is highly codified. In the prologue, the eponymous prostitute is condemned to death by legal language that does not have the courage to name the crime it condemns and to which there is no right of reply. Elisa is convicted by words where individual and group are inseparable: 'Sur mon honneur et ma conscience, devant Dieu et devant les hommes, la réponse du jury est: Oui, sur toutes les questions à la majorité' (p. 7). Nor does

---

[16] *Le Dialogue romanesque: style et structure* (Geneva: Droz, 1994), p. 95.

this formulaic language adequately express the magnitude, on a human and emotional scale, of the chain of events that it puts into motion: 'Tout condamné à mort aura la tête tranchée' (p. 9). This type of communication supports Durrer's claim that direct discourse creates narrative intrigue: 'les répliques sont, du point de vue narratif, comparables à des formes d'action' (p. 8).

In spite of their sentence, the series of events announced by the jury is never set into motion thanks to a beneficent intervention – an intervention that is not spoken and is only mentioned 36 chapters further on when Elisa thinks to herself 'une cloche, qu'on avait baptisée, dans une paroisse, le curé qui avait demandé sa grâce' (p. 113). Naturally, this detracts from the power of these isolated lines of speech to set a course of events into motion: the condemning lines are without response and are cut off from the main body of the text. What they do introduce is not made manifest until the second book. Speech that results in action – the priest's – has no place in the narrative. The transactional function of language is undermined by not representing the priest's words, as it is by not carrying through with the jury's death sentence. While Elisa is saved from having her head literally chopped off, like her saviour, she is figuratively decapitated: she is condemned to perpetual silence. The same treatment applies to written language in *Chérie*. On the one occasion that a written text is supposed to elicit a response, when Chérie sends a letter successfully inviting her friend to the opera, it is not reproduced for the reader.

Elisa's struggle to find a voice is presented as doomed to failure from the outset due to the crushing strictures of legality. Immediately following the court's decision, the heroine is presented as choking on soundless words: 'la bouche tumultueuse de paroles qui s'étranglent' (p. 9). Speech here is not intimately linked to accelerating the plot; instead, the thematic focus of the novel – the way in which society maims its members by silencing them in the name of the law – is intensified. Thus, in addition to undermining the speech-action paradigm, direct discourse in the prologue to *La Fille Elisa* sets up the theme of the discord between individual and society in terms of language. There is a strain between the rule of the law, felt in the voice of society at large, and the individual who is crushed by its power and authority.

Although Michael Macovski's interest in literary dialogue stems from an interest in the Romantic subject, particularly as manifested in poetry, his theories are pertinent to a discussion of Goncourt. Macovski positions the issue of voice and direct discourse within the context of larger cultural discourses. As a Bakhtinian who privileges notions of intertext and polyphony, he conceives of textual voice as an 'ideolectal entity' and suggests that 'literary characters interact not only with individual voices but also with other discourses themselves – political, religious, and historical'.[17] In light of this, Goncourt's characters can be considered as entertaining a dialogue with a Naturalist discourse, another *fin de siècle* discourse, or, indeed, in the case of the 1877 novel, with the law in general. *La Fille Elisa* is ostensibly a sustained rebuttal of the Auburn system of imprisonment, but on a more general note it offers a reading of the role of censors who silence authors, and who almost silenced Goncourt,[18] and a reading of the way in which language is controlled. From a metatextual perspective, Edmond de Goncourt is battling it out with these oppressive restraints, much as he is in his prefaces.

The control exerted on speech is felt in a different way in *Les Frères Zemganno*, where the majority of dialogues deal with the ordeal of finding the perfect acrobatic stunt. Dialogues are stumbling blocks that have to be overcome before the performers find a creative voice. Like Goncourt himself, the gymnasts are searching for an escape from socially coded art. They seek to articulate a truth that is inexpressible within the constraints of their art form (similarly, for Elisa, everything is inexpressible within the confines of her prison). Several features of the 1879 novel bear witness to the tension between conventional modes of communication and aesthetic expression (in this case through acrobatics). The friction between these elements in the text is comparable to the tension that existed in 1880s literary France between popular Naturalism, which was rapidly becoming canonical, and the aesthetic prerogatives of Decadence, which had yet

---

[17] *Dialogue and Literature: Apostrophe, Auditions and the Collapse of Romantic Discourse* (Oxford: OUP, 1994), pp. 3-4.
[18] *La Fille Elisa* caused quite a furore. A spoof entitled *La Fille Elisabeth* called for its repression, but was itself repressed. During the examination of *La Fille Elisabeth*, Goncourt's novel was scrupulously studied by censors but was eventually approved. See Ashley, 'Policing Prostitutes'.

to be consecrated by the public. Indeed, the parallels are connected to the dialogue that Macovski envisages between text and intertext.

The Zemgannos talk circles around their art. So inexpressible is it that it is not named by them or the narrator in the novel, regardless of the fact that the majority of discussions between the brothers concentrate on this subject. Speech does not immediately lead to revelation. The first dialogue between the brothers is a blueprint for most others, and pertains to their aesthetic crusade:

- 'Dis donc, Gianni, qu'est-ce que tu lui veux à cette chose?'
- 'Je cherche!'
- 'Qu'est-ce que tu cherches?'
- 'Ah! Voilà'. Et Gianni ajoutait: - 'Non, c'est le diable, je ne trouverai jamais!'
- 'Mais quoi donc? Dis, dis-moi-le, hein, dis-moi-le?' répétait Nello [...]
- 'Quand tu seras plus grand... tu ne comprendrais pas... Va, je cherche aussi pour toi frérot' (pp. 77-78).

The exchanges between the Zemgannos in the ensuing chapters develop the theme raised in this dialogue. All deal with artistic creation and most coincide with an impending geographical displacement. In this manner, dialogue is tied to action in a literal sense, for it is tied to the movements of the characters. However, geographical movement is not always synonymous with plot development. To be sure, in the first half of the novel, action is prevented by the fact that no matter where the brothers are, or are going, the same sort of conversation takes place: they all deal with the trials of finding the perfect jump, 'ce tour cherché par Gianni, dès sa plus tendre jeunesse' (p. 152). Subsequent to the sale of the Bescapé family circus, the brothers' conversation imparts both Nello's devotion to his sibling and the information that Gianni has plans for the pair: 'j'ai en tête des projets pour nous deux' (p. 96). What these projects are is not revealed. In chapter 26, Gianni announces to his brother that they will depart imminently for London where they will have the opportunity to revolutionise their art. Still, the exact nature of the discovery is not revealed. Another talk announces the Zemgannos' return to Paris, but nevertheless conveys little about the nature of their newfound art.[19] For all intents and purposes, their art cannot be named

---

[19] 'Nos débuts là-bas, que veux-tu, ce sera moins flatteur... mais un jour... et c'est

in the text. The fact that the theme of their conversation remains the desire to find an act 'qui fasse de nous des gens célèbres' (p. 169) shows that dialogue does not necessarily mark a progression in the plot. In point of fact, the presence of so many similar dialogues contributes to the theme of despair occasioned by the impossibility of revolutionising gymnastics and becoming consecrated artists.

The way that the Zemgannos communicate verbally is not dictated by social rules, but the presence of constricting aesthetic conventions is nonetheless felt through the inability of the conversation, and by extension their talent, to advance. Due to the fact that by chapter 54 the brothers have purportedly unravelled the secret of their art, it might be assumed that some form of creative interaction has taken place. This is not the case. What advances are made are reached regardless, or in spite of, the brothers' conversations. After years of practice, they reach the desired height for their new act. In terms of plot development, there is no need for the acrobats to converse at all. The repetition of the same subject in so many conversations accentuates at one and the same time the futility of the performers' search – will they ever pinpoint the centre of their art? – and the necessity of finding their own mode of expression – they must escape the rigidity and repetition present in their everyday life and art. The uniformity of their conversations reveals the obsessive nature of their ill-fated quest.

Numerous examples of direct discourse implicating one or more speakers show speech as being controlled by laws – be they social, aesthetic or judicial – in the same manner that novelistic discourse is constrained by accepted narrative or generic forms. Discourse in the novel and novelistic discourse adhere to certain codes from which they struggle to escape. Goncourt's last heroine, Chérie, silences her friend in the opening scene of the novel for saying something 'inappropriate'. This is a curious position for a young girl to adopt. She also distances herself from her (present or absent) interlocutors. This isolation is mirrored in the novel by the fact that the passages of direct discourse do not further the plot: they do not create elements of suspense (the reader does not worry whether or not Chérie will learn

---

bien le diable, si ce jour n'arrive pas… alors on se rattrapera… Donne-moi encore un mois, six semaines… c'est tout ce que je te demande' (p. 119-20).

her lesson, for instance); they do not purvey information to the reader other than the fact that the notion of genuine human interaction is illusory so long as conventional models are followed. Direct discourse can be used to establish relationships between characters and link them to their environment. Its rejection, whether deliberate (as is the case of Chérie) or imposed (as is the case of Elisa) results in isolation. This segregation, in turn, undermines the authority and reliability of language as a tool for interactive communication.

Fractured Discourses

Some of the most extreme forms of disruptive fracturing of direct discourse are found in *La Faustin*, where the words of several speakers, often unnamed, are gathered together. This strategy alienates characters and jeopardises the coherence of the traditional novel. Ricatte has argued that dialogue makes *Sœur Philomène* and *Renée Mauperin* almost theatrical by moments (the latter was adapted into a play).[20] Equating novelistic discourse with theatrical dialogue has been explained by Claudine Gothot-Mersch (p. 112), with regard to Flaubert, as a result of the influence of Romantic theatre, a point that would be worth pondering with regard to the Goncourts. The issue of theatricality arises in relation to *La Faustin*, in which certain dialogues are presented as though they form part of a dramatic script, transforming them into performances in their own right and disrupting the stability of the novelistic form. This generic disruption is a common feature of Decadent writing.

On one occasion in *La Faustin*, speakers are presented as the first, second, third (and so on) 'auteur dramatique' (pp. 79-80) and their words are portrayed as though it were a play, not a novel; on another, people are designated according to their roles in *Phèdre*. Additionally, a manic social life plays a considerable role in the text, where, in chapter 17, after Juliette's première as Phèdre, friends and acquaintances gather for dinner. The chapter, not quite twenty pages long, is by far the longest in the novel and its first pages are narrated. Conversation begins when the meal is served, and positively erupts

---

[20] *La Création romanesque chez les Goncourt*, p. 200.

thereafter. Speakers are not identified by name, but by tag, and this presentational method indicates that the form of the conversation is as important as who is speaking and what they are saying. As in chapter 2 of *Monsieur de Phocas*, where characters are not named straight away, individual identities remain peripheral. Spoken interventions are only needed in order to paint an accurate picture of theatrical life. No contact is made between characters. An illustrious author interrupts 'le premier interlocuteur' (p. 134), and is later referred to himself as 'l'éloquent rabelaisien' (p. 135). The narrator sets the scene thus: 'Et la fin de la tirade de l'homme d'Etat sombrait dans une fusillade de courtes ripostes, partant à droite, à gauche, comme des coups de pistolet' (p. 135). From this point onward, a profusion of voices vie for the reader's attention – just as they do in Villiers de l'Isle-Adam's 'scène où tout le monde parle' –[21] and there is not always one dominant theme to the conversation that ensues; nor is there always a logical connection between what is said. Jean-Pierre Bertrand upholds that in this novel 'la narration se fige au profit de l'instantané. Au dialogue se substitue le collage de citations conversationnelles de la plus pure contingence'.[22] The degree to which this collage effect is employed in order to reinforce the theme of alienation should not be underestimated. Arguably, it is to escape the contingent nature of her surroundings that Juliette craves a settled life, or in other words, craves William Rayne's return. As Hugues in *Bruges-la-morte* reflects: 'Que le monde, ailleurs, s'agite, bruisse, allume ses fêtes, tresse ses mille rumeurs. Il avait besoin de silence infini et d'une existence si monotone qu'elle ne lui donnerait presque plus la sensation de vivre'.[23]

The significance of the dinner scene from the point of view of narrativity is just as great, for it can be interpreted from the perspective of the dissolution of representational stability. This is the angle that Jean de Palacio adopts when he states in general terms that 'une poétique de décadence substitue la confusion à la clarté, brise les cloisons étanches, compromet les frontières'. Confusion reigns

---

[21] Quoted in Paul Verlaine, *Les Poètes maudits* [1884], ed. by Gabriele-Aldo Bertozzi (Milan: Cisalpino-Goliardica, 1977), p. 90.
[22] In Goncourt, *La Faustin*, ed. by Jean-Pierre Bertrand, p. 296.
[23] Georges Rodenbach, *Bruges-la-morte* (1892), ed. by Christian Berg (Brussels: Labor, 1986), p. 25.

supreme. As in the conversation between Lui and Elle in Rachilde's *Monsieur Vénus* (1884), the territory separating drama and novel is blurred. Here, though, individual characters are confused in a mêlée of voices. Palacio argues that the boundaries that this disrupts are 'non seulement celles du tragique et du comique, mais, de façon plus fondamentale, celles du roman et du théâtre, de la prose et du vers, du texte et de l'image, de la parole et du silence, de l'Un et du Multiple'.[24] Clearly, the dinner scene, like the rehearsal scene, participates in this explosive aesthetic.

Conclusion

In Edmond de Goncourt's novels, the transactional function of direct discourse is limited by the incoherent and superficial quality of some conversations and by the impotence of others. The texts, like their characters, are plagued by discord. Disjointed dialogue results in a disjointed narrative and dissolution of unity, both in terms of plot and characterisation. It is also, in one sense, hyper-realistic as it expresses the hopelessness of verbal language as a tool for communication. This theme was cherished from the beginnings of Romanticism, through to Flaubert who famously wrote of the inadequacy of 'la parole humaine' in *Madame Bovary*: 'la parole humaine est comme un chaudron fêlé où nous battons des mélodies à faire danser les ours, quand on voudrait attendrir les étoiles'.[25] The position is fully developed in the *fin de siècle* and gains new impetus with the advent of postmodernism and the *nouveau roman*. Allied to this is the notion that accurate representation is no longer the concern or the aim of the artist, because language can never bridge the gap between signifier and signified, between *plaisir* and *jouissance*, or, as the Decadents would have had it, the gap between possible and ideal art.

From the standpoint of narrativity, Goncourt's representations of speech are symptomatic of a dwindling confidence in traditional modes of representation. Direct discourse is shown to be an ineffective means of advancing plot, and is used to fragment the novels and

---

[24] *Figures et formes de la décadence* (Paris: Séguier, 1994), pp. 16-17.
[25] *Œuvres*, I, p. 466.

undermine their formal stability. Isolated lines of speech are rarely associated with novelistic action; instead, one of their primary functions seems to be in revealing a core of silence. Silence, in turn, is allied to incurable madness, self-imposed refusal to engage in society, restrictions placed on human interaction, and the failure of language to represent an ideal art. Dialogue involving the two protagonists in *Les Frères Zemganno* is circuitous; words cannot name their art, forcing the text into silence on the matter. In *La Faustin,* the character's double identity, and double voice – she is at one and the same time lover and actress – compete for supremacy and lead to a hyperactive creative impulse to the detriment of interpersonal communication. In *Chérie*, a lack of verbal and physical contact with other characters has as its outcome death by madness, as words spew forth from the heroine unbidden and unrestricted. Elisa, because she has neither art nor words, has no right of reply, no right to communicate, and no means of expression. As a result, she dies. In each novel there is a 'faillite de la parole', a bankruptcy of speech and words.[26] Thematically, direct discourse is presented as a vain means of apprehending others, and the inadequacies of speech are contrasted with alternative, more artistic and more individual forms of expression. Symbolists and Decadents viewed the novel as an inferior art form precisely because representation is one of its aims; whilst non-verbal arts (painting, music, gymnastics, fashion, etc.) were superior insofar as they did not necessarily rely on the exchange value of language, there was always a danger that they could become sterile through their very abstractness.

---

[26] Palacio, *Figures et formes de la décadence*, p. 18.

LANGUAGE AND THE LITERARY FIELD

> Words are the physicians of a diseased mind.
> – Aeschylus, *Prometheus Bound*, l. 378

The Goncourt brothers are renowned for having had an interest in the finer points of the French language. It has been speculated that they were keen readers of that paragon of positivism, Emile Littré, and their peer, Jules Lemaître, referred to them as 'amoureux des mots'.[1] This interest in words is reflected in Edmond de Goncourt's novels, where particular language issues are addressed both directly and indirectly. Over the course of the novels, and even within the individual novels themselves, language switches between two seemingly contradictory conceptions: the one portraying it as a utilitarian tool, the other a more aesthetically-driven position, where language is a device for the expression of higher artistic truths. In this latter conception, words become gestures, or performances, as their particularities, in advancement of Decadent exaggeration, are emphasised and exalted.

The Goncourt brothers' novels have been interpreted as lacking composition, cohesion, substance, plot, and many other qualities deemed essential to creating textual meaning.[2] They were often criticised for being too lax with their language and composition, for being too precious, for having too many mannerisms, and, frankly, for writing gobbledegook. Many, including Maupassant, took issue with Edmond's language, arguing that it lacked lucidity and clarity, and, therefore, universality. In the preface to *Pierre et Jean* (1888), Maupassant states that Realist authors should not have recourse to

---

[1] Alain Hardy, 'Un secret des Goncourt?', *Les Cahiers naturalistes*, 41 (1971), 88-95. Jules Lemaître, *Les contemporains: études et portraits littéraires, troisième série* (Paris: Société française d'imprimerie et de librairie, n.d.), p. 41.
[2] The three most vigorous critics are, chronologically, Ferdinand Brunetière in *Le Roman naturaliste*, pp. 273-96; Jean-Pierre Richard in 'Deux écrivains épidermiques: Edmond et Jules de Goncourt', in Jean-Pierre Richard, *Littérature et Sensation: Stendhal, Flaubert* (Paris: Seuil, 1954), pp. 299-321; and Lazare Prajs in *La Fallacité de l'œuvre romanesque des Goncourt* (Paris: Nizet, 1974).

'clowneries de langage' and that 'il n'est point besoin du vocabulaire bizarre, compliqué, nombreux et chinois, qu'on nous impose aujourd'hui sous le nom d'écriture artiste'.[3] It might initially appear that varied and contrasting vocabularies accurately represent reality, but as a manifestation of *écriture artiste* this practice undeniably creates difficulties on the level of interpretation and can perceived as being anti-realistic. While all of these diverse elements would seem to be simply necessary for reproducing a given social reality, they are equally the tools used to uncover what language disguises. Vocabulary has several functions in Goncourt's novels: in terms of literary realism, it is utilitarian and creates an 'effet-de-réel'; it is pan-national and multilingual; it links present artistic challenges with past endeavours; it establishes a distance between primary and secondary characters; and, finally, it accentuates appearances and peculiarities of language in an attempt to uncover a hidden truth.

New and Old Languages

In the early twentieth century, Marcel Cressot maintained that vocabulary was a tool exploited by authors of the *fin de siècle* to widen the gap between common man and an elite:

> Dès les Goncourt, la préciosité ou, si l'on préfère sa forme moderne, le 'snobisme', fait son entrée dans le roman. Tout en utilisant les ressources de la langue familière, tout en faisant feu de tout bois, l'homme de lettres est convaincu que le trait spécifique qui le distingue du vulgaire, ce doit être une langue fleurie de mots rares, de mots 'inouis'. Certes, on ne craindra pas d'offusquer le bourgeois par l'emploi d'un mot bas, mais plus volontiers encore on l'abasoudira par des mots rares, des mots qui exigeront, pour être

---

[3] Ed. by G. Hainsworth. (London: Harrap, 1966), p. 46. On the other hand, Maupassant admired *Chérie* (see 'La Jeune fille') and wrote to Goncourt in 1878 saying 'je vous relis sans cesse pour tâcher d'apprendre les secrets de votre phrase dont chaque épithète jette comme une lumière sur les choses qu'elle touche' (B.N.F. M.S.S. N.A.F., 22470 fols 20-21). In another letter, he talks of 'la puissance et la souplesse de votre style' (B.N.F. M.S.S. N.A.F., 22470 fol. 23), so consistency may not be his forte. David Baguley has noticed a comparable difference in Maupassant's public and private opinions with respect to Zola's work. See *Naturalist Fiction*, p. 21.

compris, de la méditation, et même de la manipulation de dictionnaires techniques.[4]

It is not difficult to perceive how this use of specialised vocabulary differs enormously from that of the encyclopædic Balzac, for instance, whose aim is not to dazzle his readers, but to give a faithful representation of various social groupings using their lexicons. Likewise, George Sand makes extensive use of patois in some of her rural novels, and Zola was criticised for using too much popular language, but not in a fashion that could be considered mannerist or precious.

Fin de siècle novels often contend with the pressures existing between the dominant and commercially successful literature of Naturalism and more eccentric literature that parades symptoms of art for art's sake, where language and aestheticism are ends in themselves, and where literature is infused with elitist snobbery. In both forms of literature, vocabulary has a specific, not wholly antithetical, role to play. This topic is addressed by author, linguist and critic, Remy de Gourmont, who commented on the debt post-Naturalist writing owed to Naturalism in Jules Huret's *Enquête sur l'évolution littéraire*, a collection of interviews of literary figures carried out at the end of the nineteenth century:

> L'observation exacte est indispensable à la refabrication artistique de la vie. Même pour une figure de rêve pur, un peintre est tenu à respecter l'anatomie, à ne pas faire divaguer les lignes, à ne pas plaquer d'impossibles couleurs, à ne pas s'abandonner à des perspectives chinoises… Ce besoin de l'exactitude, le naturalisme nous l'a mis dans le sang: tels son rôle et son bienfait.[5]

The desire for suitable language referred to by Gourmont is apparent in each of Goncourt's novels.

The way to renew 'ordinary' language – at least in these texts – is to make it less utilitarian. This is done by making language more precise, even if this very precision seems contradictory and can lead to confusion. At the same time as the novels engage with a Naturalist-Realist discourse, there is an unspoken prioritisation of refined and

---

[4] *La Phrase et le vocabulaire de J-K Huysmans: contribution à l'histoire de la langue française pendant le dernier quart du XIXe siècle* (Paris: Droz, 1938), p. 6.
[5] (Paris: Charpentier, 1891), p. 137.

complicated stylistic needs over linguistic comprehension. Insofar as this is the case, neology could have an important role to play in the dialogue between Naturalist and Decadent conceptions of language and literature, as the systematic invention of new words almost certainly appeals to a particularly refined or educated audience. Neologisms are a clear example of the manner in which an author seeks to find the *mot juste* – the new word being created when no existing word proves satisfactory. Words are invented to fill specific lexical gaps between language and that which it represents. This very precision, however, can undermine their mimetic function due to the fact that words can be too precise, too obscure, or too precious. Indeed, the meaning of a word could potentially be hidden from all apart from its creator.

It has long been held that the Goncourts' novels are replete with neology, but recent examination suggests that this may not necessarily be the case. Pierre Bourdat identifies a relatively restricted number of new words in the Goncourts' joint novels (as opposed to the *Journal*), and explains this result by pointing to the type of literature the brothers were writing:

> Qu'on ne s'attende pas non plus à en ramasser à foison dans les romans, leur facture naturaliste conduisant les auteurs à employer la langue de tous les jours: quatre dans *Germinie*, deux dans *La Fille Elisa*, un seul [...] dans *Renée Maupérin*. Un peu moins d'une dizaine dans chacune des autres œuvres romanesques.[6]

Implicit in this statement is that Naturalism deals with describing what exists in the language of the thing being described. The world is classifiable using a pre-established vocabulary and there is, therefore, no need to invent new words. This is not far from a view expressed in *Chérie* when the young girl's friends are introduced. The narrator takes care to describe how the children speak, both in terms of vocabulary and style. In particular, one child's mannerism – she suffixes words with *mar* – is described:

---

[6] 'Les Néologismes dans l'œuvre des Goncourt', *Les Cahiers Edmond et Jules de Goncourt*, 6 (1998), 18-47, p. 19. Alexis François also argues that there are fewer neologisms in the novels than in the *Journal*. See *Histoire de la langue française cultivée des origines à nos jours*, 2 vols (Geneva: Alexandre Jullien, 1959) II, p. 219.

> Une langue excessive aussi, que celle de cette colossale enfant. Elle dénaturait tous les mots de son vocabulaire affectionnée par l'adjonction de la terminaison en *mar*: *chicmar, chouettemar*, et ces étranges pénultièmes étaient entremêlées de 'A Chaillot! Va t'asseoir!' et suivies du dévidage de locutions drôlatiques pas du tout jeune fille (p. 213).

The narrator is well aware of the manner in which specific lexical traits are attached to certain characters, belying a consciousness of how speech and vocabulary define a person. The humorous overtones of this tactic should not be ignored. It is quite possible that Goncourt was mocking the creation of new words for its own sake, and mocking needless neology that fails to fill a lexical lacuna, is not original, and fulfils no artistic function.

Although neologisms do not blossom in Edmond's four novels according to this evaluation (and Bourdat leaves *Chérie* out of his study), it is the sheer mix and range of language that stupefies the reader and distends the narratives. For, while neologisms, following *La Fille Elisa*, return to the same frequency as in pre-1870 novels, the number of archaisms is on the rise.[7] Indeed, Goncourt's concern seems to be the resuscitation of pre-existing lexicons. Thematically, the use of archaic words isolates Goncourt's characters from their environment; stylistically, their presence alienates the reading public – possibly an end in itself – while proclaiming the author's ingenuity and erudition.

This issue is particularly pronounced in *Les Frères Zemganno*. If Gianni and Nello are not entirely fluent in popular language – or as fluent as Elisa – they are, on the other hand, versed in the historical vocabulary of gymnastics. For example, Gianni reads passages of a treatise called *Trois Dialogues de l'exercice de sauter et de voltiger* to Nello (this was the first book to be written on gymnastics and is dedicated to François 1er). Their goal is to modernise and better some of the moves outlined in this manual. In so doing, the acrobatic archaisms and stunts of yesteryear will be infused with new life and transplanted into the modern era.

Tuccaro's language belongs to a bygone era. The brothers read the book, but the archaisms remain, in a sense, a private or secret language shared by them alone. None of the other circus performers

---

[7] See Youngs, pp. 41-97.

dabble in secret languages. In fact, apart from the 'Penseur' who laments the sorry state of European circuses compared to American ones, the other performers are laconic. Certainly, in terms of the reading public, not all readers would have been familiar with the elaborate vocabulary that provides an ample dose of strangeness in the novel. A gulf separates the language of the Zemgannos and the language of their peers, just as a gulf separates the mimetic aims of the language and the linguistic disorientation that results from its use.

Juliette Faustin also turns to the past in order to uncover lost artistic genius. She seeks Racine's ancient source, Euripides, as a means of better interpreting *Phèdre*, while all the while playing word games.[8] Another character in *La Faustin*, Ragache, who is 'toujours impassible et sérieux', uses archaic words to the bemusement of others: '*Stupendum*! ainsi que s'exprime l'antiquité' (p. 17); he refers to his friend Carsonac as a 'très illustre *carcassier*' (p. 17). One person wears a 'chlamyde', a Greek jacket adopted by the Romans. Another is referred to by the archaic term for a fencer, 'spadassin' (p. 110), which is unnecessary from the point of view of *vraisemblance*.

The past and its lexicon play an important role in these two novels insofar as they appear to link the artistically minded characters with their hidden creative heritage. Brilliant aesthetic modernisation is presented as impossible without the benefit of past knowledge and vocabulary. Transposed into the nineteenth century and into literature, this could be read as a rejection of the brash modernity of Naturalism, with its faith in progress and its representation of the here-and-now. The Zemganno brothers turn their backs on modernity and return to older, more refined and established aesthetic values in order to innovate. The actual exercises described in Tuccaro's book are no longer performed in Gianni's and Nello's era, so it is through the medium of language that they must rediscover their roots. They are elitists alienated in the world of popular arts; archaic language allows them to escape. In much the same way, Edmond de Goncourt was an elitist alienating readers through the use of complex language at a time when the novel, and Naturalism, was reaching its widest public ever,

---

[8] Mireille Dottin-Orsini discusses popular language in *La Faustin* in 'Les Frères Goncourt et le "roman des actrices"', pp. 58, 62 and 66.

and when the novel was increasingly seen to be 'littérature commerciale'.[9]

In this way, refined tastes are linked to refined language, which only a select few understand; refined language belongs to an era untainted by the concerns of nineteenth-century France, and using this language can be read as an attempt to regain a lost civilisation. The emphasis on the past signals a more general *retour-en-arrière* by artists who were fascinated by the creations of their predecessors. Many authors of the period turned to the literature of the Romans, of the Middle Ages, of the Renaissance, to anything that was not mass produced or, *in extremis*, from the current century, for inspiration. A pertinent example of the fascination with older literatures and cultures is found in Huysmans's *A Rebours*, where des Esseintes outlines his preferred reading in two separate chapters. His canon is revealing because it includes not only Latin and medieval authors, but Goncourt himself, with pride of place given to *La Faustin*.

Environment-Specific Languages

While archaisms create a distancing effect, the vocabulary of Goncourt's novels also explicitly participates in a Realist discourse through the use of environment-specific vocabulary. In some places this is done to great mimetic effect; in others it either bestows an aura of eccentricity on characters and highlights the mechanisms of *écriture artiste*.

In *Les Frères Zemganno*, in accordance with the thematic axis around which the novel revolves, circus language dominates. The reader is presented with 'ring[s]' (p. 109), a 'vomitoire' (p. 142), 'travail par terre' and 'travail en l'air' (p. 148), and more 'sauts' than can be counted ('de carpe', 'de poltron', d'ivrogne', 'du singe', 'en profondeur', 'suspension horizontale en avant', 'en arrière', 'de l'Arabe', 'avec élan' or 'à pieds joints', to name but a few). In these examples, the use of specialised vocabulary seems in the first instance to be above all for utilitarian purposes, that is, in order to establish a sense of textual *vraisemblance*.

---

[9] Charle, p. 63.

All of the novels make use of vocabulary particular to the environments they portray, but this realistic vocabulary serves other more prosaic ends, as well. *Chérie* draws on the vocabulary of flora, fashion, dress and design, perfume, balls and hairstyles, all of which are related to the heroine's narcissistic decadence. In *La Fille Elisa*, the prostitute (the 'fille crottée' [p. 85], the 'femmes *en cartes*' [p. 26]), is shown 'battant son quart' (p. 68), passing 'devant la glace' (p. 103), in order to 'faire son heure' (p. 65). As in Alexandre Dumas's *Filles, lorettes et courtisanes* (1843), which touches upon the vocabulary of prostitution, a distinction is made between Parisian and provincial brothels; yet, in this case, the former is described with the (Lorraine) vocabulary of the latter: 'cette chambre, appelée le *poulailler*', 'enfin trois heures... trois heures et le *merlan*. Au *yaulement* de l'artiste capillaire dans l'escalier' (p. 63).

The reader is also privy to a guided tour of prison life. The waiting room, the courtyard, the cafeteria, the work rooms, and the dormitories are all described, but in terms that accentuate light, space and restriction. Though expressed through quite simple vocabulary, the painterly description instils an unexpected beauty on the scene: 'le carreau du réfectoire encore un peu humide du lavage du matin luisait rouge, et la lumière aigre d'une froide journée de printemps jouait crûment sur l'ocre frais des murailles et le blanc de chaux du plafond, tout récemment repeints' (p. 171). On the other hand, the 'parloir', the one place in the prison where detainees are able to speak, is described in less affective, more detached, terms: 'le parloir d'une maison centrale se compose de trois cages ou plutôt de trois grands garde-manger grillagés de fer et soudés l'un à l'autre' (p. 159). There is a clear difference in emphasis away from artistic description to a more matter-of-fact one, suggesting perhaps that this particular location is completely devoid of poetry.

The descriptions of the theatre in *La Faustin* are in many ways similar to the descriptions of the prison in *La Fille Elisa*, accentuating as they do the pictorial qualities of the scene. Balconies, statues, and scaffolding are all described in terms of light and shadow: 'un peu de pâleur blême sur les cariatides des avants-scènes' (p. 56), 'dans les frises et les trouées des échafaudages des lueurs bleuissantes' (p. 56). Noticeably absent from the novel are more disinterested depictions. Towards the end, vocabulary verges on the Gothic, and the castle is described as a 'monde vilainement fantastique' (p. 290). Realism and aestheticism coexist in all of the novels, and *écriture artiste* brings them together by merging two separate ways of seeing the world.

Shared Group Languages

In other situations, popular language, colloquialisms and slang dominate, particularly when members of a specific profession or group are presented. Nonetheless, not all characters associated with a group communicate in its language and this usually serves to distinguish the protagonists from their peers. Seldom do the main characters communicate in popular or colloquial language; when they do, it is for effect.

In the 1879 novel, popular vocabulary reflects the social status of the circus as a low form of art that is relegated to the boulevards. The vocabulary of midwifery in *La Fille Elisa* functions in much the same way. In normal circumstances, those who work in these environments communicate in their languages and it is a mark of mimetic aims to reproduce these lexicons in the novel. Curiously, however, while Gianni and Nello spend their entire existence surrounded by 'the people', they seldom utter words that could be considered popular or colloquial. When they do, it is usually Gianni when speaking to Nello, and then only after they have sold their family's travelling circus (there are, obviously, exceptions to this rule). When the two clowns sell the family's travelling show, Gianni's language temporarily changes. In contrast, the man to whom it is sold, Le Recousu, speaks in excessive colloquialisms:

> Te voilà enfin!... prends une chaise et un verre, et asseois-toi là... Il est donc dans *le champ de navets*, le père Bescapé!... je l'aimais ce vieux singe... ça m'aurait fait plaisir de *concourir à sa cérémonie*... Ah! pour un qui avait du vice, c'en était un celui-là... et comme le mâtin jouait de *l'attrape-nigaud*... Jeune homme, c'est moi, le Recousu, qui te le dis: tu as eu là un *chouette papa*... et on n'en refera plus... *la mère des humains* comme *ceusse-là* a fini d'accoucher... Bois, cochon... Et qu'est-ce que tu veux de toute ta *landière*? (p. 89).

Le Recousu utters more popularisms in this one episode than Gianni does in the entire novel, even though they live and work in the same environment. The fact that Gianni does not speak in overly popular language simultaneously signals his artistic superiority and intimates that even if he is not an aristocrat by birth, he is one by taste.

The Zemgannos' relatively restricted use of popular and colloquial language is in contrast with the eponymous heroine of *La Fille Elisa*, Goncourt's most conventionally Naturalist work. This register is a reflection of her environment: Elisa, a prostitute, is the child of a midwife from an impoverished Parisian neighbourhood. Yet, as in *Les Frères Zemganno*, italics and ellipses abound and offer examples of the way in which language is highlighted in the text, making it a spectacle:

> Elle avait plein le dos de l'existence avec sa mère... l'ouvrage du bazar était trop *abîmant*... elle ne voulait pas devenir une *tire-enfants*... voici bien des semaines qu'elle l'attendait... c'était fini, elle avait pris son parti de *donner dans le travers*... elle allait partir avec elle [a brothel owner]... si elle ne l'emmenait pas, ...elle entrerait dans une maison de Paris, la première venue... s'entendre avec sa mère, c'était vouloir *débarbouiller un mort*... Elle se sentait par moments la tête *évaporée* (p. 21).

Elisa's mother employs almost exclusively popular language, referring to her daughter as 'bernoque' (p. 15), using the term 'sortir un saint de ses gonds' (p. 17) with regard to her daughter refusing to become a midwife, and, finally, when visiting Elisa in prison, addressing her sister as a 'nigaude' (p. 160) and exclaiming 'sacré polisson de salopiat de singe' (p. 12), 'mais, vraiment, t'as bonne figure, oh! Mais c'est chouette, t'as trouvé le moyen d'engraisser tout plein' (p. 160). None of this is out of place for a 'woman of the people' and the language accurately conveys her social status as well as the author's mastery of his subject.

Much like the Zemgannos, La Faustin does not express herself in the language of her peers. While others use expressions such as 'tu steppes' (p. 79), 'tu nous courbatures l'entendement' (p. 14) (a very inventive and refined formulation), 'je suis d'attaque' (p. 26), and 'un peu de vigousse' (p. 60), her voice is different: 'elle écrivait comme une femme du siècle passé' (p. 206), 'corrigeant un mot ou un goût canaille' (p. 205). There is a distance separating Juliette from her environment. As with the Zemgannos, she is elevated above her milieu by her artistic, or at least linguistic, refinement.

Similarly, in *Chérie*, linguistic peculiarities and popularisms are committed either by those who surround the main character or by the narrator, not by the girl herself. Mme Tony-Fréneuse, who occupies an equal, if not higher, social position than the heroine, uses twice as many colloquialisms as Chérie.[10] Thus, no matter the language of their environment, the characters in Edmond de Goncourt's novels speak it differently. This is indicative of the main characters' refusal to participate in a futile process of linguistic socialisation and their desire to establish a distance between themselves and others.

Scientific Language

A fascination with medicine, anatomy and science is arguably one of the strongest links between Naturalist and Decadent output; accordingly, its use in Goncourt's novels fluctuates and evolves over time.

In *La Fille Elisa,* descriptions of the midwife's working quarters are peppered with vocabulary that reminds the reader of the nature of her work: 'éclampsie' (p. 18), 'cataplasmes' (p. 26), 'maladies de la moelle épinière' (p. 198). On the other hand, a face is described as a 'masque paralysé' (p. 199), a description that is more thematically charged. In *Les Frères Zemganno*, children must be taught in the gymnastic arts 'avant la soudure du squelette', Nello must 'fortifier les poignets et [...] habituer sa colonne vertébrale' (p. 55). Terms such as 'bandage dextriné' (p. 242), 'fracture comminutive' (p. 224) and 'solidification de l'articulation tibio-tarsienne' (p. 249), explain an injury he sustains. Conversely, anatomical language is incessantly used in elaborate descriptions of gymnastic jumps and training, and its repetition is incantatory. Terminology ranging from the mundane – 'tendons', 'fléchisseurs', 'extenseurs' (p. 86), 'une flexion oblique de la jambe', 'des courbatures des muscles sterno-pubien et dorso-acromien' (p. 184) – to the strangely prosaic – 'saillies d'omoplates étranges' (p. 132), 'biceps, pectoraux, modelages de larges attaches nerveuses aux insertions profondes' (p. 23), 'gonflements, des

---

[10] Youngs, p. 122.

dépressions défendues à une anatomie humaine' (p. 132) – sit side by side.

In *La Faustin*, medical language is used almost exclusively in relation to debauched characters and has little to do with the process of degeneration, but with degeneration itself. Selwyn, who is described as having a 'front hydrocéphale' (p. 273) of which Lombroso would no doubt be proud, suffers from an 'influx nerveux de la moelle' (p. 275); Bonne-Ame suffers from a 'fluxion de poitrine' (p. 21), a condition that is in reality quite common. Elsewhere, there is a medical description of Annandale's condition, drawn from documentary sources: 'voyez-vous, madame, les jeux bizarres du muscle risorius et du grand zygomatique?' (p. 304). One eccentric character, a translator of Darwin, speaks in a 'conversation agrémentée de termes médicaux' (p. 9), another suffers from an 'ataxie locomotrice' (p. 79). Chérie's great-grandfather dies of a 'coup de sang' (p. 21) and her grandmother is 'souffrante de la poitrine' (p. 30), yet although Chérie herself dies, her deterioration is not described in medical terms, as Elisa's is. Her brush with scarlet fever is only of interest because of the frenzy of reading it inspires. Puberty is only of interest because of Chérie's fear of menstruation and the changes that it brings about to her personality, rather than her biological make-up. Bodily functions are not described in terms that are overly technical. Medical, anatomical and scientific knowledge is integral to the representation of reality in the Naturalist novel, and contributes to the validity of the texts as scientific documents. These lexicons attest to the author's encyclopædic knowledge and grounding in science, and root the narratives in a scientific, deterministic framework. Here, though, medical vocabulary progressively loses its place in the sun and is by 1884 employed to paint eccentricities of character rather than processes of physiological degeneration.

Foreign Languages

In Goncourt's four novels, language use is also closely linked to sensuality, often to the detriment of meaning. This is particularly obvious with respect to the presentation of foreign languages.

In order to better portray Phèdre, Juliette Faustin visits the Greek sage Athanassiadis. There the actress is read Euripides' *Hippolytus* in the original, and, crucially, Greek is not a language she understands. The actress tells him:

> Je suis curieuse de vous entendre lire de cette *Phèdre* dans l'original... Ça éveillera peut-être des idées chez moi... Voilà... Je voudrais revenir de chez vous, comme une Barbare d'autrefois... qui aurait passé deux heures dans la Grèce de Périclès... et avec un peu du bruit de la langue dans mon oreille (p. 34).

Foreign words do not alienate her from the play; on the contrary, they bring her closer to the core of Phèdre's being. Feeling is more important than linguistic comprehension, though once the reading is over, Athanassiadis offers his view of the role: 'le commentateur donnait à la tragédienne moderne, la tentation d'accents nouveaux à introduire dans le rôle rajeuni, renouvelé, compris historiquement' (pp. 40-41). In much the same manner, in the closing scenes of *Chérie*, the protagonist listens, enraptured, to *Lucia di Lammermoor* 'à travers une succession de demi-évanouissements' (p. 333). The exact words – 'T'amo ingrata, t'amo ancor' (p. 332) – though they are reproduced, seem secondary to the effect that is created. The effect the opera has on her is caused by the mixture of musical and verbal language.

It is a combination of the sensation words create and their foreignness that is vital both to characters and readers, not the words themselves, and certainly not their meaning. In this context, words are akin to performances or displays of linguistic virtuosity, fundamentally sensual tools. The ability of a word to signify through something other than its referent is discussed by Pierre Sabatier who clearly sees the Goncourtian word as contributing to a new *fin de siècle* aesthetic that is very different from the typical Naturalist one: 'Pour eux, comme pour nos poètes symbolistes et décadents, tout mot, par ses sonorités, renferme une puissance de suggestion, une richesse d'évocation, qu'il s'agit seulement de mettre en valeur par une savante disposition' (p. 403).

In *La Faustin*, the obverse of this use of foreign language for effect is the fact that for a significant portion of the novel, the eponymous actress is sequestered with her British lover and his sadistic friend

Georges Selwyn, but there is relatively little use of English. Sabatier's comments offer a possible explanation as to why this is the case: if words are meaningful due to their sonority, then this is all that is required of them, be they foreign or French. The narrator, in contrast, accounts for the lack of English in their conversations in another way: 'Il y a encore chez l'Anglais le dédain de la parole inutile, et comme une pudeur, très distinguée d'ailleurs, à ne pas souligner les marques de son amour avec du verbiage' (p. 212). It is added that 'l'Anglais n'a pas le vocabulaire d'amour' (p. 212). The vocabulary of love or a love of vocabulary? For Goncourt, English is perhaps not sensuous or sonorous enough to evoke through sound alone.

When Gianni and Nello move to London to train, the manner in which foreign words are transcribed, rather than the Zemgannos' use of them, is remarkable. One episode is drawn directly from a chapter on the acrobat Alhambra Joe in *Circus Life and Circus Celebrities*. It furnishes a graphic illustration of how the *document humain* and *écriture artiste* can overlap, and draws attention to the particularities of language and vocabulary. Translated from the English, words are transcribed in different ways: some are in italics, some are capitalised, and others hyphenated where they are not in the original.

> Il existait dans Victoria-Street un endroit nommé *Les Ruines*. C'était un immense terrain, où la commission des AMÉLIORATIONS MÉTROPOLITAINES avait fait démolir trois ou quatre cents maisons, un espace désert tout parsemé d'écroulements [...]. Les Ruines, depuis plusieurs années, étaient le rendez-vous, le gymnase en plein air de tous les acrobates, gymnastes, *trapézistes* du trapèze volant ou du trapèze fixe, clowns, jongleurs, danseurs de cordes, équilibristes sans emploi, de tous les gens nés dans la *sciure de bois* ou désireux d'y vivre. (p. 104).[11]

On another note, the demolition site as circus arena is a travesty of the life led by aesthetes. It is conceivably the farthest one can get from conceptions of high art and refined cultural activity. It is also an allegory of the Goncourts' own wanderings into the life of the working class, which they sought to portray both artistically and realistically.

Complicated vocabulary does not always result from a complicated scenario or setting. Books dealing with 'base' environments have

---

[11] Cf. Frost, p. 227.

sophisticates and elegant vocabularies that stand out against the backdrop of their subject matter. In these four texts, the contrast between vulgar and refined, and between base and elevated, is a reflection of the historical circumstances of the novel. The use of foreign words in these works, however, is not entirely accounted for by the changing nature of French vocabulary. Italian was widely used around the 1880s in discussions of art, while English was growing in usage in matters of industry and economics, not to mention sport, racing and other pastimes;[12] but, these are not always the uses to which these languages are put by Goncourt. The use of foreign vocabulary here illustrates that the criteria of both Naturalism and Decadence are in play. For, while certain foreign words may realistically portray an environment, they may also signal the author's erudition through needless lexical explanations (sometimes in footnotes) and repetitive highlighting that leads to disruptive narrator intrusions and prevents narrative progression.

Treacherous Language

This brief overview of some of the lexical issues raised in Goncourt's novels is related to broader questions regarding language and lexical usage in the late-nineteenth-century novel.

The unabashedly over-the-top scene that takes place when Lord Annandale is on his deathbed is without doubt one of the most dramatic uses of foreign language in any of Goncourt's novels. Juliette, the consummate actress, studies Annandale as though he were not a living being, much less her dying lover. In a brief moment of lucidity before his death Annandale screams, twice, and his resounding words are the last of the novel: 'Turn out that woman!' (p. 307). There is a symbolic return to the mother tongue here, marking the distance that has come to stand between the two lovers. It also, of course, adds to the stereotype of the eccentric and corrupt British gentleman, already introduced in the text in the form of the sinister

---

[12] See L. Petit de Julleville, *Histoire de la langue et de la littérature française des origines à 1900*, 8 vols (Paris: Armand Colin, 1899), III: *Dix-neuvième siècle, période contemporaine (1850-1900)*, pp. 811-40, and Remy de Gourmont, *Esthétique de la langue française* [1899] (Paris: Editions Ivrea, 1995), chapter 8.

Georges Selwyn, who holidays in a castle named after a character of the Marquis de Sade's. Nevertheless, theatre and acting are gulfs that separate Juliette and William, and this is accentuated by the histrionic and melodramatic nature of these English imperatives from the deathbed.

Mireille Dottin-Orsini has addressed the question of language in this episode on a broader level, by comparing it to the finale of Wilde's *Salomé*:

> Quant au cri final de la pièce de Wilde ('Tuez cette femme!' S'écrie Hérode…), il se souvient de celui de l'Anglais agonisant aux dernières pages de *La Faustin*, dans toute l'horreur que leur geste (baiser une bouche morte, imiter *La Faustin*. Salomé comme Juliette une agonie) inspire au regard masculin […]: 'Turn out that woman!'. Dans les deux cas, il s'agit de punir une insulte faite à l'homme aimé, le sacrilège d'un irrespect envers la mort.[13]

It would be more accurately Decadent to state that Annandale has realised that Juliette, as a woman, can only ever be a duplicitous and deceptive actor: 'Une artiste… vous n'êtes que cela… la femme incapable d'aimer!' (p. 244). Regardless, this particular example seems to be exceptional as regards the use of English or any foreign language in Goncourt's novels.

In *Les Frères Zemganno*, Gianni and Nello, unlike Edmond and Jules – though this is hotly contested with regard to the Goncourts – do not succeed in their attempt to revolutionise their art. None of Goncourt's protagonists do: the doomed nature of creativity is an aesthetic necessity in Edmond's novels, as it is in much *fin de siècle* literature. The Zemgannos' *tour de force* is sabotaged when one prop is replaced by another. Gianni suspects all is not well, hesitates, and Nello breaks his legs in a suspicious accident. The fate that awaits Gianni, and particularly Nello, is provoked by two causes. The first cause, which has been addressed in an earlier chapter, is the *femme fatale*, the American equestrian – an aristocratic art form if ever there was one. The second is the word that Gianni whispers to his brother in order to launch their performance, a word that is conventionally used by all circus performers to get the show rolling, but that has no particular symbolism in its language of origin: 'Go!', 'ce solennel "Go", l'appel que l'un fait à l'autre de venir le retrouver à travers le

---

[13] '*La Faustin*, les paons blancs et l'agonie sardonique', p. 255.

vide, – pour ce "Va" qui est peut-être la mort' (p. 213). When Gianni calls Nello, it is with a '"Go" hésitant, inquiet, désespéré, et qui avait l'intonation de ces "à la grâce de Dieu" poussés en un de ces instants mortels où il faut prendre un parti, sans qu'il vous soit donné le temps de reconnaître, d'interroger le danger' (p. 220). Importantly, even after Nello's legs are broken in the fall, and the clowns have resigned themselves to busking and fiddling for a living, Nello's only desire is to read his sixteenth-century gymnastic manual. The conviction remains that the process of innovation chosen by the brothers is suitable, even if it is hazardous. This belief seems to be shared by aspiring authors of the time, for the rise of the Decadent novel, which develops many of the linguistic risks thrown up by Edmond de Goncourt's novels, follows his works by only a few years.

In *La Fille Elisa*, a simple word is *mis-en-abîme* in much the same manner, and likewise attains a degree of symbolism otherwise unattached to it. Moreover, the same narrative technique is employed to accentuate the importance of the monosyllable. After the jury deliver their verdict of guilty in Elisa's murder trial, the narrator repeats the condemning word almost lyrically: 'En le saisissement de ce mortel "Oui, sans circonstances atténuantes", de ce "oui" redouté, mais non attendu – du froid passe dans tous les dos, et le frisson des spectateurs remonte jusqu'aux impassibles exécuteurs de la loi' (p. 7). Even the most banal words have the power to influence situations and change the course of events, if used at the wrong time or in the wrong way.

Conclusion

Each of the protagonists in the three final novels seeks artistic innovation in an environment that no longer fulfils their aesthetic demands. Mirroring this yearning for originality, the novels adopt several different vocabularies in an attempt to renew and extend literary language. Attempts to transcend artistic norms are presented as extremely perilous enterprises. Goncourt's artists have difficulty reconciling high art with popular art forms. Gianni and Nello wish to transform the circus into something it is not: elevated and cultivated. Juliette Faustin must create while simultaneously entertaining the masses, remaining true to herself by using vocabulary that spans centuries and civilisations (she unsuccessfully attempts to give this up altogether in the name of love). Chérie has difficulty reconciling her artistic inclinations with the superficial world in which she moves. Difficulty also arises due to the very nature of the arts portrayed: the circus and the theatre are both popular. Refinement is one of the primary concerns of Goncourt's novels, but so too are the doomed ambitions of characters whose artistic and personal aspirations inevitably result in decline and disaster.

The fact that none of the protagonists succeed in living artistic lives and transcending the restraints of the body without disastrous (sometimes fatal) consequences reflects a general disillusionment of the late nineteenth century. The characters are suspended on a tightrope between, at the one extreme, the need for specialised art forms and, at the other, the environments in which they wish to innovate and live, environments with specific vocabularies essential to understanding them. The impossibility of art appears to be an absolute end, as ideal art can never be adequately expressed through the language at hand. In terms of literary language, a consequence of this kind of uncomfortable balancing act is a privileging of 'paraître' over 'être', of surface appearance over essence. Although the excessive lexical cultivation of the novels may suggest that language is attempting to pinpoint an essential, higher truth, it is at the very moment of lexical searching that words are denied deeper meanings – because they are too elusive or enigmatic – and become significant for their beauty rather than their meaning. This closely echoes the way in which Edmond de Goncourt is constrained by the pull between consecration as a member of the Naturalist movement and the desire for aesthetic innovation. His specialised vocabulary is supposed to help the reader approach artistic truth, but risks alienating him from both public and peers. In this sense, words are not so much the physicians of the diseased mind, but the symptoms of decadence.

Natural and Artificial Expression

> CAMPAGNE. Les gens de la campagne meilleurs que ceux des villes.
> – Flaubert, *Dictionnaire des idées reçues*[1]

If Edmond de Goncourt's characters fail in terms of communication, and if the link between direct discourse and plot development is weakened in the novels, it is due to a privileging of aesthetic expression over utilitarian communication. With the notable exception of *La Fille Elisa*, each of the novels features characters who are, in one way or another, artistic: the Zemganno brothers are circus performers, La Faustin is an actress, and Chérie transforms her body into art through her obsession with fashion and dress. Significantly, the protagonists' creativity is not necessarily expressed in verbal language, but through other art forms. None of the characters choose written language as their medium; instead, they focus on the visual or performing arts. Even where the art form is oral – for example, where the theatre is concerned – attention is put on the manner in which things are said rather than on what is being expressed. Verbal language is portrayed as sensual rather than meaningful, and this sensuality is indicative of a cleavage within language itself, where the aesthetic and the utilitarian coexist. As evidenced by the creative channels left open to the protagonists, notions of natural sensuality and civilised aestheticism are constantly opposed in these novels.

The tension between competing visions of art is in part a result of the opposition between rural and urban life in Edmond de Goncourt's fiction. The Zemgannos' desperately doomed artistic search begins once they leave their idyllic travelling circus. In *Chérie*, the main character's eccentric and affected artistry is contrasted with the sensuality of her childhood language, a language that must compete with more 'refined' and 'civilised' forms of expression. When Chérie overhears two girls speaking the 'langue de son enfance' (p. 153), it is presented as inextricably linked to the sensual. Although the reader

---

[1] (Paris: Librio, 1997), p. 15.

does not read the patois, its effects on Chérie are noted, as though 'ce parler de caresse' (p. 153) had physically touched the eavesdropper. On another occasion, Chérie's governess, Lizadie, tells the girl a fairytale about three men – a mayor, his deputy, and a schoolmaster – from a village called Ruaux-les-Fous. These dignitaries wish to learn French. However, after an unfortunate incident where their French is misunderstood, they are imprisoned for speaking it inappropriately and inadvertently confessing to murder. By not understanding the language that is spoken to them and its function, the fairytale characters are forced from an idealised conception of language, based in the realm of the imaginary, and foisted into the positivist realities of a world where language is transactional and communicative. With the help of the timely intervention of a fairy, they return to their native Lorraine never to leave, nor speak an urban, civilised language, again: 'ils mouraient bien des années après n'ayant, jusqu'au jour de leur mort, jamais plus parlé que patois' (p. 71). Unlike the three fairytale characters, Goncourt's heroine returns to her native Lorraine, but speaks a foreign language: French. She is condemned to an expressive prison from which she can only escape through other modes of expression. Her escape will be mostly based on appearances, and goes some way to accounting for the predominance of description over dialogue in the novel.

In *La Fille Elisa*, there is an incompatibility between base subject and refined writing. There is even a tension between base environment and language and cultivated inner spirit. For this reason, it is amazing that Elisa, who is initially presented as a foul-mouthed street urchin, is transformed into the most desirable of women once in a provincial brothel. This improbability is accounted for by the simple fact that she is from Paris, and speaks an urban language:

> Parmi ces femelles, la plupart originaires du Bassigny, Elisa apportait dans sa personne la *femminilité* que donne la grande capitale civilisée à la jeune fille élevée, grandie entre ses murs. Elle avait une élégante tournure, de jolis gestes; dans le chiffonnage des étoffes légères et volantes habillant son corps, elle mettait de la grâce de Paris (p. 37).

Paris influences even its most deprived inhabitants, and a new word is used to describe this unlikely, yet legendary quality that the city bestows on its daughters: *femminilité*. When Elisa's speech is described from the point of view of the people in Lorraine, it is perceived as quite different from the popular, crass language examined earlier:

> Elle parlait presque comme le monde qui parle bien, écoutait ce qui se disait avec un rire intelligent, se répandait certains jours en une verve gouailleuse d'enfant du pavé parisien, étonnant de son bruit le mauvais lieu de la petite ville (p. 37).

As in *Les Frères Zemganno*, the countryside has an idealising, edenic quality which impacts on those new to it. The countryside is associated with happiness and fulfilment, with love and with elevation of spirit – not so much for those who live there on a permanent basis, but for those who visit. Within this framework, the descriptions of brothel life are all the more effective: Elisa seems refined, but the people who surround her, though oddly immersed in the good country air, are not similarly affected.

The rejuvenating power of the countryside is a theme in *Chérie*, as well, as is plain when the protagonist is reminded of the language of her youth. The French language is painted as though it imprisons its speakers within a system, while Lotharingien (and, one assumes, other provincial dialects) connotes liberty. The obverse of Chérie's expression through fashion is her link to a provincial language. The artificiality of Parisian society is accentuated by the sensuality associated in the novel with the Lorraine language.

> Dans la chaleur et l'odeur d'Orient de la journée, les deux fillettes, tout en épongeant la sueur de l'entre-deux de leurs seins, causaient en patois, – dans ce parler de caresse et de musique et de l'enfance d'un pays, – causaient de la douceur du premier baiser d'amour donné sur la bouche (p. 153).

Chérie is 'étonnée de se rappeler si bien la langue de son enfance' (p. 153) and eavesdrops on the conversation. This language and its vocabulary are both hidden from the reader. Nonetheless, they penetrate the young protagonist's psyche and become inextricably linked with pastoral pleasure and lazy summer days (both of which are absent in Paris). In order for Chérie to be fulfilled, the gulf between town and country needs to be lessened. Frustration reigns, however, and the gap is never narrowed.

The opposition between urban (or civilised) and rural (or natural) linguistic and artistic realities is somewhat different in *La Faustin*. In this novel, the heroine's obsession with the theatre is underlined once she is removed from its environs. Juliette Faustin is taken over, haunted even, by her theatrical passion the moment letters from Paris reach her at her retreat on Lake Constance. In chapter 47, which takes place at the rural retreat, the actress says but two lines, one of which comes to pass during a bout of sleepwalking in which she acts out the role of Hermione. In the chapter that follows this nocturnal incident, the actress addresses herself and orders herself to change her ways:

> L'actrice, à la suite d'impatiences muettes, se mettait tout à coup à crier avec des piétinements colères, comme si elle s'adressait à une autre créature qu'elle-même: 'Non! non! puisque je vous dis que c'est fini, fini, à tout jamais fini!' (p. 266).

La Faustin is aware that she is a subject divided between art and reality, and this reading of actresses, cherished during the second half of the nineteenth century, was positively worshipped by the Decadents. Nowhere is the innate duality of artists more succinctly summed up than in *The Decadent Imagination*, where it is maintained that the artist is:

> [A] victim of a fatal duality inherent in his personality [...] he is doomed to be constantly torn between the two sides of his own nature, one experiencing with great intensity, and even pain, all the impressions life has to offer, the other lucid and disillusioned, coldly observing and judging them.[2]

Juliette herself is an example of this: she struggles to banish the conflict between theatrical and private discourses. If Juliette somnambulistically lapses into theatrical mode even without an audience, it demonstrates that theatre has become for her a purely artistic act (it has been separated from its popular environment) and has no relation to communication. Her personal voice is inseparable from the voices of the heroines she portrays and will be forever intermingled with that of a non-existent fictional other. Torn between playing a role in the theatre and playing the role of lover, in chapter 54 she is brusquely brought back to reality and out of her imagined theatrical world by the use of English, in which foreign language she must respond ('Oh yes, yes wait', p. 282). In this novel, nature

---

[2] Pierrot, pp. 50-51.

perverts the characters and only makes their need for artistic expression greater. Deprived of a creative forum, the thespian withdraws into herself and disconnects from her pastoral environment by, for all intents and purposes, severing communicative links with her lover. Annandale's attempts to separate Juliette from her fatal artistic drive by taking her away from Paris are in vain.

On a thematic level, the dichotomy in the actress testifies to a cleavage between natural and artificial language, a rift between two contrasting states of existence. The theatre so dominates Juliette's life that certain chapters read like plays. A passage in chapter 10 is presented as a drama would be, except that the actress' voice becomes confused with the voice of her character. Three speakers are involved in an exchange during a rehearsal: 'l'actrice', 'le metteur en scène' and 'le directeur'. The actress reads her lines from *Phèdre* (which are written as direct discourse in the novel) and the two others comment on her performance and coach her. The reader is thus left to imagine how 'l'actrice' portrays her role and speaks her lines, as well as what the others' visions of the play are. It is only at the end of the rehearsal that the actress is named, but confusingly, she is designated by her nickname while her interlocutor retains his dramatic name:

> Et la Faustin, apostrophant Hippolyte, lui disait sur un ton agressif: 'Mais je ne peux pas cependant aller chercher votre épée sous votre tunique... le geste est pour moi horriblement difficile... il faut que par votre position... vous me fournissiez un mouvement qui ne soit ni un mouvement commun, ni un mouvement canaille (p. 98).

The conversation accentuates the protagonist's duality by giving her, but not the others, two names, and by showing how the reality of life as an actor divides her. This offers yet another illustration of how direct discourse contributes not so much to the development of plot in this instance, but to characterisation. Juliette is, fatally, a creature of artifice.

In reproducing a theatrical rehearsal – and a considerable amount of space is devoted to describing how the actress learns to perform – gestures and feeling are emphasised so as to minimise the importance of linguistic meaning. In the 1882 novel, the narrator must recreate theatrical performances and rehearsals in such a way that words become gestures, and the same lines are not repeated *ad infinitum*. In an argument with her director, La Faustin, unable to say her lines correctly, asks him: 'Comment le diriez-vous, vous?' (p. 90). This is his reply: 'LE METTEUR EN SCÈNE: "Je désire ne pas le dire... je voudrais ce que ce fût vous... et dans l'intonation que je sens..."' (p. 90). The director's response is offset as though it were part of the play itself. Verbal language is a stimulus rather than a tool for interaction; pitch and tone are of utmost importance in gaining entry to a hidden world of symbolic meaning. This confirms that functional language is sidelined in favour of a conception of art that goes beyond denotation.

In *Chérie*, too, art is felt and not thought. The main character detects beauty 'au moyen de son délicat et susceptible système nerveux' (p. 201). When she reads she puts perfume on her books. Music is a drug to her. When she plays piano she is affected by a 'joie fiévreuse' and it gives her a fittingly Decadent

> Bien-être exalté, [...] un fouettement des facultés imaginatives, une augmentation de son être sensitif, enfin un petit rien des jouissances surnaturelles que procurent aux hommes les stupéfiants: car la musique n'est peut-être point autre chose que le *haschisch* des femmes (pp. 104-05).

This feeling only comes to pass when music is not associated with lessons and is not the domain of the intellect and intellectualising music teachers.

Whereas Juliette's spoken voice is often confused with the voice of the heroines she embodies, in *Chérie* the protagonist's spoken voice is replaced by the pen in terms of communication and by fashion in terms of art. Chérie only expresses her inner self through verbal language in private situations. Two chapters of the 1884 novel reproduce in their alleged entirety documents purportedly written by the heroine, but it is through the visual that the Parisian really manages to express her artistry. Her teacher, Jodocus Cochemer, predicts that 'elle écrira très joliment, Mlle Haudancourt' (p. 98). The reader, however, is never shown a written specimen of Chérie's 'côté imaginatif' (p. 97), nor her 'aptitude à forger des histoires' (p. 97). The only samples of the main character's written expressive skills deal with genres that are usually considered as purely non-fiction, rather than imaginative: firstly, a personal code of conduct; secondly, extracts of her journal; and, thirdly, a note expressing anguish over a secret love, found by her grandfather after her death.

What is termed by the omniscient narrator as Chérie's 'goût à la composition de style' (p. 97) is only witnessed in matters of dress and fashion. Numerous glimpses of the girl's aptitude to graft a style onto her body are provided (like the Zemganno brothers, Chérie's body has its own gesticular language that transcends the purely verbal). At times, Chérie objectifies herself, a fact that is made manifest stylistically by the way that oral discourse appears in isolation, so that it does not form part of a linguistic exchange between two characters. As a young girl, the heroine falls and cries 'je suis cassée, je suis cassée' (p. 73), as though she were a doll. She also refers to herself in the third person, emptying her being of its 'self': 'Chérie a fait ça' (p. 42). When she is older, she is a mannequin who only discusses what colours, at a given instant, suit her, and what colours will create the greatest, most splendid, effect. The frivolity of this attitude is apparent just as much in her words that make reference to a precious metal – 'Non, le rose ne me va pas décidément aujourd'hui... Il ne me fait pas la peau argentine, mais du tout...' (p. 255) – as in the narrator's description, which repeats four times words based on 'teint', two times the word 'jour', three times the word 'nuance', three words derived from light ('lumière' and 'lumineux'), and also makes reference to the girl's 'photogénité' (p. 255). In keeping with the general tenets of *écriture artiste*, this description transforms the child into a painting. It is not a person that is described, but an object (this mirrors Chérie's own inclinations to turn herself into an object). The heroine's voice is not the voice of *écriture artiste*, she does not speak in what could be called 'parole artiste'; however, her words deal with visual appearances (her speech is not elaborate, but the appearances she describes are).

Paul Bourget discusses the style of the Goncourts in terms that can crystallise the issue of individual artistic style in Edmond's characters: 'Le style d'un écrivain, c'est l'expression et comme le raccourci de toute sa manière habituelle de penser et de sentir. Se découvrir un style, c'est tout simplement avoir le courage de noter les mouvements de son *moi*' (p. 336). The movements of Goncourt's 'moi' are of little import here, and, in any event, they are made available to all in his own *Journal: mémoires de la vie littéraire*. But if 'style' is replaced by 'voice' in the above passage (if they are not essentially similar), the cause of Chérie's downfall is named. Chérie is unable to achieve self-knowledge in her writings because they reflect a widespread worldview at the time of publication of the novel: that women were incapable of self-analysis. To quote Maupassant in 'La Jeune fille': 'Comment découvrir les délicates sensations que la jeune fille elle-même méconnaît encore, qu'elle ne peut ni expliquer, ni comprendre, ni analyser, et qu'elle oubliera presque entièrement lorsqu'elle sera devenue femme'. This view is at the heart of *Chérie*, a novel that is ripe with these sorts of stereotypes. In fact, the inability to arrive at the 'truth' may, from a Decadent perspective, be a truth unto itself. There is thus a link between the inabilities of women and the impotence of art.

Chérie's writings, therefore, are not where her *fin de siècle* penchant for aesthetic refinement is best expressed. This is confirmed by the narrator who explains that Chérie's fundamental artistry, like that of any woman, is expressed through fashion:

> Au fond, la toilette pour une femme, c'est le moyen de témoigner de l'artiste qui habite en elle, [...] c'est le moyen d'exposer sa grâce, sa gentillesse, sa beauté, parmi l'arrangement, le coloris, l'harmonie d'un heureux tableau; c'est le moyen de faire de sa personne, dans les sociétés civilisées, à travers les incessants changements de modes et d'ajustements, un charmant et frêle objet d'art, toujours renouvelé, toujours nouveau (pp. 252-53).

Like a dandy, she searches for sensation and constant novelty through appearance, as is illustrated when she is described as 'déraisonnablement mondaine' (p. 247). Chérie moves from self-denial to self-indulgence: she gains an in-depth knowledge of the art of fashion in all its guises, including dress, perfume, and make-up, to name but a few. She shares these concerns with many a Decadent character, for instance, Lorrain's Princesse Ilsée, '[qui] n'aimait qu'elle-même':

> Toute sa somptueuse existence se passait à se baigner, à se parfumer, à se peigner, à se parer, à essayer des bijoux, des tuniques et des voiles, à se sourire à elle-même et à rêver la robe nouvelle, l'attitude imprévue ou l'étoffe inconnue qui la distinguerait de la foule et la ferait différente des autres femmes. C'était, en somme, une petite créature assez futile, férocement égoïste et follement éprise d'elle-même, mais elle portait à ravir les tuniques transparentes des îles Canaries, les colliers de coquillages de l'Extrême-

Orient, et personne dans le royaume ne possédait une taille aussi souple: la princesse Ilsée n'aimait que les miroirs et les fleurs.[3]

Des Esseintes also shares Chérie's preoccupations, so much so that Edmond de Goncourt considered him her soulmate. He comments in the *Journal* that des Esseintes was like the 'silhouette du futur mari de Chérie' (16 May 1884) and remarked to Huysmans, 'mais savez-vous que cela a un peu l'air de la monographie du mari que devrait épouser Chérie'.[4] A knowledge of fashion and appearances enables the socialite Chérie to always be the centre of attention and to always be an *objet-d'art* to interpret and behold in all its beauty: 'Il lui arrivait à *soigner*, à la façon d'une actrice, ses entrées, et d'appartenir cœur et âme, tout le temps qu'elle passait dans le monde, à la production d'*effets*' (p. 247). The production of external effects hides a core of absence, masks the void at the heart of her existence.

Chérie suffers from 'une sorte de spiritualité du chiffon' (p. 250) that makes her to want to be more refined, more civilised, and more eccentric. The style of her dress and coiffure reflects the level of civilisation of society, and the prerogatives of Decadence dictate that refinement is linked to knowledge of cultures distant in both time and space. So, like the Zemganno brothers who create new performances by building on earlier gymnastic knowledge, Chérie dons dresses – costumes even – that draw on multiple fashion sources. In the privacy of her own room she wears an eighteenth-century dress ('la fanfreluche, le pasquillage argentés de la broderie', p. 257) that has been crossed with a '*haïck*, ce vêtement de l'Orient' (p. 256). As if this were not enough, 'Chérie se faisait coiffer par sa femme de chambre avec des gazons, de grandes herbes vertes tressées en couronne au-dessus de ses cheveux épars…' (p. 276). Concerned solely with 'des adorations paresseuses de sa personne' (p. 257) she sinks into debased depravity. These costumes convey the child's indulgence and Decadent love of artifice. Artificiality, according to A.E. Carter, 'is not only urban and modern, but sickly […] decadent'.[5]

---

[3] 'La Princesse au Sabbat', in Jean Lorrain, *Princesses d'ivoire et d'ivresse* [1902], ed. by Virginie Fauvin (Paris: Gallimard, 2002), pp. 29-35 (pp. 29 and 30).
[4] *Corres. Huys-Gonc.*, letter 13, 21 May 1884, p. 80, n. 1.
[5] *The Idea of Decadence in French Literature, 1830-1900* (Toronto: University of Toronto Press, 1958), p. 17.

As Carter's comment attests, Chérie's artistry can be tied to a much larger thematic issue in *fin de siècle* fiction.

The eccentricity of Chérie's appearance is mirrored in the eccentricities of language that many critics have identified in *écriture artiste*. The paradox is that *écriture artiste* is an ideal medium to describe this kind of visual embellishment, as it is itself so concerned with appearances, with portraying that which is seen rather than felt. Likewise, fashion is presented as a language in its own right, but a language that focuses on outward appearances. Goncourt's language, too, reflects fashion and outward appearances, and this very modern materialism bespeaks a fundamental cultural shift away from essentialism and the perceived dogmatism of mimetic representation.

The world of appearance is precisely what Pierre Saint-Amand believes both the Goncourts loved about fashion. He contends that 'ce que les Goncourt célèbrent dans la mode, c'est le triomphe de l'ostentation, les signes les plus éloquents du paraître, la célébration totale de l'artifice'.[6] Indeed, in the three final novels, the characters masquerade as something or somebody else, manifesting a very Decadent propensity for disguise, otherness, and possibly even debauchery: Juliette Faustin earns her living by travestying herself; Chérie chooses to do so in order to distance herself from the repetitive *ennui* of everyday existence; Nello, the reader is told, takes great pleasure in his disguises.

The significance of the divide between aesthetics and communication, and between verbal language and other art forms, permeates Goncourt's three final novels, and is a reflection of both his own artistic beliefs and the transformation that the literary field was undergoing at the end of the nineteenth century. As previously stated, one of the commonly accepted traits of *écriture artiste* is the manner in which it concentrates on the mechanisms of seeing and writing, that is to say on the process of creation. In these texts, the alternative modes of expression favoured by characters accentuate the visual over other senses, and, in this way, the thematic interests of the novels mirror those of *écriture artiste*. *Ecriture artiste* sought to rejuvenate language in order to make it less common and less popular. The commercialisation of literature was thought to jeopardise authors'

---

[6] 'La Passion de l'éphémère', *L'Esprit créateur*, 37 (1997), 21-33 (p. 21).

individual styles. The Goncourt brothers' style is in many ways a backlash against this, a means of guaranteeing individuality in a world – and a market – with ever-expanding borders. Similarly, the central characters in *Les Frères Zemganno*, *La Faustin* and *Chérie* are artists, and they are all driven by their art: Gianni and Nello seek a means by which to revolutionise acrobatics; Juliette Faustin cannot escape her art, which eats into, and divides, her consciousness; Chérie, finally, lives amidst swirls of exotic fabrics and fashions in order to forget or repress the demands of a repetitive and fatigued society. There is a connection between Goncourt's own artistic concerns – as well as the concerns of his characters – and Max Nordau's reactionary, yet influential, reading of the *fin de siècle* artist as a degenerate whose illness has been mistaken for 'a sensitive nature yearning for aesthetic thrills' (p. 5). In Edmond de Goncourt's solo novels, the thrills gained from gesture and effect far outweigh the joys of meaning.

CONCLUSION

Conclusion

> Artiste... tu es prêtre. Artiste... tu es roi. Artiste... tu es mage.
> – Joséphin Péladan, *Le Vice suprême*[1]

Approaching Edmond de Goncourt's novels *La Fille Elisa*, *Les Frères Zemganno*, *La Faustin* and *Chérie* through a Naturalist and Decadent framework provides a potent illustration of the instability that prevails in definitions of literary movements. Indeed, study of these four works consistently affirms the overlap between Naturalism and Decadence in the last decades of the nineteenth century. Many characteristic traits of Naturalism are reinvented and reinterpreted by Goncourt in his solo novels and given a new lease of life under the auspices on what some would term Decadence.

The study of Goncourtian titles furnishes an important starting point for an analysis of continuity and change from pre- to post-1870 novels. Eponymous titles were common in nineteenth-century literature, yet the Goncourts' systematic use of them is almost unique. In pre-1870 novels, titles that initially relate to types evolve into ones relating to individuals representative of their type (the servant, the journalist), illustrating the brothers' singular perspective on literary Naturalism and their penchant for 'cas pathologiques'. While Edmond remained true to this general pattern, by *Chérie* in 1884, possibly as early as 1879 with *Les Frères Zemganno*, the titles of his novels had little to do with announcing typical patterns of behaviour and focused much more on names – like Zemganno, Faustin, Chérie – that draw heavily on imaginary rather than observed realities. The evolution of Goncourtian titles therefore provides the first indications of a modification in Edmond de Goncourt's literary aesthetic.

If the titles to the four novels quietly suggest an aesthetic shift, their prefaces loudly plead for such an evolution. Using *Germinie Lacerteux* and its preface as the starting point, and linking the output of the Goncourt brothers to the output of Emile Zola, the prefaces to

---

[1] (Paris: Editions des autres, 1979), p. 13, n.1.

Les Frères Zemganno, *La Faustin* and *Chérie*, rather than explaining the novels they allegedly introduce, call for a transformation of the literary field. By building on the successes of the past and creating an interprefatorial dialogue, Goncourt is able to call for a renewal of literature, which is exposed as healthy only if it is in a state of permanent modernisation. The novels of the Goncourt brothers are presented as founding texts of the Naturalist movement; simultaneously, however, the surviving Goncourt is presented as a moderniser: someone attempting to distance himself from themes generally associated with Naturalist production in favour of a more cultivated vision of art, both formally and thematically.

There are suggestions in the use of documentation that the part in the writing process formerly played by Jules de Goncourt was subsequently shared amongst other contributors, be they friends asked for information or women solicited for confessions. In addition, in what is sometimes a complex intertextual relationship, other texts are researched for detail. *La Fille Elisa* is the only text by Edmond de Goncourt whose genesis has been established and it is thus useful for examining the process of literary creation. Evidence suggests that although extensive research was carried out for the novel by both brothers, Edmond adapted a new method of collaborative writing following Jules's death. The increase in correspondence relating to novels post-1877 seems to confirm this. *La Fille Elisa* is the most conventionally Naturalist of Goncourt's novels: it portrays a prostitute and her environment and attempts (somewhat half-heartedly at times) to link her downfall to her social situation and to her hereditary faults; subsequent novels paint more refined characters and pay less attention to the advent of faults as to the faults themselves. The social significance of *La Fille Elisa*, together with the condemnation of the Auburn system of imprisonment that it contains, also links it to a specific moment in time, transforming its author into a polemicist. In contrast, the three later novels have little to do with the political or social *actualité* of the 1880s.

In the Goncourtian aesthetic, the author is in many ways equated with the historian. In the 1879, 1882 and 1884 novels, fiction and non-fiction documents, in the form of letters and books as well as notes in the *Journal*, are accumulated and incorporated into the texts in the same way that they would be for works of history. Even so, while the process of gathering documents conforms to Naturalist methods of creation, the documents are used in service of themes that have much in common with Decadence. On the surface, for example, *Les Frères Zemganno* appears to paint a popular environment, when in fact it paints the refined artistic quest of two idealistic gymnasts. Although it can be considered a sentimental autobiographical novel, the verisimilitude that such a genre would seem to imply is disrupted by discordance between the use of, on the one hand, personal memories that are far from objective and verifiable and, on the other, observed facts relating to the world of the circus and drawn from diverse sources. The novel swings between realism in the portrayal of the circus, the author researching the environment as would a historian, and Decadence in the portrayal of the main characters' artistic quest and the *femme fatale*, Tompkins. The relationship between documentation and imagination in this novel is representative of wider cultural changes in the 1880s, when Decadence was slowly encroaching on Naturalism's territory. This helps to explain how arch-Decadent Robert de Montesquiou could reminisce about his 'passion pour l'œuvre de l'auteur des *Frères Zemganno*'.[2]

In *La Faustin*, as in *Chérie*, secondary characters are easily located in the Goncourt *Journal*, which in retrospect appears to have been a repository for possible future novels. Main characters, by contrast, are much more elusive. In *La Faustin* this is largely accounted for by Goncourt's over-familiarity with the theatrical world, past and present, on which he had already extensively written, and the likelihood that Juliette Faustin is a prolongation of an earlier Goncourtian character, Armande, who is herself modelled on Rachel Félix. This would also account for the almost complete absence of background information pertaining to Juliette in the novel. The link between *Les Actrices* and *La Faustin* is one example of continuity between pre- and post-1870 works. Those documents that do date from the period of writing, particularly relating to the male characters Annandale and Selwyn, tie in to Decadent themes like debauchery and moral and physical degeneracy. By virtue of its aestheticism, *La Faustin* was, as J.-H. Rosny

---

[2] In Alain Barbier Ste-Marie, 'De quelques-uns...', *Les Cahiers Edmond et Jules de Goncourt*, 4 (1995-96), 52-60 (p. 58).

put it, a 'livre destiné au petit nombre'.[3] Indeed, for many, it was a testimony to Edmond de Goncourt's aesthetic shift: in an 1890 letter to Pierre Louÿs, for example, Paul Valéry cites it as proof of Goncourt's decadence.[4] While decline is portrayed in the Naturalist novel as a means to denounce degeneracy, in *La Faustin* it is an end in itself, as Decadent themes foreground the end result of decay rather than its causes. There is no moral or social function in the text, only an all-powerful artistic drive.

Chérie is also closely related to the emerging Decadent aesthetic, as the main character, repulsed by her body, fatally chooses not to marry and, therefore, not to reproduce. While her friends devote their lives to marriage, Chérie devotes hers to the production of artistic effects and attempts to transform herself into a work of art. The Decadent vision of a fragmented, eccentric and sickly woman depicted in *Chérie* has little relation to the picture of women contained in Goncourt's documentary sources, be they letters, books, or *Journal* entries. This suggests that he had a precise vision of how he wanted to portray his character before he solicited documents from his readers, and in this he differs considerably from the practices of the historian. In addition to being permeated by Decadent themes such as the inability, or unwillingness, to consummate love, the collage-like structure of the text announces twentieth-century literature, in particular Modernism. Documents are collected and used out of context (if they exist at all), and pasted into a text to disrupt its stability. Paradoxically, Goncourt's novel retains a historical documentary approach while casting off Naturalist documentary aims. Equally important is the evidence that documents contribute to less realistic themes. Ultimately, his works display a fundamental shift away from a mimetic representation of reality, even though they are allegedly grounded in it.

The disintegration of unity visible in terms of characterisation and themes, and the diminishing importance of causality and hereditary frameworks, inseparable from the evolution from Naturalism to Decadence, is also visible in terms of the form and the language of

---

[3] 'Edmond de Goncourt' (1896), *Les Cahiers Edmond et Jules de Goncourt*, 4 (1995-96), 21-29 (p. 26).
[4] In Alain Barbier Ste-Marie, 'La Génération des "cadets"', *Les Cahiers Edmond et Jules de Goncourt*, 4 (1995-96), 61-70 (p. 61).

Goncourt's novels. In *La Fille Elisa*, *Les Frères Zemganno*, *La Faustin* and *Chérie*, Naturalist frameworks gradually disappear to be replaced by unsubstantiated, generalising suppositions. Narratives contain fewer and fewer events and those events that are related are often described using language that immobilises the progression of the stories. Consequently, time becomes static, the novels cease to advance according to a cause and effect logic, and the author's voice intrudes in the narrative in a way that is incongruent with a Naturalist programme requiring objectivity and impersonality. Traditional modes of representation lose their authority and the novels become, increasingly, novels about nothing, novels for and about the exaltation of art.

It is not only in terms of narration that the texts eschew Naturalist causality. There is much less direct discourse in Edmond de Goncourt's solo novels than in the joint novels of the Goncourts. What discourse there is frequently stands in isolation from the main body of the text and fragments it, playing no role in advancing plot. There is also a lack of trust in the representation of speech in these four works, where silence and the inefficacy of communication contribute to some of the central themes, including duplicity, alienation and the impossibility of artistic expression. The diminishing place of direct discourse is allied to a diminishing faith in the efficacy of verbal language as a means of communication. Whereas traditional mimetic novels rely on a transactional conception of language, in Edmond de Goncourt's novels this no longer seems to be the case.

Vocabulary also participates in the playful aesthetic repositioning from mimetic to poetic literature. Each of the texts portrays a specific environment and the vocabulary deployed in them attests to a desire to represent this environment accurately, whether it is through the use of modern or ancient, foreign or French, medical, theatrical, gymnastic or other lexicons. The quest to find the *mot juste*, which is essentially mimetic but also typical of *écriture artiste*, can, however, turn in on itself when language becomes so obscure and rarefied as to inhibit lexical comprehension and prevent interpretation. Refinement, in this case, is an end in itself, and words are important not so much for their meaning as for their sound, their appearance (which is often highlighted, marking certain words out as other), and their unusualness. This non-utilitarian conception of language has no real place in Naturalism, and the language deployed by Edmond de Goncourt seems in many ways closely associated to Decadent experimentation.

The style of these novels everywhere rejects the link between verbal language and communication. The texts, however, are not so pessimistic as to not replace this bond with something else. For this reason, in the three final works the protagonists emphasise visual art – be it gymnastics, acting, or fashion – over the written word, and are more concerned with feeling and sensation than with representation. There is, in this respect, a clear transformation toward Decadence. Art is their reality, as many thought it was for Goncourt himself. Like his characters who are all unable to love, to interact socially, and to detach themselves from their artistic fervour, so it was for Goncourt. As Octave Mirbeau notes: 'Edmond de Goncourt eut une passion exclusive, héroïque et violente: la littérature. Il y sacrifia tout, comme un prêtre à sa foi'.[5] There is no point arguing, as René Doumic does, that Goncourt had little to lose in so doing ('Nous aimerions à savoir quels sacrifices a jamais coûté à M. de Goncourt son culte pour les lettres').[6] The point is that it did exist, or was almost universally perceived as existing, if the 300-strong banquet of 1 March 1895 in his honour is anything to go by. Even police records of the time confirm him in his role as a patrician of letters:

> Ce n'est pas un écrivain populaire; quioque ses creations soient presque toujours d'un réalisme brutal, il est artiste en littérature, et n'est goûté que par un public spécial. Il a du reste des goûts et des manières très aristocratiques.[7]

Goncourt's two final narratives take place in refined environments, but the final three novels describe characters desperately in search of novelty. This aesthetic disposition, and its implicit link to the failure to reconcile art and life, betrays an ideology of despair. Koenraad Swart's remark that 'the only recourse open to the individual [in the *fin de siècle*] was to escape into the world of art and beauty' (p. 168)

---

[5] 'Edmond de Goncourt' (1896), *Les Cahiers Edmond et Jules de Goncourt*, 4 (1995-96), 9-12 (p. 10).
[6] 'Revue littéraire: M. Edmond de Goncourt', *La Revue des deux mondes*, 15 August 1896.
[7] Quoted in Jean-Jacques Lefrère, 'Le Centenaire de la mort de Monsieur de Goncourt', *La Quinzaine littéraire*, 699 (1-15 Sept. 1996), 15-18 (p. 16).

nowhere rings more true. In Edmond de Goncourt's solo novels, the thrills gained from effect far outweigh the joys of meaning. Insofar as this is the case, Naturalism, in these works, is in the process of being superseded by a Decadent aesthetic born of a reinvention of the roles of the *document humain* and *écriture artiste*. There are clear distinctions between the joint *œuvre* of the Goncourt brothers and Edmond's solo *œuvre*, which reinterprets Naturalism and is allied to larger modifications in the nineteenth-century literary field.

Goncourt is by no means the 'homme de génie' (p. 28) that Rosny claimed he was; he was, however, an author obsessed with novelty and originality in literature. He repeatedly lamented his lack of public recognition and the fact that other authors outsold him while using his innovations, all the while failing to recognise that this was in itself significant and that this implicated him very closely with the repositioning of the novel at the *fin de siècle*. In order to ensure that his name was linked to contemporary literature after his death, he instituted the Académie Goncourt to award the Prix Goncourt to novels that represented 'tentatives nouvelles et hardies de la pensée et de la forme'.[8] Perhaps in time his own novels will themselves be seen as innovative in terms of both thought and form, and their role in the mediation between Naturalism and Decadence will be more fully realised.

---

[8] Jacques Robichon, *Le Défi des Goncourt* (Paris: Denoël, 1975), p. 348.

BIBLIOGRAPHY

Goncourt Brothers

Goncourt, Edmond de, *A bas le progrès!*, Paris, Charpentier et Fasquelle, 1893
–, 'Chérie', *Gil Blas*, 11 March 1884-17 April 1884
–, *Chérie*, Paris, Charpentier, 1884
–, *Chérie* [1884], ed. by Jean-Louis Cabanès and Philippe Hamon, Paris, La Chasse au Snark, 2003
–, 'La Faustin', *Le Voltaire*, 1 Nov. 1881-8 Dec. 1881
–, *La Faustin* [1882], ed. by Jean-Pierre Bertrand, Arles, Actes sud, 1995
–, *La Fille Elisa* [1877], ed. by Gérard Delaisement, Paris, La Boîte à documents, 1990
–, 'La Fille Elisa (fragment)… Alexandrine Phénomène', *La République des lettres. Revue littéraire et politique*, n.s. 2 (4), 18 March 1877
–, *Les Frères Zemganno* [1879], ed. by Pierre-Jean Dufief, Geneva, Slatkine, 1996
–, 'Une passionnette de petite fille', *La Revue indépendante*, 1 May 1884
–, 'Une préface', *Le Figaro*, 17 April 1884
Goncourt, Edmond and Jules de, *Charles Demailly* [1860: *Les Hommes de lettres*], ed. by Nadine Satiat, Paris, 10/18, 1990
–, *En 18…*, Paris, Dumineray, 1851
–, *Germinie Lacerteux* [1864], ed. by Philippe Desan, Paris, Librairie Générale Française, 1990
–, *Henriette Maréchal*, Paris, Librairie internationale Lacroix Verbœckhoven, 1866
–, *Journal: mémoires de la vie littéraire* [1887-96], ed. by Robert Ricatte, Bouquins, 3 vols, Paris, Robert Laffont, 1989
–, *Les Actrices (Armande)* [1856], ed. by Mireille Dottin-Orsini, Toulouse, Editions ombres, 2000
–, *Les Goncourt: l'œuvre romanesque*, Paris, Bibliopolis, 1999 [cd-rom]
–, *Madame Gervaisais* [1869], ed. by Marc Fumaroli, Paris, Gallimard, 1982
–, *Manette Salomon* [1867], ed. by Stéphanie Champeau, Paris, Gallimard, 1991
–, *Œuvres*, 46 vols, Paris, Flammarion, 1921-36
–, *Œuvres complètes*, 21 vols, Geneva, Slatkine, 1985-86

–, *Préfaces et manifestes littéraires* [1888], ed. by Hubert Juin, Geneva, Slatkine, 1980
–, *Renée Mauperin* [1864], ed. by Nadine Satiat, Paris, Garnier Flammarion, 1990
–, *Sœur Philomène* [1861], ed. by Pierre-Jean Dufief, Tusson, Du Lérot, 1996

Manuscripts

Correspondance addressée aux Goncourt, Paris, Bibliothèque nationale de France, Manuscrits, Nouvelles acquisitions françaises, 22450-479
Goncourt, Edmond de, 'La Faustin I', Bibliothèque de l'Arsenal, Manuscrits, 14363, fol. 3
Régnier, Marie de, 'Les Paons', Bibliothèque de l'Arsenal, Manuscrits 14363, fols 68-69

Correspondence

Goncourt, Edmond de and Alphonse Daudet, *Correspondance Edmond de Goncourt et Alphonse Daudet*, ed. by Pierre-Jean Dufief, Geneva, Droz, 1996
Goncourt, Edmond de and Gustave Flaubert, *Correspondance Flaubert-Goncourt*, ed. by Pierre-Jean Dufief, Paris, Flammarion, 1998
Huysmans, J.-K., *Lettres inédites à Edmond de Goncourt*, ed. by Pierre Lambert and Pierre Cogny, Paris, Nizet, 1956
Lorrain, Jean and Edmond de Goncourt, *Correspondance de Jean Lorrain avec Edmond de Goncourt, suivie d'un choix d'articles de Jean Lorrain consacrés à Edmond de Goncourt*, ed. by Eric Walbecq, Tusson, Du Lérot, 2003

Other Sources

Adam, Paul, *Chair molle*, Brussels, Auguste Brancart, 1885
Ashley, Katherine, 'Authority and Intertext in the Goncourt Prefaces', *Trivium*, 32 (2000) 59-72
–, 'Policing Prostitutes: Adaptations and Reactions to Edmond de Goncourt's *La Fille Elisa*', *Nineteenth-Century French Studies*, 33-1/2 (2004-05), 135-46

Auerbach, Erich, *Mimesis: The Representation of Reality in Western Literature*, trans. by William Trask, Princeton, Princeton University Press, 1953
Baguley, David, 'Le *Journal* des Goncourt, document naturaliste', in *Les Frères Goncourt: art et écriture*, ed. by Jean-Louis Cabanès, Bordeaux, Presses universitaires de Bordeaux, 1997, pp. 105-14
–, *Naturalist Fiction: The Entropic Vision*, Cambridge, CUP, 1990
Baju, Anatole, *L'Anarchie littéraire: les différentes écoles: les décadents, les symbolistes, les romaines, les instrumentistes, les magiques, les magnifiques, les anarchistes, les socialistes, etc.*, Paris, Léon Vanier, 1904
–, *Le Décadent*, 1-15 February 1888
Baldick, Robert, *The Goncourts*, London, Bowes and Bowes, 1960
Balzac, Honoré de, *La Comédie humaine* [1831-47], ed. by P.-G. Castex and others, Pléiade, 12 vols, Paris, Gallimard, 1976-81
Banville, Théodore de, *Œuvres poétiques complètes*, ed. by Peter J. Edwards, 8 vols, Paris, Champion, 1994-2001, II: *Odelettes*
Barbier Ste-Marie, Alain, 'De quelques-uns…', *Les Cahiers Edmond et Jules de Goncourt*, 4 (1995-96), 52-60
–, 'La Génération des "cadets"', *Les Cahiers Edmond et Jules de Goncourt*, 4 (1995-96), 61-70
Baudelaire, Charles, 'De l'essence du rire et généralement du comique dans les arts plastiques' [1855], in Charles Baudelaire, *Critique d'art, suivi de critique musicale*, ed. by Claude Pichois, Paris, Gallimard, 1992, pp. 185-203
Bayle, Marie-Claude, *'Chérie' d'Edmond de Goncourt*, Naples, Edizioni scientifiche italiane, 1983
Becker, Colette '*La Fille Elisa*, ou comment tuer le romanesque: "une stupide absence d'elle-même"', *Les Cahiers Edmond et Jules de Goncourt*, 7 (1999-2000), 194-204
–, *Lire le réalisme et le naturalisme*, Paris, Dunod, 1992
Becker, Colette and Anne-Simone Dufief, eds, *Relecture des 'petits' naturalistes*, Paris, RITM, Université de Paris X, 2000
Bergerat, Emile, *Théophile Gautier: entretiens, souvenirs et correspondance*, Paris, Charpentier, 1879
Bever, Pierre van, 'Signification du "décadentisme"', *La Revue des langues vivantes*, 34 (1968), 366-72
Bigne, Yolaine de la, *Valtesse de la Bigne ou Le Pouvoir de la volupté*, Paris, Librairie académique Perrin, 1999

Bordas, Eric, 'Interactions énonciatives dans *Charles Demailly*', in *Les Frères Goncourt: art et écriture*, ed. by Jean-Louis Cabanès, Bordeaux, Presses universitaires de Bordeaux, 1997, pp. 209-23

Bouilhet, Louis, *Faustine,* Paris, Michel Lévy frères, 1864

Bouillaguet, Annick, 'Proust lecteur des Goncourt: du pastiche satirique à l'imitation sérieuse', in *Les Frères Goncourt: art et écriture*, ed. by Jean-Louis Cabanès, Bordeaux, Presses universitaires de Bordeaux, 1997, pp. 339-48

Bourdat, Pierre, 'A propos d'Annandale, hypothèse d'une source indienne de *La Faustin*', *Les Cahiers Edmond et Jules de Goncourt*, 4 (1995-96), 245-48

–, 'Les Néologismes dans l'œuvre des Goncourt', *Les Cahiers Edmond et Jules de Goncourt*, 6 (1998), 18-47

Bourdieu, Pierre, *Les Règles de l'art: genèse et structure du champ littéraire*, Paris, Seuil, 1992

Bourget, Paul, *Essais de psychologie contemporaine: études littéraires*, ed. by André Guyaux, Paris, Gallimard, 1993

Brévannes, 'La Fille Elisabeth: un chapitre du roman de l'année prochaine', *Le Tintamarre*, 1 April 1877

Bridgeman, Teresa, *Negotiating the New in the French Novel: Building Contexts for Fictional Worlds*, London and New York, Routledge, 1998

Brunetière, Ferdinand, *Le Roman naturaliste*, Paris, Calmann Lévy, 1892

Burns, Colin, 'Documentation et imagination chez Emile Zola', *Les Cahiers naturalistes*, 24-25 (1963), 69-78

Cabanès, Dr., 'Journal médical des Goncourt', *Le Journal de médecine de Paris*, 22 March 1891

–, 'La Documentation médicale dans le roman des Goncourt', *La Chronique médicale*, 1 August 1896

Cabanès, Jean-Louis, ed., *Les Frères Goncourt: art et écriture*, Bordeaux, Presses universitaires de Bordeaux, 1997

Caffier, Michel, *Les Frères Goncourt: un déshabillé de l'âme*, Nancy, Presses universitaires de Nancy, 1994

Calinescu, Matei, *Five Faces of Modernity: Modernism, Avant-Garde, Decadence, Kitsch, Postmodernism*, Durham, Duke University Press, 1987

Caramaschi, Enzo, *Réalisme et impressionisme dans l'œuvre des frères Goncourt*, Pisa, Libreria Goliardica, 1971

Carter, A.E., *The Idea of Decadence in French Literature, 1830-1900*, Toronto, University of Toronto Press, 1958

Castex, P.-G., 'L'Univers de *La Comédie humaine*', in Honoré de Balzac, *La Comédie humaine* [1831-47], ed. by P.-G. Castex and others, Pléiade, 12 vols, Paris, Gallimard, 1976-81, I, pp. ix-xix

Céard, Henry, '*La Faustin*, par Edmond de Goncourt', *La Vie moderne*, 28 January 1882

Champsaur, Félicien, *Dinah Samuel*, Paris, P. Ollendorf, 1889

–, *Lulu, roman clownesque*, Paris, Fasquelle, 1900

Chardin, Philippe, 'Fins comparées de quelques artistes fictifs de la fin-de-siècle', in *Fins de siècle: terme-évolution-révolution? Actes du congrès de la société française de littérature générale et comparée, Toulouse 22-24 septembre 1987*, ed. by Gwenhaël Ponnau, Toulouse, Presses universitaires du Mirail, 1989, pp. 231-39

Charle, Christophe, *La Crise littéraire à l'époque du Naturalisme: roman, théâtre et politique: essai d'histoire sociale des groupes et des genres littéraires*, Paris, Presses de l'Ecole Normale supérieure, 1979

Citti, Pierre, ed., *Fins de siècle: colloque de Tours 4-6 juin 1985*, Bordeaux, Presses universitaires de Bordeaux, 1990

Collister, Peter, 'Marie Bashkirtseff in Fiction: Edmond de Goncourt and Mrs Humphrey Ward', *Modern Philology*, 82 (1984-85), 53-69

Compagnon, Antoine, 'Zola dans la décadence', *Les Cahiers naturalistes*, 67 (1993), 211-22

Cressot, Marcel, *La Phrase et le vocabulaire de J.-K. Huysmans: contribution à l'histoire de la langue française pendant le dernier quart du XIXe siècle*, Paris, Droz, 1938

Daudet, Julia, 'Départ', *La Vie moderne*, 7 April 1883

–, 'La leçon de lecture', *La Vie moderne*, 17 June 1882

–, 'Le Mensonge', *La Vie moderne*, 24 March 1883

–, 'L'Enfance d'une Parisienne - fragments III', *La Vie moderne*, 19 May 1883

–, *Œuvres de Madame A. Daudet 1878-1889: L'Enfance d'une Parisienne; Enfants et mères*, Paris, Lemerre, 1892

–, *Souvenirs autour d'un groupe littéraire,* Paris, Charpentier, 1910

Delzant, Alidor, *Bibliothèque des Goncourt, livres modernes. Vente à Paris, Hôtel Drouot 5-10 avril 1897*, Paris, Imprimerie de Motteroz, n.d.

–, *Les Goncourt*, Paris, Charpentier, 1889

De Quincey, Thomas, *Confessions of an English Opium Eater* [1822], ed. by Grevel Lindop, Oxford, Oxford Paperbacks, 1998

Derrida, Jacques, *La Dissémination*, Paris, Seuil, 1972

Desprez, Louis, *L'Evolution naturaliste*, Paris, Tresse, 1884

Dickens, Charles [Boz], *Memoirs of Joa Grimaldi*, 2 vols, London, R. Bentley, 1838

Didier, Béatrice, *Journal intime*, Paris, PUF, 1976
Dottin-Orsini, Mireille, '*La Faustin*, les paons blancs et l'agonie sardonique', in *Les Frères Goncourt: art et écriture*, ed. by Jean-Louis Cabanès, Bordeaux, Presses universitaires de Bordeaux, 1997, pp. 247-60
–, 'Les Frères Goncourt et le "roman des actrices"', *La Revue des sciences humaines*, 259 (2000), 55-74
Doumic, René, 'Revue littéraire: M. Edmond de Goncourt', *La Revue des deux mondes*, 15 August 1896
Dufief, Pierre-Jean, 'Edmond de Goncourt et son cercle de "petits" naturalistes', in *Relecture des 'petits' naturalistes*, ed. by Colette Becker and Anne-Simone Dufief, Paris, RITM, Université de Paris X, 2000, pp. 21-33
–, 'Les Goncourt précurseurs de la décadence', *Les Cahiers Edmond et Jules de Goncourt*, 3 (1994), 13-22
Dumas, Alexandre, *Filles, lorettes et courtisanes* [1843], Paris, Flammarion, 2000
Duquette, Jean-Pierre, *Flaubert, ou l'architecture du vide*, Montréal, Presses de l'université de Montréal, 1972
Durrer, Sylvie, *Le Dialogue romanesque: style et structure,* Geneva, Droz, 1994
Duval, Georges, 'Le Roman nouveau', *L'Evénement*, 22 April 1884
Enne, Francis, 'Au hasard: la préface de *Chérie*', *La Nation*, 27 April 1884
Fabre, Yves-Alain, 'Vanités décadentes', in *Fins de siècle: terme-évolution-révolution? Actes du congrès de la société française de littérature générale et comparée, Toulouse 22-24 septembre 1987*, ed. by Gwenhaël Ponnau, Toulouse, Presses universitaires du Mirail, 1989, pp. 355-63
Flaubert, Gustave, *Dictionnaire des idées reçues*, Paris, Librio, 1997
–, *Œuvres*, ed. by A. Thibaudet and R. Dumesnil, Pléiade, 2 vols, Paris, Gallimard, 1951
Forster, E.M., *Aspects of the Novel* [1927], ed. by Oliver Stallybrass, Harmondsworth, Penguin, 1974
Fosca, François, *Edmond et Jules de Goncourt*, Paris, Albin Michel, 1941
François, Alexis, *Histoire de la langue française cultivée des origines à nos jours*, 2 vols, Geneva, Alexandre Jullien, 1959
Freud, Sigmund, 'On Dreams', in *The Freud Reader*, ed. by Peter Gay, London, Vintage, 1995, pp. 142-72
Frost, Thomas, *Circus Life and Circus Celebrities*, London, Tinsley Brothers, 1875
Gautier, Théophile, *Histoire de l'art dramatique en France depuis vingt-cinq ans, deuxième série* [1858-59], Geneva, Slatkine, 1968
Geffroy, Gustave, 'Les livres: *La Faustin*', *La Justice*, 21 March 1882

–, 'Revue littéraire: les Goncourt', *La Justice*, 10 November 1884
Genette, Gérard, 'Le Journal, l'anti-journal', *Poétique*, 47 (1981), 315-22
–, *Palimpsestes: la littérature au second degré*, Paris, Seuil, 1982
–, *Paratexts: Thresholds of Interpretation*, trans. by Jane E. Lewin, Cambridge, CUP, 1997
–, *Seuils*, Paris, Seuil, 1987
–, 'Structuralisme et critique littéraire', in Gérard Genette, *Figures I*, Paris, Seuil, 1966, pp. 145-70
Genette, Gérard and Tzvetan Todorov, *Théorie des genres*, Paris, Seuil, 1986
Gold, Arthur and Robert Fizdale, *The Divine Sarah: A Life of Sarah Berhardt*, New York, Alfred A. Knopf, 1991
Gothot-Mersch, Claudine, 'Le Dialogue dans l'œuvre de Flaubert', *Europe*, 485-87 (1969), 112-21
Goulemot, J.M. and others, 'Les Siècles ont-ils une fin?', in *Fins de siècle: colloque de Tours 4-6 juin 1985*, ed. by Pierre Citti, Bordeaux, Presses universitaires de Bordeaux, 1990, pp. 17-33
Gourmont, Remy de, 'Du style ou de l'écriture', in Remy de Gourmont, *La Culture des idées* [1900], Paris, 10/18, 1983, pp. 15-52
–, *Esthétique de la langue française* [1899], Paris, Editions Ivrea, 1995
–, *Le Deuxième Livre des masques* [1898], Paris, Mercure de France, 1917
Grivel, Charles, *Production de l'intérêt romanesque: un état du texte (1870-1880), un essai de constitution de sa théorie*, Paris, Mouton, 1973
Guibert, Noëlle, *Portrait(s) de Sarah Bernhardt*, Paris, Bibliothèque nationale de France, 2000
Hamon, Philippe, 'Autour de *Chérie*', in *Les Frères Goncourt: art et écriture*, ed. by Jean-Louis Cabanès, Bordeaux, Presses universitaires de Bordeaux, 1997, pp. 275-85
Hardy, Alain, 'Un secret des Goncourt?', *Les Cahiers naturalistes*, 41 (1971), 88-95
Hélin, Maurice, 'Les livres et leurs titres', *Marche romane*, 6-3/4 (1956), 139-46
Hennequin, Emile, 'Les Romans de M. Edm. De Goncourt', *La Revue indépendante*, 1 May 1884
Hotier, Hugues, 'Le Vocabulaire du cirque et du music-hall en France', unpublished doctoral thesis, Université de Lille, 1972
Houbre, Gabrielle, 'Le Mauvais procès de *La Fille Elisa*', *Francofonia*, 21 (1991), 87-96
Hugo, Victor, *Cromwell* [1828], ed. by Annie Ubersfeld, Paris, Flammarion, 1990
Huret, Jules, *Enquête sur l'évolution littéraire*, Paris, Charpentier, 1891

Huysmans, J.-K., *A Rebours* [1884], ed. by Pierre Waldner, Paris, Garnier Flammarion, 1978
–, *Marthe: Histoire d'une fille; Les Sœurs Vatard* [1876, 1879], ed. by Hubert Juin, Paris, Union générale d'éditions, 1975
Ignotus, 'Goncourt', *Le Figaro*, 4 March 1885
Jesse, John Heneage, *Memoirs of Celebrated Etonians: including Henry Fielding, the Earl of Chatham, Horne Tooke, Horace Walpole, George Grenville, Thomas Gray, George Selwyn, Lord North, Earl of Bute, Earl Temple, etc.*, 2 vols, London, R. Bentley, 1875
Jones, Louisa, *Sad Clowns and Pale Pierrots: Literature and the Popular Comic Arts in Nineteenth-Century France*, Lexington, French Forum, 1984
Laforgue, Jules, *Moralités légendaires* [1887], ed. by Daniel Grojnowski and Henri Scepi, Paris, Flammarion, 2000
Lefrère, Jean-Jacques, 'Le Centenaire de la mort de Monsieur de Goncourt', *La Quinzaine littéraire*, 699 (1-15 Sept. 1996), 15-18
Lemaître, Jules, *Les contemporains: études et portraits littéraires, troisième série*, Paris, Société française d'imprimerie et de librairie, n.d.
Lemonnier, Camille, *Le Mort* [1882], Paris, Dentu, 1891
'Les Influences d'un sentiment', <www.ac-reunion.fr/pedagogie/lyvergerp/FRANCAIS/2nde6/Cedric_symbolisme/influences.htm> [accessed 26 July 2004]
Levaillant, Jean, 'Flaubert et la matière', *Europe*, 485-87 (1969), 202-09
Levallois, Jean, 'Causerie Littéraire', *Le Télégraphe*, 28 April 1884
Levin, Harry, 'The Title as Literary Genre', *Modern Language Review*, 72 (1977), xxiii-xxxvi
Lévi-Strauss, Claude, *La Pensée sauvage*, Paris, Plon, 1962
Lloyd, Christopher, *J.-K. Huysmans and the fin-de-siècle Novel*, Edinburgh, EUP, 1990
Lorrain, Jean, *Histoires de masques* [1900], ed. by Hubert Juin, Paris, Belfond, 1966
–, *Monsieur de Phocas* [1900], ed. by Hélène Zinck, Paris, Flammarion, 2001
–, *Princesses d'ivoire et d'ivresse* [1902], ed. by Virginie Fauvin, Paris, Gallimard, 2002
Macovski, Michael, *Dialogue and Literature: Apostrophe, Auditions and the Collapse of Romantic Discourse*, Oxford, OUP, 1994
Mallet, Joséphine, *Les Femmes en prison: causes de leurs chutes, moyens de les relever*, Paris, Desrosiers, 1843
Mann, Thomas, *Doctor Faustus* [1947], trans. by H.T. Lowe Porter, Harmondsworth, Penguin, 1971

Marchal, Bertrand, 'Fin de siècle et temps nouveaux ou l'évangile selon Zola', in *Fins de siècle: colloque de Tours 4-6 juin 1985*, ed. by Pierre Citti, Bordeaux, Presses universitaires de Bordeaux, 1990, pp. 325-36
Marquèze-Pouey, Louis, *Le Mouvement décadent en France*, Paris, PUF, 1986
Martino, Pierre, *Le Roman réaliste sous le Second Empire*, Paris, Hachette, 1913
Mathet, Marie-Thérèse, 'La Parole des personnages dans l'œuvre romanesque des frères Goncourt', in *Les Frères Goncourt: art et écriture*, ed. by Jean-Louis Cabanès, Bordeaux, Presses universitaires de Bordeaux, 1997, pp. 237-45
Maupassant, Guy de, 'La Jeune fille', *Le Gaulois*, 27 April 1884
–, 'Les Femmes de théâtre', *Le Gaulois*, 1 February 1882
–, *Pierre et Jean* [1888], ed. by G. Hainsworth, London, Harrap, 1966
Mendès, Catulle, *La Vie et la mort d'un clown*, Paris, Dentu, 1879
Minhar, Raoul and Alfred Vallette, *A l'écart* [1891], ed. by Sophie Spandonis, Paris, Champion, 2004
Mirbeau, Octave, 'Edmond de Goncourt' [1896], *Les Cahiers Edmond et Jules de Goncourt*, 4 (1995-96), 9-12
–, *Sébastien Roch* [1890], ed. by Hubert Juin, Paris, Union Générale d'Editions, 1977
'Miscellanées', *Les Cahiers Edmond et Jules de Goncourt*, 6 (1998), 296-97
Mitterand, Henri, *Le Discours du roman*, Paris, PUF, 1980
–, *Le Regard et le signe*, Paris, PUF, 1987
Moncelet, Christian, *Essai sur le titre en littérature et dans les arts*, Paris, BOF, 1972
Moréas, Jean, *Les Premières armes du symbolisme*, ed. by Michael Pakenham, Exeter, University of Exeter Press, 1973
Mortier, Daniel, 'Quelques questions posées au concept "fin de siècle"', in *Fins de siècle: terme-évolution-révolution? Actes du congrès de la société française de littérature générale et comparée, Toulouse 22-24 septembre 1987*, ed. by Gwenhaël Ponnau, Toulouse, Presses universitaires du Mirail, 1989, pp. 336-43
Mounoud-Anglés, Christiane, *Balzac et ses lectrices: l'affaire du courier des lectrices de Balzac. Auteur/lecteur: l'invention réciproque*, Paris, Indigo & Côté-Femmes, 1994
Mylne, Vivienne, *Le Dialogue dans le roman français de Sorel à Sarraute*, ed. by Françoise Tilkin, Paris, Universitas, 1994
Noiray, Jacques, 'Déconstruction du romanesque: la subversion du modèle balzacien dans *Charles Demailly*', in *Les Frères Goncourt: art et*

écriture, ed. by Jean-Louis Cabanès, Bordeaux, Presses universitaires de Bordeaux, 1997, pp. 167-80

–, 'Tristesse de l'acrobate: création artistique et fraternité dans *Les Frères Zemganno*', *La Revue des sciences humaines*, 259 (2000), 91-110

Nordau, Max, *Degeneration* [1892], Lincoln and London, University of Nebraska Press, 1993

Palacio, Jean de, *Figures et formes de la décadence*, Paris, Séguier, 1994

–, 'Le Silence des Goncourt', *La Revue des sciences humaines*, 259 (2000), 27-39

Parent-Duchâtelet, A.J.B., *De la prostitution dans la ville de Paris* [1837], ed. by Adolphe Trébuchet and others, Paris, Bibliothèque nationale de France, 1995 [electronic document]

Péladan, Joséphin, *La Décadence latine: éthopée* [1884-1908], 9 vols, Geneva, Slatkine, 1979

–, *Le Vice suprême* [1884], Paris, Editions des autres, 1979

Petit de Julleville, L., *Histoire de la langue et de la littérature francaise des origines à 1900*, 8 vols, Paris, Armand Colin, 1899, III: *Dix-neuvième siècle, période contemporaine (1850-1900)*

Peylet, Georges, 'L'Art maniériste d'Edmond de Goncourt dans *La Faustin* ou la déviation du modèle naturaliste', in *Les Frères Goncourt: art et écriture*, ed. by Jean-Louis Cabanès, Bordeaux, Presses universitaires de Bordeaux, 1997, pp. 261-74

Pierrot, Jean, *The Decadent Imagination 1880-1900*, trans. by Derek Coltman, Chicago and London, University of Chicago Press, 1981

Poictevin, Francis, *Ludine* [1883], ed. by Jean de Palacio, Paris, Séguier, 1996

Ponnau, Gwenhaël, ed., *Fins de siècle: terme-évolution-révolution? Actes du congrès de la société française de littérature générale et comparée, Toulouse 22-24 septembre 1987*, Toulouse, Presses universitaires du Mirail, 1989

Pontmartin, Armand de, 'Semaines littéraires DLXXIII, M. Edmond de Goncourt, *Les Frères Zemganno*', *Gazette de France*, 11 May 1879

Prajs, Lazare, *La Fallacité de l'œuvre romanesque des Goncourt*, Paris, Nizet, 1974

Praz, Mario, *The Romantic Agony*, trans. by Angus Davidson, London, OUP, 1970

Proust, Marcel, *A la recherche du temps perdu* [1913-27], ed. by Jean-Yves Tadié, Pléiade, 4 vols, Paris, Gallimard, 1987-89

–, 'A propos du style de Flaubert', in Marcel Proust, *Contre Sainte-Beuve, Pastiches et mélanges, Essais et articles*, ed. by Pierre Clarac, Pléiade, Paris, Gallimard, 1971, pp. 586-600

–, 'Les Goncourt devant leurs cadets', in Marcel Proust, *Contre Sainte-Beuve, Pastiches et mélanges, Essais et articles*, ed. by Pierre Clarac, Pléiade, Paris, Gallimard, 1971, pp. 641-43

Pykett, Lyn, ed., *Reading Fin de Siècle Fictions*, London and New York, Longman, 1996

Quidam, 'Les Goncourt', *Le Figaro*, 25 April 1884

Rachilde, *La Marquise de Sade* [1887], Paris, Mercure de France, 1981

–, *Monsieur Vénus* [1884], Paris, Flammarion, 1977

Raimond, Michel, *La Crise du roman des lendemains du Naturalisme aux années vingt*, Paris, José Corti, 1966

Ricatte, Robert, 'Autour de *La Fille Elisa*', *La Revue d'histoire littéraire de France*, 48-1 (1948), 69-83

–, *La Création romanesque chez les Goncourt 1851-1870*, Paris, Armand Colin, 1953

–, *La Genèse de 'La Fille Elisa'*, Paris, PUF, 1960

Richard, Jean-Pierre, 'Deux écrivains épidermiques: Edmond et Jules de Goncourt', in Jean-Pierre Richard, *Littérature et Sensation: Stendhal, Flaubert*, Paris, Seuil, 1954, pp. 299-321

Richepin, Jean, 'Autour de *La Faustin*', *Gil Blas*, 1 February 1882

Robichon, Jacques, *Le Défi des Goncourt*, Paris, Denoël, 1975

Rodenbach, Georges, *Bruges-la-morte* [1892], ed. by Christian Berg, Brussels, Labor, 1986

Rosny, J.H., 'Edmond de Goncourt' [1896], *Les Cahiers Edmond et Jules de Goncourt*, 4 (1995-96), 21-29

Rouff, Marcel, *La Vie et la passion de Dodin-Bouffant* [1924], Paris, Serpent à Plumes, 1994

Sabatier, Pierre, *L'Esthétique des Goncourt*, Geneva, Slatkine, 1970

Sade, Marquis de, *La Philosophie dans le boudoir* [1795], ed. by Yvon Belaval, Paris, Gallimard, 1976

Saint-Amand, Pierre, 'La Passion de l'éphèmère', *L'Esprit créateur*, 37 (1997), 21-33

Sangsue, Daniel, 'L'excentricité fin-de-siècle', in *Dieu, la chair et les livres: une approche de la décadence*, ed. by Sylvie Thorel-Cailleteau, Paris, Honoré Champion, 2000, pp. 459-82

Sauvage, Marcel, *Jules et Edmond de Goncourt: précurseurs*, Paris, Mercure de France, 1970

Schmid, Marion, 'From Decadence to Health: Zola's *Paris*', *Romance Studies*, 18-2 (2000), 99-111

Simon-Bacchi, Catherine, *Sarah Bernhardt: mythe et réalité*, Paris, Presses universitaires de la S.E.D.A.G., 1984

Starobinski, Jean, *Portrait de l'artiste en saltimbanque*, Paris, Flammarion, 1970
Stephan, Philip, *Paul Verlaine and the Decadence 1882-1890*, Manchester, Manchester University Press, 1974
Stevenson, Robert Louis, *The Strange Case of Dr Jekyll and Mr Hyde* [1886], ed. by Robert Mighall, Harmondsworth, Penguin, 2003
Swart, Koenraad, *The Sense of Decadence in Nineteenth-Century France*, The Hague, Martinus Nijhoff, 1964
Symons, Arthur, 'J.-K. Huysmans', *The Fortnightly Review*, March 1892, on <http://www.huysmans.org.uk/fortnightly.htm> [accessed 26 July 2004]
Tadié, Jean-Yves, *Introduction à la vie littéraire du XIXe siècle*, Paris, Bordas, 1970
Thorel, Sylvie, 'Naturalisme, naturaliste', *Les Cahiers naturalistes*, 60 (1986), 76-88
Thorel-Cailleteau, Sylvie, ed., *Dieu, la chair et les livres: une approche de la décadence*, Paris, Champion, 2000
–, *La Tentation du livre sur rien: naturalisme et décadence*, Mont-de-Marsan, Editions interuniversitaires, 1994
Toussaint du Wast, Nicole, *Rachel, amours et tragédie,* Paris, Stock, 1980
Verlaine, Paul, *Les Poètes maudits* [1884], ed. by Gabriele-Aldo Bertozzi, Milan, Cisalpino-Goliardica, 1977
Via, Sara, 'Une Phèdre décadente chez les naturalistes', *La Revue des sciences humaines*, 153 (1974), 29-38
Wallace, Jeremy, 'Les Goncourt, La Bruyère et l'art du portrait', *Les Cahiers Edmond et Jules de Goncourt*, 6 (1998), 74-94
Weir, David, *Decadence and the Making of Modernism*, Amherst, University of Massachusetts Press, 1995
Wilde, Oscar, *The Picture of Dorian Gray* [1890], ed. by Isobel Murray, Oxford, Oxford Paperbacks, 1998
Williams, Roger, *The Horror of Life*, London, Weidenfeld and Nicolson, 1980
Youngs, Michael, 'The Style of the Goncourts in their Novels: Vocabulary and Imagery', unpublished doctoral thesis, University of Leeds, 1964
Zola, Emile, 'Edmond et Jules de Goncourt' [1875], in Emile Zola, *Du Roman: sur Stendhal, Flaubert et les Goncourt*, ed. by Henri Mitterand, Brussels, Complexe, 1989, 247-84
–, 'La Formule critique appliquée au roman' [1879], in Emile Zola, *Du Roman: sur Stendhal, Flaubert et les Goncourt*, ed. by Henri Mitterand, Brussels, Complexe, 1989, pp. 51-58

–, *Les Rougon-Macquart: histoire naturelle et sociale d'une famille sous le Second Empire*, ed. by Armand Lanoux and Henri Mitterand, Pléiade, 5 vols, Paris, Gallimard, 1960

–, *Œuvres complètes*, ed. by Henri Mitterand, 15 vols, Paris, Cercle du livre précieux, 1966-69

–, 'Revue dramatique et littéraire', *Le Voltaire*, 25 March 1879

Zola, Emile and others, *Les Soirées de Médan* [1880], Paris, Grasset, 1955

Zulli, Floyd, 'Edmond de Goncourt's American Equestrienne', *French American Review*, 3 (1978-79), 53-56

INDEX

Abbatucci, Marie, 130, 144
Adam, Paul, 151
Aeschylus, 195
Alhambra Joe, 94, 208
Allard, Julia *see* Daudet, Julia
Apollinaire, Guillaume, 139
Ashley, Katherine, 81, 187
Auerbach, Erich, 17
Baguley, David, 19, 31, 71, 80, 196
Baju, Anatole, 22-23, 30
Bakhtin, Mikhail, 187
Baldick, Robert, 152
Balzac, Honoré de, 17, 35, 39-40, 43, 48, 127, 197
Banville, Théodore de, 87
Barbey d'Aurevilly, Jules, 123
Barbier Ste-Marie, Alain, 229, 230
Barthes, Roland, 64
Bashkirtseff, Marie, 131
Baudelaire, Charles, 20, 123, 125, 183
Bayle, Marie-Claude, 127, 128, 130-31, 132, 138, 176
Becker, Colette, 19, 21, 170, 172
Berg, Christian, 191
Bergerat, Emile, 110
Bernard, Claude, 72
Bernhardt, Sarah, 108, 110, 112-13, 117, 126
Bertozzi, Gabriele-Aldo, 191
Bertrand, Jean-Pierre, 19, 127, 191
Bever, Pierre van, 181-82
Bigne, Valtesse de la, 131

Bigne, Yolaine de la, 131
Bonaparte, Princess Mathilde, 131
Bonnetain, Paul, 98
Bordas, Eric, 176
Bouilhet, Louis, 45
Bouillaguet, Annick, 24
Bourdat, Pierre, 115, 198, 199
Bourdieu, Pierre, 66
Bourget, Paul, 26, 27, 167, 219
Braquemond, Félix, 91, 126
Bridgeman, Teresa, 52
Brunetière, Ferdinand, 59, 195
Burns, Colin, 109
Burty, Philippe, 122
Cabanès, Dr. Augustin, 72
Cabanès, Jean-Louis, 20, 24, 39, 44, 71, 118, 127, 176
Caffier, Michel, 88, 123, 126
Calinescu, Matei, 28
Caramaschi, Enzo, 75-76, 78
Carter, A.E., 221-22
Castel, Pierre-Henri, 72
Castex, P.-G., 40
Céard, Henry, 18, 98, 107
Champfleury, 31, 48
Champsaur, Félicien, 103, 112, 151
Charcot, Jean-Martin, 72
Chardin, Philippe, 15
Charle, Christophe, 56, 59, 201
Child, Theodore, 115-16, 120, 121
Citti, Pierre, 29
Clarac, Pierre, 24, 166
Colette, 46

Collister, Peter, 131
Coltman, Derek, 117
Compagnon, Antoine, 30
Corneille, Pierre, 121
Courmont, Nephthalie de, 110
Cressot, Marcel, 196-97
D'Annunzio, Gabriele, 123
Darwin, Charles, 206
Daudet, Alphonse, 42, 43, 47, 84, 130, 139
Daudet, Julia, 43, 88, 116, 130, 135, 137, 139-41, 142-43, 144, 171
Daudet, Léon, 130
Daudet, Lucien, 142
Davidson, Angus, 121
Delzant, Alidor, 93, 144
Derrida, Jacques, 61
Desan, Philippe, 25
Descaves, Lucien, 21
Desprez, Louis, 47, 99
Dickens, Charles, 94, 96
Didier, Béatrice, 80
Donizetti, Gaetano, 120, 125, 141, 207
Dottin-Orsini, Mireille, 44, 46, 108, 112, 117, 200, 210
Doumic, René, 232
Dufief, Anne-Simone, 21
Dufief, Pierre-Jean, 21, 88-89, 91, 92, 107-108, 141
Dumas, Alexandre, 78, 96, 202
Dumesnil, René, 125
Duquette, Jean-Pierre, 166
Durand, Marie, 131
Durrer, Sylvie, 185, 186
Duval, Georges, 62
Edwards, Peter J., 87
Enne, Francis, 62
Euripides, 110-11, 200, 207
Fabre, Yves-Alain, 22

Faucou, Lucien, 141
Fauvin, Virginie, 221
Félix, Dinah, 112
Félix, Lia, 112
Félix, Rachel, 108-11, 112-13, 124, 126, 229
Fizdale, Robert, 112
Flaubert, Gustave, 16, 38, 42, 43, 44, 76, 120, 125, 127, 163, 166, 184, 190, 192, 213
Forster, E.M., 149
Fosca, François, 20, 79, 131
Foucault, Michel, 135
François 1er, 199
François, Alexis, 198
Franconi, Charles, 91
Franconi, Victor, 92
Freud, Sigmund, 152
Frost, Thomas 94-95, 208
Gautier, Théophile, 31, 96, 110-11
Gay, Peter, 152
Geffroy, Gustave, 62, 107
Genette, Gérard, 38, 39, 52, 64, 79-80, 81, 128, 135, 141
Gold, Arthur, 112
Got, Edmond, 109
Gothot-Mersch, Claudine, 184, 190
Goulemot, J.M., 29
Gourmont, Remy de, 27, 66, 175, 197, 209
Grivel, Charles, 38-39
Guibert, Noëlle, 112
Guyaux, André, 26
Hahn, Reynaldo, 29
Hainsworth, G., 196
Hamon, Philippe, 20, 127
Hanlon-Lee (brothers), 92
Hardy, Alain, 195
Hélin, Maurice, 43

Index 251

Henkey, Frédéric, 123
Hennequin, Emile, 149
Heredia, José Maria de, 112
Hoffmann, E.T.A., 31
Hotier, Hughes, 101
Houbre, Gabrielle, 77, 78
Hugo, Victor, 58, 77
Huret, Jules, 30, 197
Huysmans, Joris-Karl, 16, 23-24, 27, 28, 49, 53, 97, 98-99, 103, 120, 123, 126, 151, 163, 174, 201, 221
Ignotus, 65
Janin, Jules, 126
Jesse, John Heneage, 121
Jones, Louisa, 97, 101, 102
Jouvenot and Micard, 29
Juin, Hubert, 51, 53, 54, 56
Junges, Catherine, 131, 132-34, 136, 139, 144
Kipling, Rudyard, 115
Krelage, 23
Kroeker, Anna, 131
La Bruyère, 25, 129
Laforgue, Jules, 117
Lanoux, Armand, 52
Lassailly, Charles, 39, 41
Leblanc, Léonide, 131
Lefrère, Jean-Jacques, 232
Lemaître, Jules, 195
Lemonnier, Camille, 24
Levaillant, Jean, 166
Levallois, Jean, 136
Levin, Harry, 35
Lévi-Strauss, Claude, 135
Lewin, Jane, 52
Littré, Emile, 195
Lloyd, Christopher, 98
Lombroso, Cesare, 206
Lorrain, Jean, 24, 27, 29, 112, 117, 151, 160, 177, 191, 220-21
Loti, Pierre, 29
Louÿs, Pierre, 230
Lucas, Prosper, 72
Macovski, Michael, 187, 188
Malingre, Rose, 76
Mallarmé, Stéphane, 28, 29, 167
Mallet, Joséphine, 78
Manet, Edouard, 37, 41
Mann, Thomas, 45
Marchal, Bertrand, 29
Marquèze-Pouey, Louis, 20, 22, 26
Martino, Pierre, 75
Masson, Frédéric, 92, 94
Mathet, Marie-Thérèse, 176
Mathurin, C.R., 125
Maupassant, Guy de, 98, 107, 118-19, 122, 163, 195-96, 220
Mendès, Catulle, 103
Menken, Adah Isaacs, 96-97
Minhar, Raoul, 116
Mirbeau, Octave, 24, 27, 28, 232
Mitterand, Henri, 17, 22, 27, 52, 53, 55
Moncelet, Christian, 38
Montesquiou, Robert de, 23, 29, 117, 229
Moore, George, 116
Moréas, Jean, 25
Mortier, Daniel, 29
Mounoud-Anglés, Christiane, 127
Mylne, Vivienne, 176-77
Nietzsche, Friedrich, 64
Nisard, Désiré, 93
Nittis, Line de, 131
Noiray, Jacques, 39, 95, 160, 165
Nordau, Max, 21, 31-32, 71, 114, 223

Pakenham, Michael, 25
Palacio, Jean de, 162, 175, 182, 191, 192, 193
Parent Duchâtelet, A.J.B., 78
Passy, Blanche, 76
Pater, Walter, 23
Péladan, Joséphin, 151, 227
Petit de Julleville, L., 209
Peylet, Georges, 118
Pichois, Claude, 125
Pierrot, Jean, 117, 137, 216
Plato, 89
Poictevin, Francis, 24, 27, 151, 162
Ponchet, Georges, 84, 124
Ponnau, Gwenhaël, 15, 22, 29
Pontmartin, Armand de, 103-04
Popelin, Claudius, 112
Prajs, Lazare, 195
Praz, Mario, 121, 122-23
Proust, Marcel, 24, 166
Pykett, Lyn, 104
Quidam, 62
Quincey, Thomas de, 118
Rachilde, 115, 151, 192
Racine, Jean, 55, 110-11, 119, 121, 126, 181, 190, 200, 217
Raimond, Michel, 174
Régnier, Marie de, 107, 117
Réjane, 108
Renan, Ernest, 91
Ricatte, Robert, 41, 76-77, 81, 83, 85, 112, 131, 157, 175-76, 179, 190
Richard, Jean-Pierre, 195
Richepin, Jean, 45
Rimbaud, Arthur, 167
Robert the Bruce, 117
Robichon, Jacques, 233
Rodenbach, Georges, 27, 29, 191
Rosny, J.-H., 229-30, 233

Rouff, Marcel, 53
Ruskin, John, 23
Sabatier, Pierre, 71, 207-08
Sade, Marquis de, 121, 210
Saint-Amand, Pierre, 222
Sainte-Beuve, C.-A., 110
Saint-Victor, Paul de, 124, 126
Sand, George, 48, 96, 197
Sangsue, Daniel, 151
Sari, Léon, 92
Sauvage, Marcel, 18, 127
Schopenhauer, Arthur, 115, 137, 154
Schmid, Marion, 32
Schwob, Marcel, 24
Scott, Walter, 119-20
Selwyn, George, 121-22
Sérieux, Paul, 72
Shakespeare, 114
Simon Bacchi, Catherine, 112
Spandonis, Sophie, 116
Stallybrass, Oliver, 149
Starobinski, Jean, 103
Stendhal, 48
Stephan, Philip, 15, 27, 73-74
Sterne, Laurence, 151
Stevenson, Robert Louis, 120
Swart, Koenraad, 22, 23, 93, 232
Swinburne, Algernon Charles, 96, 122, 123
Symons, Arthur, 23, 163
Tadié, Jean-Yves, 24, 156
Taine, Hippolyte, 18, 73, 130, 152
Thibaudet, Albert, 125
Thompson, William, 44
Thorel-Cailleteau, Sylvie, 16, 19, 45, 64, 72, 82, 114, 151
Tilkin, Françoise, 177
Todorov, Tzvetan, 64
Tolstoy, Nikolai, 131

Index

Toussaint du Wast, Nicole, 108, 110
Tuccaro, Archangelo, 92, 93, 199, 200
Turgenev, Ivan, 96
Valéry, Paul, 230
Vallette, Alfred, 116
Véri, Léonine, 131
Verlaine, Paul, 21-22, 191
Via, Sara, 111
Villemessant, J.H.A. de, 126
Villiers de l'Isle-Adam, A., 191
Waldner, Pierre, 24
Wallace, Jeremy, 25, 129
Weir, David, 21, 23, 26-27, 30, 155-56
Wilde, Oscar, 117, 155, 210
Williams, Roger, 15, 23, 184
Youngs, Michael, 176, 178, 199, 205
Zeller, Pauline, 131-32, 136, 139, 144
Zola, Emile, 17-19, 23, 25, 29, 31-32, 36, 37, 39-40, 48-49, 52, 53-54, 56, 58-60, 63, 71, 72, 73-74, 76, 83-84, 98, 99, 109, 111, 114, 123, 130, 150-51, 161-63, 172, 196, 197, 227
Zulli, Floyd, 96-97